Short Histories of Europe

3

H.V. LIVERMORE

PORTUGAL

a short History

EDINBURGH
UNIVERSITY
PRESS

◆

EDINBURGH UNIVERSITY PRESS
22 George Square, Edinburgh
ISBN 0 85224 207 7
North America
Aldine-Atherton, Inc.
529 South Wabash Avenue, Chicago
Library of Congress
Catalog Card Number 71-159594
Printed in Great Britain
by W & J Mackay Limited, Chatham

PREFACE

In accepting the publisher's invitation to contribute a book on Portugal to the present series of short histories, I have been faced by the fact that I have already written a longer *History of Portugal* and a more compact *New History of Portugal*. In order to avoid at least the vanity of repetition, it seemed best to attempt to deal with the evolution of Portuguese society. Since a purely social or economic history would require considerable length and would necessarily pass over many aspects of Portugal readers might expect to find in a short history, I have included in the following pages the main events of political history with some account of social organization.

H. V. Livermore *São Miguel (Azores), London, Vancouver*

CONTENTS

ILLUSTRATIONS

The publisher is indebted to the Portuguese National Office for permission to reproduce illustrations 8, 11, 14, 16, 18, 20, 22, 25; to the Secretaria de Estado da Informação e Turismo, Lisbon for illustrations 1, 3, 4, 7, 23; to the Radio Times Hulton Picture Library for illustrations 2, 13, 19, 24.

I

ORIGINS OF PORTUGAL,
PRE-ROMAN TO AFONSO HENRIQUES

I: PRE-ROMAN. Portuguese territory was occupied in the Middle Palaeolithic by groups of Neanderthaloid people and has yielded traces of Upper Palaeolithic man, including the cave-paintings at Escoural (Alentejo) of the period 18000–13000 B C. Like the cave-art of northern Spain and central France, these refer to the great hunting-cultures of the end of the last ice-age. These cultures declined as the last glaciation receded northward. In the warm period that followed groups of gatherers left mounds of shells (the Asturian culture) in the north-west of the Peninsula, and similar vast shell-middens occur on the lower course of the Tagus (the 'moitas' of Muge, c 5000 B C). These last sites were occupied over a long period.

But these small settlements scarcely provide antecedents for the modern Portuguese. The first signs of a fixed and institution-alized life are associated with the appearance of agriculture, stock-raising and the associated arts, which emerged in the Near East after 9000 B C and reached south-eastern Spain after 5000. The first Neolithic cave-dwellers using decorated pottery appear at Almería, and their innovations march westwards across Andalusia into central Portugal. After 4000 the practice of constructing tombs for collective burials spread from Almería into south-central Portugal, which is rather rich in cave-burials and dry-stone cists. The grave-goods include plaque 'idols' or amulets of bone or slate and stone axe-heads and hoes. In the Alentejo the foundation of pastoral and agrarian societies was laid before 2500, and by 2000 the tradition of megalithic passage-graves had spread to northern Portugal and Galicia. There the passages tend to disappear, leaving only a polygonal chamber with less varied contents, but from 2500 the region of Lisbon and the Alentejo had acquired its own style of collective tomb, a rock chamber pierced at the top by a man-hole covered by a slab which could be removed to make new burials. The grave-goods were copious, and included ritual objects, stone axe-heads, copper tools, beads and bowls. The site of Vila Nova de São Pedro (not far from Santarém) bridges the gap from rock-cut tombs to a fully developed fortified township. It was occupied for a long period, and its inhabitants possessed flint sickles and hoes, a large potter's kiln and a form of loom. They cultivated wheat, barley and beans, the olive and flax, and their stock included the horse, oxen and sheep. The original settlement was later surrounded by a massive rampart of limestone and clay covered by a rough wall. Huts were built outside this, and contained by an outer wall. The expanded site contained many objects of copper.

The onset of the age of metals perhaps doomed these Neolithic townships. The destroyers may have been pastoral nomads who possessed flint- or copper-tipped arrows and copper daggers. They used gold to adorn their weapons and make jewellery. The step from copper to bronze was made in south-eastern Spain after 1700 and must soon have reached Portugal. The practice of communal burial gave way to interment in separate cists or pits. The covering slabs are sometimes carved with axes, and later with swords and shields. The focus in Portugal seems still to be the valley of the Tagus, Alentejo and Estremadura.

From about 1000 the Peninsula was in direct contact with the civilizations of the Near East. The Phoenicians reached the mouth of the Guadalquivir and traded for gold, silver or tin, and Punic influences appear in the pottery of central Portugal. But now the Celtic Iron Age, spreading throughout Europe, crossed the Pyrenees and introduced new industries (700–600). The mesetas of central Spain, hitherto little occupied, were settled by Celts, and in the north-west the culture of hilltop forts, the *castros*, became strongly established. Some *castros* were surrounded by enclosures for stock defended by walls or banks and ditches. The largest, the Citânia de Briteiros, which continued to be occupied after the Roman invasion, contains both circular and rectangular huts with walled spaces and paved streets, the whole surrounded by concentric defence systems. In eastern Portugal, the chief activity was pastoral: it belongs to the culture of the *verracos*, crude stone figures of boars or bulls which apparently served as tutelary deities (e.g. the boar of

Murça). In the south, urbanization had developed under the influence of the Tartessian civilization at the mouth of the Guadalquivir. We know nothing of the origin of Lisbon, but its name Olissipo has a common Tartessian ending (-ipo): so too does Ossonoba (now Faro).

The successors of the Phoenicians, the Carthaginians, succeeded in excluding their rivals from the Straits of Gibraltar and monopolizing the trade of the western shores. They explored the Moroccan coast, and must also have known the Portuguese seaboard, though there is no record of their doings. After their defeat by the Romans in the First Punic War (241), they occupied southern Spain, and wintered their troops in the Portuguese Algarve. They may have recruited men among the Celtic tribes of central Portugal.

Rome defeated Carthage in Spain and Africa, but a generation passed before she penetrated the central part of the Peninsula. The Celtic peoples formed federations to resist her, and one of these, the Lusitanians, found a great leader in Viriathus, the 'Hannibal' of the native peoples. His home was in the Serra da Estrela of central Portugal, where his people grazed their flocks and sold protection to the richer agricultural population of the Tagus valley. He conducted expeditions that ranged deep into the Roman south, but when he was murdered, the native opposition quickly collapsed. There seems to have been no organized resistance when in 137 D. Junius Brutus marched northwards from Olissipo, fortified a camp near Viseu, crossed the Douro, and reached the Lima and Minho. Beyond this he found peoples called Callaeci, whence his own cognomen of Callaecus: the region was to be known as Callaecia or Gallaecia, then later Galicia.

II: ROMAN PORTUGAL. In northern Portugal, the indigenous population had been moulded by the Celtic invasion. In the south, Punic influences were now followed by the process of Romanization. The indigenous cities below the Tagus were rather easily adapted to Roman ways. The settled peoples of the Tagus valley, formerly at the mercy of the Lusitanians, also submitted. In mid-Portugal the first Roman settlements were military camps, one of which can still be seen adjoining the airfield to the south of Coimbra. Beyond this, many hill-peoples were removed to lower ground and obliged to alter their way of life. It was long before the *castros* of the north were much modified.

In 60 Julius Caesar was pro-praetor in the west, and was faced by a revolt of the Lusitanians. He operated from Lisbon, whose fidelity he rewarded with the title of Felicitas Julia. It was the only city in the area to enjoy Roman rights. He bestowed Latin rights on Ebora (Évora) and Myrtilis (Mértola), and was also the founder of Pax Julia, whose name has been transmuted through Arabic into Beja. Caesar put down colonists at Scallabis (Santarém) in the Tagus valley. These places became the chief Roman centres in Portugal.

It fell to Augustus to resume the war on the still unsubdued Asturians in the north. After the campaigns he rewarded his veterans with grants of land near the new city of Emerita Augusta, now Mérida in Spain, which became the capital of a new province named Lusitania. This province corresponds neither to the tribal territory of the Lusitanians nor to modern Portugal, the word Lusitania being adopted as a classicism for Portugal by the antiquarians of the sixteenth century. According to Pliny, Roman Lusitania possessed five colonies (Mérida, Medellín and Cáceres, in Spain; and Santarém and Beja, in Portugal), and four *municipia* (Lisbon, Évora, Mértola and Alcácer do Sal). There were also thirty-six tribute-paying townships, making forty-five *populi* in all. The whole province was divided into three *conventus*, whose capitals were at Mérida, Santarém and Beja. It is probable that all the townships, like those of neighbouring Baetica, had adopted Roman dress and the Latin language by the beginning of the Christian area. Roman agriculture brought the typical Mediterranean landscape. The essential crops were wheat and barley, olives and the vine. The coins of Mérida display oxen ploughing; those of Évora show jars for oil or wine; those of Salacia (Alcácer do Sal) wheat and fish; those of Myrtilis and Ossonoba show fishes and merchant-ships; and those of Baesuris (Castro Marim) olive-branches and fish. Copper was worked at Vipasca (Aljustrel), where an in-scribed panel records the regulations governing the autonomous mining industry.

It is likely that to the inhabitants the *conventus* was at least as real as the province. Thus the *conventus* of Beja may be equated

with the Alentejo of southern Portugal and that of Santarém
with the Tagus valley. Farther north, the process of Romanization was less advanced. Nearer the coast, Roman influence was
strong as far as the Mondego, but beyond this the land had affini-
ties with the culture of the *castros* above the Douro. Inland, the
town of Egitania (Idanha) was a centre for the administration of
the native peoples, linked by road with Mérida. Farther north,
the Callaeci who had submitted to Junius Brutus had been divided into two *conventus*, that of the Callaeci Lucenses, with their
capital at Lugo in Galicia, and that of the Callaeci Bracarenses,
with theirs at Bracara (Braga). Their neighbours, the Asturians,
formed a separate *conventus*, administered from the site of
Augustus' former camp, Asturica Augusta, or Astorga. These
three *conventus* were put together to form a new province in
about 212 A D. It was the Provincia Antoniniana, the dynasty of
Caracalla, but it was generally called Callaecia. There was little
Roman settlement in this area. The VII Legion had been established at León by Galba in 69. But the three capitals of Braga,
Lugo and Astorga have together yielded fewer Roman inscrip-
tions than any one of the larger cities of the south. The number
of *populi* in the *conventus* of Braga was nine, as compared with
sixteen in Santarém and nineteen in Beja. This does not necessarily imply a lower density of population, but indicates less concentration in Roman capitals and towns and a higher proportion
of those still living in tribal fashion. The toponyms show the survival of many tribal or sub-tribal units, and the north-west is full
of reminiscences of native deities, such as the crude colossal
figure now in the museum of Guimarãis: by contrast, the south
has few traces of indigenous religions. There is little evidence
about the economy of the *castros*, but it is likely that the high
levels and slopes were tilled by communal strip methods, and
were enclosed by ramps and ditches, while the valley bottoms
were used for grazing.

The Roman system of roads remained in service until the
Middle Ages. From Mérida there were three roads to Lisbon,
two south of the Tagus and one north. They joined Santarém,
Alcácer, Évora and Setúbal. Alcácer and Évora were linked with
Beja, and Beja had two routes to Baesuris (Castro Marim) near
the mouth of the Guadiana. The main routes from Mérida to the
north ran outside Portuguese territory to Salamanca and Astorga,

but one route crossed the Tagus at Valencia de Alcántara by a notable bridge, still extant, and reached Egitania (Idanha). From Santarém a road ran northward by way of Conimbriga (Condeixa-a-Velha) and Aeminium (Coimbra) to reach the Douro at Cale (Oporto). From Braga roads ran north to Lugo and Astorga. The general effect was of one southern network between Lisbon and Mérida, and a smaller net linking the three northern capitals. The two systems were joined by an outer route used to convey metals from the north to Mérida, and by the Lisbon-Santarém-Braga route, apparently of minor importance.

The period of urban prosperity lasted until the first and second centuries A D. It was then that the curial class displayed its local patriotism by building public works and monuments. During the anarchy of the third century the Roman world almost fell apart, as rival 'tyrants' vied for the purple. We have no evidence of Peninsular pretenders, but bands of barbarian marauders, Franks and Alamans, destroyed Tarragona and other places in eastern Spain. The towns of the northern meseta hastily erected fortifications, among them Lugo in Galicia. At the same period, Roman Clunia (not far from Aranda, Burgos), the capital of a *conventus*, was abandoned. Its disappearance isolated Gallaecia from Tarraconensis, and at some stage the frontiers of Gallaecia were extended eastwards to incorporate its territory.

The reconstitution of the Empire by Diocletian led to the creation of new provinces, which were arranged in groups, the dioceses, each placed under a *vicarius*, subordinate to the praetorian prefect. The Iberian Peninsula formed a diocese at first attached to Italy or Africa, but later to the praetorian prefect of the west, resident in Gaul. The *vicarius* of the Hispanic diocese had his headquarters at Seville. The provincial governors were now civilians with a training in law. The Peninsula appears to have had only small garrisons, and nothing is known of any of the factories which supplied the Empire with arms and armour, or of mints.

Christianity had perhaps reached the southern coast of the Peninsula in the first century. It spread to the Romanized cities in the third, but it was still professed by only a small minority when Constantine legalized it. Its success at the Imperial court influenced officials and members of the curial class. But Con-

1. The Citânia de Briteiros, near Guimarãis: *ref.* p. 2

2. Roman temple at Évora, traditionally called the 'Temple of Diana'

stantine failed to reconcile the divisions between Catholics and the followers of Arius of Alexandria. The Spaniard Hosius of Córdoba passed over to Arianism, and so did Potamius, the first recorded bishop of Lisbon (fl. c 360). The two professions co-existed until Theodosius, a native of Gallaecia, became Emperor of the East (379) and ordered the repression of Arianism. But the mood of fervour and asceticism which accompanied the campaign for orthodoxy produced a new variant in the province of Gallaecia. A wealthy young nobleman, Priscillian, devised a system of spiritual practices which included continence and Bible-study: it was in fact a monastic rule. The orthodox bishops denounced Priscillian to the secular authorities, and he was tried and put to death. Because of his martyrdom, his teachings took firm hold in the province of Gallaecia, where they persisted until the sixth century.

III: THE SUEVI. The isolation of Gallaecia, whether political or economic, and its spiritual aberrations, perhaps explain the arrival there of several barbarian peoples early in the fifth century. Since the death of Theodosius, the two parts of the Empire had been at odds. When a large force of barbarians forced its way into Italy, troops had been summoned from Gaul, and for this reason other barbarian peoples were able to cross the Rhineland frontier and press into Gaul. They were Suevi, two branches of the Vandals, and Alans. The Roman forces in Britain, perhaps alarmed at the prospect of being cut off, proclaimed an anti-emperor, Constantine III, who crossed to Gaul and advanced as far as Arles. The barbarians meanwhile found their way through western France, living off the land; and when the quarrels of the Roman rulers or their own persistence enabled them to cross the Pyrenees at the western end, they made for the cornlands of the Castilian meseta. After a year or two they were awarded territories in the west. The Suevi occupied the *conventus* of the Bracarenses between the Minho and the Douro, the future *territorium* of Portugal. By tradition farmers, they quickly took root in their new abode, becoming the only one of the four peoples to remain permanently in the place assigned to them. The Asdingian Vandals were placed next to them on the north bank of the Minho in the *conventus* of Lugo. The location of the Alans was in Lusitania and that of the Silingian Vandals in Lusitania and Baetica, though their precise places are not known. In any case, they did not remain long. Both began to maraud in Roman territory, and the Empire replied by contracting another and larger tribe, that of the Visigoths, to bring them under control. The Visigoths, who had entered Italy from the east and had sacked Rome itself, had passed on to southern Gaul, where lack of supplies obliged them to take service with the Empire in return for a promise of land in Aquitania. They duly crushed the Silingian Vandals and Alans. The Alans were so reduced that they decided to merge with the Vandals: the Silingian Vandals joined the Asdingians. This done, the Visigoths departed to occupy the land promised them between Toulouse and Bordeaux.

It was not long before the Suevi quarrelled with their Vandal neighbours, and as they were about to come to blows, the Roman authorities decided to move the Vandals southward. We are told that they passed through Braga, but not where they went, probably to territory lately evacuated by the Silingians and Alans. But after raiding the Roman settlements in the south, they defeated a Roman army, overran Seville, and finally migrated to North Africa, where they founded the Vandal kingdom of Carthage (429).

As a result of these events, the Suevi were for a time the only barbarian people settled in the Peninsula. Most of what is known of their monarchy derives from the annals of Hydatius, who was bishop of Aquae Flaviae or Chaves, on the edge of their territory, and negotiated with them on behalf of the Romans. They held court at Braga, perhaps in the suburb of Dume, the royal estate, and at Portucale (Oporto), just as the Visigoths held Toulouse and the port of Bordeaux. Their king Hermeric ruled from their first entry until he became incapacitated in 438. It does not appear that the Suevic court had an elaborate following of Roman administrators as had the Visigothic. When the king received a messenger from the Romans and desired to consult his nobles, they were summoned for a parley: after it, they dispersed to their villages or estates. They had come straight from the Rhineland to northern Portugal in a few years without any previous experience of Romanization. They came as a people on the move, their leaders mounted, the warriors marching, the women, children and possessions transported in wagons and carts. They were still pagans, free men, warriors and farmers. Once they arrived in the fields between the Minho and Douro, they settled. There is little doubt that the Suevi stand in a similar relation to Portugal as the Visigoths do to Spain. From the settlement of Germanic military peoples on the territory of the Roman Empire emerge the foundations of modern societies and nations.

But the contribution of the two barbarian peoples is not precisely the same. Firstly, the Visigoths had their seat of authority in Aquitania until the beginning of the sixth century: although they intervened in the Peninsula increasingly as the Empire weakened, they did not transfer their seat there until nearly a century after the Suevi. Secondly, the Visigoths had long experience of the Romans both as rivals and as federates: they had slain a Roman Emperor in battle, had sacked Rome itself, had carried off an Emperor's sister to be the bride of their king, and had accepted Christianity, though in its Arian form. Alone among the barbarian peoples they had thought themselves capable of replacing Romania with 'Gothia'. This they could hardly do, but after they had played a prominent part in the defeat of Attila and his Huns in 451, they remained the strongest force in the west. Though content to use Romans as administrators, they maintained their proud aloofness as a military caste. There is no indication that the Suevi shared their thirst for authority or their segregationism. Both peoples surrendered their Germanic language, which was never written down. But it is no coincidence that the Visigoths are commemorated by their personal names which have passed into Spanish and to some extent into Portuguese, while the Suevi survive in place-names: the proportion of Germanic toponyms in northern Portugal is far higher than anywhere else in the Peninsula.

The Suevic tribespeople were thus settled, mainly in the countryside, in Entre-Douro-e-Minho. The Romans remained in control of the townships. The territory of Orense (the southern part of Spanish Galicia), which had been occupied by the Vandals, appears to have been returned to the Romans on their departure, and the Suevi disputed it. They also carried off Gallaeco-Romans, perhaps as serfs or for ransom. Hydatius of Chaves was called upon to act as mediator in respect of his catholic flock. He refers to a Roman governor or *rector* at Lugo, but this seems to have been a civil official with no forces. Such Roman troops as there still were appear to have been commanded by a count or *comes*, one Censorius, whom Hermeric pursued and captured at Mértola.

Hermeric's son and successor, Rechila, occupied Seville and collected tribute in Baetica and Carthaginensis. The court then advanced to Mérida, where he must have been in touch with the bishop Antonius, now the senior Roman official in the province. Rechila himself remained a pagan, but his son and successor Rechiarius (448 – 456) was a Catholic, possibly the son of a Catholic mother. This was the first time that a barbarian monarch had embraced the orthodox faith of the Romans, and it precedes by more than a generation the conversion of Clovis. There is no reason to suppose that the Suevi, who had now been nearly half a century in northern Portugal and knew no other home, had not intermarried with their more or less Romanized neighbours.

For Hydatius, and for later writers, the western Empire was considered to have ended with the murder of Valentinian III, the last ruler of the house of Theodosius: the Emperors who followed were mere puppets set up and torn down by barbarian commanders. When the general Avitus was proclaimed in his native Gaul, he received the support of the Visigoths. But the Iberian Peninsula, the home of the Theodosians, seems to have looked rather to Byzantium, where there were still legitimate Emperors. Rechiarius refused to acknowledge Avitus, who sent the Visigoths to impose order on him. The Visigothic king, Theodoric II, marched with a large barbarian army across the northern meseta, and confronted Rechiarius and the Suevi on the river Orbigo near Astorga. Rechiarius was defeated and fell back on Braga. Theodoric occupied the city, and his men captured Rechiarius at Portucale. In December 456 Theodoric put Rechiarius to death and appointed Agiulf, a Varn, to govern the Suevi. He himself occupied Mérida and then returned to Gaul. From this time the Visigoths had permanent garrisons in northern and western Spain, and the Suevi were confined to the western seaboard.

Soon after Theodoric's departure, the Suevi began to rebel. Agiulf tried to hold their allegiance by proclaiming himself their king, but he was overthrown and killed. However, the Suevi divided into two factions, perhaps one purely tribal and the other Romanized. In 460 Frumarius and Rechismund disputed the succession, the former holding the tribal area and the latter Orense and part of Galicia. Frumarius sent a party to capture Hydatius, who was held prisoner for three months. Then a detachment of Goths arrived and he was released. From this time a Visigothic garrison seems to have held Lugo, and Hydatius records various missions between Goths and Suevi. At the same period the Goths, who already held Mérida, advanced to Santarém, thus penning in the Suevi from north and south.

With the eclipse of the Roman emperors, the Visigothic king Theodoric was the arbiter of Gaul. One Palogorius was sent to explain the troubles of the Gallaeco-Romans, and he sent his general Cyrilla to return with him. On the way they met a mission of Suevi making for Toulouse. It accompanied Cyrilla to Lugo, where the Goth judged between the Suevi and Gallaeco-Romans. When he left, the disputes were renewed, but finally Frumarius was killed, and his rival obtained power and made submission to Theodoric, who sent him arms, money and a bride. At the same time there arrived Visigothic missionaries, and the Suevic court embraced the Arian religion.

But although Roman Gallaecia was now garrisoned by Visigoths, the Suevi were not easily to be contained. They already held land to the south of the Douro, and Hydatius accuses them of entering Conimbriga (Condeixa) by a trick, and capturing the leader of its Roman population, one Cantaber. The Visigothic king sent a mission to negotiate, but at this moment he himself was murdered and power was seized by his brother Euric (466–484), who finally severed the theoretical dependence of the Visigothic monarchy on the puppet emperors of Rome. The Eastern Emperor reacted by sending a prominent member of his court, Anthemius, to rule the West. This was seen by the Visigoths as an intrusion and a threat, but it was perhaps not unwelcome in the Spains. Although Euric had sent a mission to announce his succession to the Suevi, they seem to have refused to recognize him and to have ejected the Visigothic garrison from Orense. The association of the Suevi with the Roman population is shown by the fact that they were admitted into Lisbon by its Roman governor Lusidius. Conimbriga, which had been garrisoned by the Visigoths, was devastated and its walls destroyed (its bishop migrated to the stronghold of Æminium). In return, Euric decided to overthrow the Suevic monarchy. Although the Suevic king Remismund appealed directly to the Eastern Emperor, no help was forthcoming. Hydatius' annals come to an end with the appearance in the west of Euric's army, amidst many portents, and the departure of Lusidius to make a final appeal to Byzantium. Perhaps Hydatius died in the course of the invasion (469). From this point we hear nothing of the Suevic kingdom until 550. It seems probable that on the departure of the Visigothic troops, or on the death of Euric, the Suevi again freed themselves and restored their line of rulers.

The Suevi were now firmly established in the old *conventus* of Braga. Their attempts to expand northwards into Galicia had been resisted by their Gallaeco-Roman neighbours, who had called on the Visigoths to garrison Lugo. Thus the limit of Suevic territory was set at the Minho, the present frontier of Portugal. But to the south, as Roman power declined, they had crossed the Douro and overrun part of Lusitania. Although the Visigoths had occupied Mérida and even Santarém, the Suevi had been able to seize Condeixa, and even reached as far south as Lisbon, thus foreshadowing the southward expansion of the future county of Portugal.

We know little of Suevic society, but it is probable that the amalgamation of the barbarian monarchy with the Romanized population was already well advanced. One of the Suevic kings professed the Roman religion and in Braga coins were produced for the Suevi in imitation of those that had circulated in the Empire. We do not know how long the Germanic language survived: it was never written down, and has left few traces in modern Portuguese, which proceeds from the Latin spoken in the territory of Braga. As Visigothic power replaced Roman, the Suevi seem to have wavered between the influence of the stronger Germanic people and that of their Roman neighbours. For a time they hesitated and were divided, but when the Visigoth Euric rejected Roman authority, the Suevi joined with the Roman governor of Lisbon in opposing him. We do not know what happened after Euric's invasion, but once the Suevi made common cause with the Romans against a more powerful rival the process of assimilation was hastened.

Meanwhile, the Visigothic empire of Toulouse was shaken by

the rise of the Franks, who defeated and killed Alaric, the successor of Euric, and occupied their territory. The Visigothic tribe was forced to migrate from Aquitania, and held Narbonensis only through the intervention of the ruler of Italy, Theodoric the Ostrogoth. Much of the Visigothic tribal mass was transplanted to Spain, founding settlements across the northern meseta, and especially in what is now Castile.

Inasmuch as the modern nations of the Peninsula descend from Germanic settlements in the Roman Empire, the barbarians of Portugal are the Suevi and the barbarians of Spain the Visigoths. But, as we have seen, the former had been established for almost a century when the main body of the Visigoths was finally transplanted into the Peninsula. While the Suevi were thus already much influenced by their Roman habitat, the Visigoths retained their Germanic customs and organization and had made Arianism into a national religion which separated them from the Romanized population. However, after their defeat by the Franks, their prestige was severely shaken, and they owed their survival to the help of their Ostrogothic cousins.

The Hispano-Roman population, deprived of the military and administrative intervention of the Empire, had long been thrown on its own resources. The landowning or senatorial class retained its wealth and exercised local authority. But the imperial administration had been lost. In the north, the settlement of the Germanic peoples had overlaid the provincial divisions on which Roman administration had been based. In the south, the cities retained their importance, but the leaders of Roman society were now the bishops. In the sixth century, the healing of a breach between the Papacy and the Eastern Empire paved the way for a revival of the Roman church, and the Pope conferred the title of *vicarius* of Baetica and Lusitania on the bishop of Seville. Eastern clergy began to find their way to the west. Thus the *Lives of the Fathers of Mérida* shows that two successive bishops were Greeks, one of whom had been a doctor in the city, the founder of a hospital or hostel for strangers. Eastern merchants again repaired to Mérida. The church comprised not only the cathedral, but numerous monasteries and sanctuaries on the roads outside. It was strongly supported by the ruling class of *senatores*, owners of neighbouring estates.

The ecclesiastical revival began to stir also in the Suevic

territory farther north. In 538 Pope Vigil addressed a letter to
Profuturus, bishop of Braga, in which he alludes to the super-
stitions that were rife in the region. Now Justinian overthrew
the Vandal kingdom of Africa and occupied the port of Ceuta,
fortifying it and rebuilding its church which he dedicated to the
Virgin. Byzantine ships frequented Ceuta, where a small fleet
was kept, and it may have been by this route that new ecclesiastical influences reached the west. Ships from Alexandria carried
Egyptian wheat to Britain in exchange for tin, and they must
have put in at the Portuguese ports.

Before 550 a Pannonian monk named Martin had arrived at
the Suevic court of Dume outside Braga, where his preaching
caused the Suevic king to embrace Catholicism. Martin is said
to have saved the life of the king's son, who on his succession
brought the Suevic people into the Catholic church. This ruler
was Theodemir (c 558–9). Barbarian princes had usually reserved the right to authorize the celebration of councils of the
Catholic church; and the holding of such a council at Braga in
563 shows that the episcopal restoration of Suevic Gallaecia had
been achieved. The assembly was presided over by Lucretius,
bishop of Iría, and attended by eight bishops, whose sees are
not named. It defined the errors of the Priscillianists: probably
these traditional beliefs did not long survive. A *parochiale* dating
from 569 describes the parochial organization of both the Suevic
area and adjoining Galicia. The whole province consisted of
thirteen sees. The first of these, Braga, comprised thirty
churches—the *cathedra*, seventeen *ecclesiae* or subordinate
churches, and twelve *pagi* or rural parishes. The neighbouring
see of Oporto had its *sedes* in the 'new fort' (the *castro novo*—the
old having been destroyed by the Visigoths?), and contained
eighteen *ecclesiae* and seven *pagi*. The other sees are much smaller: Dume, which is described simply as *familia servorum*, the
royal estate, and those south of the Douro, Lamego with five
subordinate churches, Viseu with eight, Conimbriga with six,
and Egitania with two. Evidently the two main dioceses of Braga
and Oporto were more highly organized and thickly populated
than these outlying sees, and this can only be ascribed to a dense
settlement of the Suevi in the area. The sees to the south of the
Douro show the expansion of the Suevi into the old province of
Lusitania.

The document also mentions the six sees of Roman Galicia—
Lugo is a *civitas*, but it has only three subordinate *ecclesiae*;
Orense has ten; Astorga nine; and Iría seven. This implies that
Galicia had less churches and was much more sparsely populated
than northern Portugal. Only Tuy, just beyond the Minho, has
ten *ecclesiae* and six *pagi*, perhaps due to the settlement of barbarians, either Suevi or residual Vandals, at the mouth of the
Minho. Only Braga, Oporto and Tuy show the distinction between *ecclesiae* and *pagi*, perhaps discriminating between Roman
and Suevic settlements.*

The reorganization of the province of Gallaecia shows what
could be achieved when the church was supported by a Catholic
semibarbarian monarch. Yet the revival was not simply a resur-
rection of the Roman province of late Imperial days. Dume, the
royal see of the Suevi, was unknown in ancient times, and the
sees of Viseu, Lamego, Coimbra and Idanha had formerly belonged to Lusitania. Conversely, although the Suevic rulers
authorized the council, they had never held authority in the
conventus of Lugo and Astorga, the modern Galicia. At the following council of Braga of 572 this latter difficulty was recognized by arranging all the sees in two groups or synods, one
including those of the Suevic kingdom, and the other Lugo and
the remaining Galician sees.

This division was the work of St Martin, the apostle of the
Suevi, now metropolitan of Braga. He must be counted among
the famous restorers of Romanism. He founded or rebuilt a
church at Dume dedicated to St Martin of Tours, and the invo-
cation was later adopted for many churches in northern Portugal. As a proof of his influence Martim-Martins is today one
of the commonest Portuguese names. His works include the *De
correctione rusticorum*, in which he refers to pagan beliefs still
widespread among his people. When he died in 580 an inscrip-
tion in Latin verse was placed on his tomb. He was the great

* The remaining see of the province is the colony of Britons
established about their devotional centre, the monastery of
Maximus, at or near the modern Mondoñedo. These were
Christian Celts, either brought direct from Britain, or
transplanted from Brittany. The date of their arrival is un-
certain.

conciliator of barbarians and Romans, and his works deserve to be regarded as a conscious contribution to the Portuguese spirit.

St Martin had attempted to create a new kingdom, Germanic in its secular power, and Roman in religion and tradition, the true forerunner of the modern state rising from the anarchy and localism that followed the fall of the Empire. The significance of the work has been largely ignored, because the Suevic monarchy was overthrown within a few years of his death.

With the fall of the Visigothic kingdom of Toulouse, Theodoric the Ostrogoth had saved the Visigoths from destruction. Their nobles and part of the tribe had remained in Narbonensis, perhaps in the hope of recovering Toulouse: most of the tribal mass had been deposited on the meseta of Castile. When Justinian had occupied North Africa, it had been feared that he would invade Spain from Ceuta, and Gothic nobles had been summoned to put garrisons in Seville and other cities of the south. In fact, Justinian had chosen to attack Italy. But one of the Visigothic nobles, Athanagild, appealed to Byzantium for military aid, which he used to seize power for himself. The Byzantines were permitted to occupy Córdoba and other cities in the south-east. Athanagild became king of the Goths, making a capital in Toledo. He then repudiated the Byzantine alliance, seeking instead to cultivate the Franks, hitherto the hated and successful foes of the Visigoths. The revival of the Gothic monarchy, thus begun, was continued by Leovigild (568–586), who introduced the trappings of Byzantine imperialism to Toledo, mobilized the tribal Visigoths of the meseta and set about making his authority run the length and breadth of the Peninsula, driving the Byzantines out of almost all the south and defeating the Vascones and mountain peoples of the north.

It was not to be expected that such a ruler would fail to reincorporate Galicia into his territories. Theodemir, the Suevic king, had died in 570: his son Miro became involved in a conflict with the Ruccones, a tribe in the territory of Astorga or Cantabria, whom he conquered: perhaps, as a Catholic king, he aimed at a protectorate over Roman Galicia. But Leovigild soon extended his power westward across the 'Gothic fields' of the northern meseta to Sabaria, reducing the people known as Sappi (in the region of Zamora). He then moved northward and subdued the Cantabrians. In 575 he was ready to enter

Galicia, where he suppressed the autonomy of a leader named Aspidius, who held the mountains of Orense on the frontier of the Suevic territory. He then made a truce with Miro. Both the Suevic and the Visigothic kingdoms had evolved from tribal monarchies towards mixed states which combined barbarian and Roman elements. But while the Suevi had taken the essential step of embracing Catholicism, Leovigild, despite his many borrowings from Byzantium, was dependent on the military resources of the tribal Visigoths, who still adhered to the national Arian church. He himself had been married to a Catholic, and he allowed his elder son Hermenegild to wed a Catholic, a Frankish princess: he then sent the young couple to govern the Catholic south in his name. But when Hermenegild reached Seville, he openly embraced Catholicism, disobeying his father's orders to return to Toledo. Leovigild, fearful of Frankish or Byzantine intervention, sought to reconcile the two churches, but the rebel prince sent emissaries to Mérida and other places, which declared for him. Leovigild finally marched on Seville, defeated Hermenegild and took him prisoner.

Hermenegild had appealed for help to various Catholic courts, including that of Miro, who alone marched with an army to his relief. The intervention was too late, and Miro died while returning to his own country. Once Leovigild had resolved his own domestic problems, he turned against the Suevic kingdom. Miro had been succeeded by a young son Eboric (583), some of whose nobles were in favour of a settlement with Leovigild, while others wanted a heroic resistance. These last received support from Leovigild's enemies in France. Frankish ships sent to help the extremist party were dispersed by a Gothic fleet, but some of the men were able to land. Eboric himself was deposed, tonsured and shut up in a monastery. His rival, one Andeca, married Miro's widow and prepared to face Leovigild's invasion. But the Visigoths entered Braga and Oporto and captured the new king, who was in turn tonsured and secluded in a monastery at Beja (586). The Suevic monarchy was then finally suppressed, and its territory was annexed to the Visigothic empire.

The Suevic state had endured, amidst many vicissitudes, for a century and three-quarters. We have little information about Suevic society from the overthrow of the monarchy until the Muslim invasion of 711. Nevertheless, there are several references which suggest that the Visigoths continued to treat 'Galecia' as a separate province from their own 'Spania'. The confessional difference disappeared when Leovigild's younger son and heir Reccared announced his conversion to Catholicism and persuaded part of the Arian clergy to follow him. At the III Council of Toledo (589), the king and his nobles and clergy witnessed the subscription of the Arians to Catholicism. Those present included the clergy of Gallaecia. But the ecclesiastical organization of the north-west as established in the time of St Martin endured until the middle of the seventh century.

These years saw a great revival of Roman traditions in religion, law and society under the leadership of St Isidore of Seville. Although St Isidore seemed to 'proceed out of antiquity', he envisaged a new nation in which the military might of the Goths was combined with the faith and culture of the Roman south. He set himself the task of harnessing the proud and unruly semibarbarians who held sway in Toledo, but the work was still far from complete when he died in 636. Gothic nobles regularly rebelled against their rulers and seized power. It fell to Khindaswinth to crush the pretensions of the nobles with a fearful persecution, in the wake of which his son Recceswinth (653–672) promulgated a new code of laws inspired by the teachings of St Isidore and intended to apply equally to all his subjects, Roman, Gothic and Suevic alike. This code is the great monument of the Roman revival of the seventh century, and it remained the law of the Christian states even after the Muslim conquest, being replaced only in the thirteenth century. However, whether Recceswinth's code was immediately received is more doubtful. Although it proclaims a single system of law, it clearly foresees the continuance of the administration of justice by Germanic nobles, the *comites* or counts, and others. It superseded older codes and expressly forbade the use of any other book of laws; but it did not put an end to Germanic laws, which were customary, and not committed to writing.

Although the Visigoths suppressed the Suevic monarchy, it is unlikely that they assimilated the society that had been ruled by the Suevic kings. It was not so much the secular ambitions of the neighbouring Germanic monarchy as the retrospective fervour of the Hispanic church that sought to dismember the realm of King Miro. The introduction of a general law implied an attempt to restore the administrative practices and divisions of Roman times. In 660 the bishop of Mérida applied to Recceswinth to have the ancient boundaries of Lusitania restored by divesting St Martin's church of the sees of Lamego, Viseu, Coimbra and Idanha. It is clear that this was not easily achieved. The metropolitan of Braga was removed from his office. The peaceable Recceswinth himself died at a settlement called Gerticos or Gothicos, perhaps in the midst of an expedition. His successor Wamba was elected by the nobles and army: he was an elderly soldier who had governed Lusitania and seems to have been responsible for applying the territorial reform solicited by the bishop of Mérida.

Wamba's reign opened with a rebellion at the other end of his kingdom, in Gothic Gaul. When he had repressed it, he issued a drastic law on military service which required the presence of all nobles and churchmen with their contingents whenever the country or public order was endangered. The effect of this law seems to have been to restore the Gothic tradition of military localism. The last years of the Gothic monarchy are filled with rumours of strife.

IV: THE MUSLIMS. The Gothic state was a Roman restoration, but it owed much to the example of the Eastern Empire. This had long been engaged in a violent struggle with the rising power of Islam, which had burst out of Arabia and conquered Egypt, Palestine and Syria. The Byzantines still retained control of Carthage and the old Vandal kingdom of Africa, but in about 682 a Muslim expedition ranged across North Africa and reached the Straits of Gibraltar. It was only a reconnaissance, and a quarter of a century passed before the Muslims invaded the Magrib and seized Tangier. But news of the plight of the Eastern Empire and the arrival of Byzantine refugees reached Gothic Spain. As the Eastern Emperors desperately sought to impose unity on their subjects by pressing on the Jewish population, thought to be sympathetic to the Muslims, the Gothic monarchy reinforced the existing legislation against the Jews in the Iberian Peninsula.

We know little of how the gathering storm may have affected the Atlantic seaboard of the Peninsula. Mérida was now an important centre for the Gothic nobility: it alone offered strong resistance to the Muslims after their invasion. There are also indications of Gothic settlements in Galicia. Gothic nobles occupied places on the strategic road from Astorga to Lugo, and a Gothic monastic reformer, St Fructuosus, founded monasteries in the Bierzo, before becoming bishop of Braga. A medieval source tells us that King Egica (687–698) appointed his son Witiza to govern in the north-west, so that the father might rule the Goths and the son the Suevi. The prince's residence was at Tuy, on the Galician bank of the Minho, and he was supported by a Gothic *dux*. His presence is attested by the minting of coins at Tuy (as well as at Braga, Lugo and Astorga).

On the death of his father, Witiza became king in Toledo. The monarchy was not hereditary, but the ruling family was increasingly reluctant to be dislodged from the thousands of estates which the crown had accumulated, often by confiscations from its enemies. It was upheld by a palatine class of *duces* and *comites*, whose privileges had been made hereditary. It could also remove the metropolitan of Toledo, now the head of the Peninsular church, who in turn could remove other bishops. The burden of taxation fell on the indigenous population, and there were numerous seizures for debt. We have little specific evidence about the consequences of this apparently oppressive system on the societies of the West: but there is no reason why they should have been especially zealous in its defence.

The praetorian government of Toledo collapsed suddenly before the Muslims. In the last years of the seventh century Carthage fell to them, and a new caliph authorized the annexation of the African north-west: his governor, Mūsa ibn Nuṣair, took Tangier, but the stronghold of Ceuta passed under the Goths, and Witiza sent it supplies from Spain. On Witiza's death in 710, there was a struggle in Toledo. The praetorium refused to be ruled by his young sons and gave power to a *dux*, Roderic. The family of Witiza fled from the capital and opened negotiations for Muslim military help. The Muslims demanded the cession of Ceuta and the provision of ships to cross the Straits, promising to restore the Witizans to the royal estates. Roderic's army was defeated in a single battle fought near Medina Sidonia, and the king was killed. The Muslims then marched directly on Toledo and occupied it. Mūsa himself arrived and laid siege to Mérida, which capitulated only after a long resistance. Thereafter the conquest consisted rather of a tour to receive the capitulation of the local governors and nobles. Mūsa himself marched from Mérida to Toledo, and thence to Saragossa. He is said to have then crossed the northern meseta to Astorga and Lugo, where he received the capitulation of the Galician authorities. His son ʿAbduʾl-ʿAziz annexed Beja and Évora in an expedition from Seville. We are not told if the Muslims entered the Suevic region at this time.

The Muslims did not restore the Gothic crown to the sons of Witiza, but they did return to them the royal estates, consisting of more than 3,000 villages. The eldest son, Olmund, received the estates in the west and resided in Seville. According to a late account, Witiza, when prince at Tuy, had quarrelled with and killed the *dux* Fafila: a son of this *dux* named Pelagius (Pelayo) had been a supporter of Roderic and was held prisoner by the Muslims at Córdoba. He now escaped and made his way to Galicia, but failing to find support, he withdrew to the fastnesses of the Asturian mountains. One version says that Olmund accompanied a Muslim force sent to reduce Pelayo and appealed to him to submit, but Pelayo refused and beat off the Muslims: Olmund died in Galicia. This was the modest beginning of the Christian reconquest.

For a long period the Portuguese area is enveloped in silence. The Muslims had established their military colony at Córdoba. Many Arab leaders dwelt in the cities or on estates in the south: the attempt to carry the expansion into Gaul took others to Saragossa and the valley of the Ebro. But the majority of the Muslims were recently converted Berber tribespeople from North Africa, and part of these occupied the central meseta, where they pursued a pastoral and nomadic existence. It is likely that detachments of troops were posted in Lugo and Braga, but some of the Berbers were soon removed to strengthen the eastern Pyrenean frontier, and others returned to Africa after the great Berber rebellion of 740. This revolt was a protest against Arab supremacy. All North-West Africa threw off the Arab yoke, and the movement spread to the Peninsula, where the Berbers marched on the cities of Córdoba and Toledo, in which the Arabs sought refuge. The caliph of Damascus raised an Arab army, which was defeated near Tangier, but entered the Peninsula, suppressed the revolt and then seized power in Córdoba. As a result, the newcomers, known as 'the Syrians', were given land in Andalusia, southern Portugal and Murcia. The upheaval was followed by a serious famine, as a result of which many of the Berber tribespeople returned to their native Africa. In the East, the overthrow of the Ummaiyad caliphate of Damascus forced the one surviving prince of the house to flee to the West: he was received by the 'Syrians' of Andalusia, and presently established an Arab monarchy at Córdoba (756).

These chaotic experiences divided the Peninsula on new lines. The Muslim governors held the Roman south and east, but they made their seat not at Seville, but at Córdoba, which had been the capital during the Byzantine occupation. The monarchy of Toledo was utterly destroyed, and many of the Gothic settlements on the upper meseta were abandoned. Many Goths fled to the northern mountains, the Cantabrians or Pyrenees. By contrast, the other Germanic people, the Suevi, now almost assimilated with their Gallaeco-Roman neighbours, were probably much less disturbed. However, the *duces* and *comites* were swept away; many of the towns, including Braga, were sacked, and some at least of the sees disappeared. There is no indication that either Arabs or Berbers made any serious attempt to colonize northern Portugal. It is likely that Berbers, perhaps nomadic, reached the Serra da Estrela, and a garrison and governor were installed as far north as Coimbra.* Arabs, intermarried with Peninsular families, settled as landowners in the valley of the Tagus, and on the Roman wheat-belt of Évora and Beja. One of the Arab contingents, part of the *jund* of Egypt, settled in the Algarve, where they made their capital at Silves.

The Muslim invasion was a military intervention from the south. The newcomers rather easily adapted themselves to the forms of life they found in the ancient cities and on the large estates of the Romanized part of the Peninsula. They found little to attract them in the more tribal north, deeply impregnated with Germanic traditions. Thus Coimbra became the northern limit of Muslim influence. Beyond it, a tract of territory on the Vouga appears to have capitulated, but to have been left un-

* The ancient Conimbriga had been destroyed, but its bishopric and name were transferred to the site of the Roman Æminium (Gothic Eminio) on a hill overlooking the Mondego, the present Coimbra.

3. Nuno Gonçalves, Adoration of St Vincent, painted *c.* 1465. Panel of the friars

occupied by the invaders. The region to the north of the Douro was attacked by the Berbers, who sacked Braga, but made no attempt to settle there.

A document shows that they also attacked Lugo and carried off its bishop and numbers of his followers to the south. When these men were released and returned to the north, their bishop, Odoarius, rewarded his companions by granting them *villae* in the territory of Lugo, and also in that of Braga, whose see remained unoccupied. The new settlers were supplied with workers, cattle and equipment. But while steps were taken to repair the depopulation that had occurred and to reoccupy and cultivate abandoned estates, there is little evidence of an administrative revival, whether secular or ecclesiastical. It seems that the *comites*, administrators and governors, had been effaced. The Peninsular church still acknowledged the metropolitan of Toledo as its head: Cixila, metropolitan in 744–753, is called a restorer of churches, but we are not told what he was able to accomplish.

The collapse of the centralized Gothic state left an administrative vacuum. In the Asturian mountains Pelayo had set up a small kingdom, which more resembled a Germanic county than the Gothic empire of Toledo. During the Muslim anarchy, his successor, Alfonso I, succeeded in entering almost all the old cities of the north-west and the northern meseta, but he lacked the resources to occupy them, and could only carry off the residual population to settle in his mountain fastness: among the places he visited were Braga and Oporto, whose depopulation he may have completed. But it does not appear that he or his successors exercised jurisdiction outside their mountain kingdom, unless in the northernmost corner of Galicia. The restored church of Lugo may have continued the task of reorganization, but there is no sign of a restoration at Braga. The Asturian territory itself had no cities or sees, and the leaders of the Asturian clergy were not bishops of specific dioceses: the ecclesiastical revival therefore came rather through the foundation of monasteries.

In the last quarter of the eighth century, the Asturian kingdom was drawn into the orbit of the Frankish empire of Charlemagne. Alfonso II executed a raid on Lisbon and sent part of the proceeds to Charles. In the Asturian church the influence of Toledo was replaced by impulses from France. Some of the

4. Adoration of St Vincent. Panel of the knights

Galician sees were revived. From that of Iría-Padrón arose the supposed discovery of the tomb of the Apostle St James, for whom a new shrine was erected at Santiago de Compostela. Meanwhile, the Christian populations of the capitals of the south began to rebel against the new taxes imposed by the Muslims and the growing Syrianization of the administration. The Frankish rulers encouraged this unrest, and we find Louis the Pious urging the inhabitants of Mérida to resist the Muslims and if necessary to emigrate to the north. But the Muslims refortified Mérida, and this act perhaps accounts for the removal of many Christian relics from the Lusitanian capital to the new shrine of Santiago.

It is possible that the inhabitants of the north-west were shaken out of their isolation, not by struggles between Christians and Muslims, but by the attacks of the Norsemen, whose longships appeared in the creeks of Galicia in 844: they went on to the Tagus and the Guadalquivir, where the Muslims finally defeated them. By now northern Galicia had acquired a civil and ecclesiastical organization: its sees were being restored and its leading families held the office of *comes* as members of the Asturian court. The great protector of the cult of St James was Alfonso III (866–912), who visited the shrine at the beginning of his reign.

v: THE TERRITORY OF PORTUCALE. The same prince took the decision to annex the territory between the Minho and Douro. The task was entrusted to one Vimara Peres, perhaps a magnate from neighbouring Galicia (868). Braga was still abandoned, and Oporto may also have been unoccupied. The region was known as the 'territorium Portugalense', the 'territory of Portucale'. We do not know what Vimara achieved, but it seems likely that he established a new settlement not far from Braga which was given the name of Vimaranes or Guimarãis. It remained the focus for the reorganization of the old Suevic territory for the following two centuries. Vimara himself died in Galicia soon after, but another enterprising frontiersman named Hermenegild began to occupy and reorganize the territory below the Douro.

The occupation of these lands between the Minho and the Mondego was made possible by a long crisis in the affairs of the

Muslims of Córdoba, whose state seemed to be in danger of collapse in the last third of the ninth century. For a time Alfonso III hoped to restore the Gothic empire in the Peninsula, but his plans were frustrated and Córdoba recovered. In the tenth century, its rulers, now calling themselves caliphs, struck back and almost vanquished the Christian kingdom of the north. The county of Portugal stretched from the Minho to the Douro and the sea to the Marão. It was long governed by counts drawn from a local family. They can be traced from Hermenegildo Gonçalves and his wife Mumadona, the foundress of the monastery of Guimarãis (fl. c 931). When her husband died, she held the territory for her two sons, Gonçalo and Diogo. Gonçalo Mendes acquired great influence at the Asturo-Leonese court under Ordoño III (951–957): he joined with the counts of Galicia and the bishop of Santiago in defending Ordoño's son Vermudo II against his rivals. Gonçalo's son, Mendo Gonçalves, became tutor to Vermudo's heir, the future Alfonso v (b. 994). The leading family of Portugal thus appears as a prominent supporter of the neo-Gothic monarchy.

The settlement at Guimarãis was a burgh in the Germanic tradition, not a Roman *civitas*. It consisted of the palace or castle of the governing family and the great monastery. A document of 953 shows that the count had founded the fishing-port of Vila do Conde, which was then sold by Flamula Deo-vota to the monastery. Her parents, Pelagius and Iberia, had installed clients or serfs at Vila do Conde, and the place had fisheries, orchards and a fig-plantation. The land was divided into contiguous estates, each named after its founder or owner, Villa Fromarici, Villa Tauquinia, Villa Argundi, Villa Anserici. Most of the names are Germanic. The estates are near the road to the south, the 'carraria Maurisca'. The payments include mules, a decorated and gilded vessel, and garments made of Muslim silks. Farther south, there was another notable monastery at Lorvão to the north of Coimbra. A document of 978 says that Mumadona's father, Veremundus, had intended to endow Lorvão. His widow Onneca and her children gave it a *villa* in the suburbs of Coimbra to provide the monks with food and clothing.

But this 'neo-Suevic' revival was halted in the later part of the tenth century when the caliphs of Córdoba, bringing in large contingents of Berber cavalry, smote the Christian north with devastating blows. This renewed Holy War reached its height under al-Manṣūr. Although not all of his campaigns are chronicled, he marched into Portugal in the 'campaign of the cities' (986 or 987) and in 997, when his men sacked Santiago and carried off its bells and gates to adorn the great mosque of Córdoba. It is usually held that Coimbra was reconquered by the Muslims and lay abandoned for several years. But this may not be accurate, for after Coimbra was recovered by the Christians in 1064 one Zuleiman Alafla deposed that when the Muslims took it in the time of al-Manṣūr his grandfather Ezerag of Condeixa went to the Muslim commander, professed Islam, and went with thirty Muslims into the woods where the Christians from the villas were hiding, and cried: 'Come out, good people, I have made peace with the Moors.' The Christians emerged, but the Muslim governor sold them and sent the money to al-Manṣūr, who rewarded Ezerag with a grant of water-mills and villas near Coimbra.

Coimbra was and remained a centre for Mozarabs, or Christians living under Muslim rule. It received Christian migrants from the Muslim cities of the south. Thus a document from Lorvão shows the abbot Primus sending to Coimbra for a bridge-builder named Zacarias of Córdoba to make crossings over the river Alviaster. No documents from Lorvão survive for the years 988–97, but after the Muslim reconquest records of donations were resumed, only they are no longer confirmed by Christian counts.

The Count of Portugal, Mendo Gonçalves, acted as tutor to the future Alfonso v of Leon and enjoyed great influence at court. During his absence he entrusted the government of Portugal to a delegate named Magister Everardus. But in 1008 the Vikings again raided the region, and Mendo died in a campaign against them. His county passed to his widow, Tuta Mendes. Their daughter and heiress was married to one Nuno Alvito, whose father had governed Vermoim. Nuno was a warrior, called *dux magnus*, and he died in 1028. His widow Ilduara governed for their young son Mendo Nunes, who died in battle (1050–3). Ilduara then governed on behalf of her grandson Nuno Mendes. Thus the county of Portugal was transmitted within a single family.

Meanwhile, on the death of al-Manṣūr, the caliphate of Córdoba became unable to control its Berber armies and fell into confusion. Such was the disorder that the citizens of the capital suppressed the caliphate in 1031, and the rest of the Muslim territories split up into small kingdoms, the *taifa* states. The Leonese empire had been so badly battered that it could take little advantage of this sudden collapse. Its eastern region, unified as the county of Castile, proved better equipped for the crisis. It passed under the influence of Sancho III, king of Navarre (1000–1035), who then overthrew the so-called emperors of Leon. The last of these was Alfonso v, the pupil of Mendo Gonçalves, who in 1028 attempted to recover Viseu from the Muslims and was killed by a bolt from its walls. It was the last royal campaign in the west for thirty years. Sancho III installed his son Ferdinand as count of Castile, and in 1037 Ferdinand made himself the first king of Castile, and wrested the old Leonese 'empire' from the dynasty of Alfonso I. In Portugal, the house of Mendo Gonçalves, so powerful under the old regime, fell into eclipse. The new dynasty seems to have appointed its own nobles from Castile or Navarre to administer it. In 1050 an *infanção*—a member of the lesser nobility—named Gomes Eitaz appears as governor in Guimarãis, and other officials held the 'land of Portugal' in 1062. In 1063 Portugal was governed by *maiorini* or *vicarii*, administrators from Ferdinand's court.

The collapse of Córdoba rapidly weakened the Muslim hegemony through the frontier region. One Gonçalo Trastemires seized the castle of Montemór-o-Velho on the Mondego, thus cutting off Coimbra from the sea. In 1057 Ferdinand I came to the west and occupied Lamego and Sena (Seia): he took Viseu in 1058, and the smaller places in the region surrendered. In 1064 he embarked on the conquest of Coimbra. It fell on July 9 after a siege of six months. It was entrusted to Sisenand ibn Dawd, a native of Tentugal who acted as an intermediary between Ferdinand and the taifa-states of the south. Thus Coimbra passed from the control of the Muslims to that of the Mozarabs, or Arabized Christians. There was probably no great exodus of population; and in marked contrast to Portugal, Coimbra continued in its appearance, speech, customs and industry to bear many signs of the Islamic occupation. The gateway to its *madina*, the Arco de Almedina, still survives, as do the *couraças*, or avenues of access built under the shadow of the walls.

2

THE FORMATION OF PORTUGAL

All this territory was soon to be overrun by the movement of adventurers and conquerors pressing southward. The practice of seizing unoccupied land had long been exercised by nobles and prelates; the occupier became a *presor* and the land *presúria*. Much of the original territory of Portugal had been annexed and colonized in this way by the enterprise of individuals. The victims of the process were not only Muslims. Even the great monastery of Lorvão seems to have been despoiled by adventurers: such at least appears to be the implication of the flight of some of the brothers who went north and were sheltered by the monks of Leça.

Ferdinand I of Castile and Leon died in 1065. Following a practice derived from Carolingian France, but foreign to Peninsular customs, he divided his realms between his three sons, giving Castile to the eldest, Sancho II, and Leon to the second, Alfonso VI, and creating for the third, García, a kingdom of Galicia with its capital at Santiago. It was the first time that Galicia had had its own ruler, and the experiment did not last long. In 1071 the two elder brothers partitioned Galicia; and when Sancho II was murdered and Alfonso took over Leon and Castile, he suppressed the kingdom of Galicia and held García captive until he died.

The emergence of this kingdom was a recognition of the preeminence Santiago had won as the apostolic shrine of the Spains. It had, of course, not existed in Roman times, when Braga had been the seat of the metropolitanate in the north-west. The see of Braga was restored in 1070, when it was the only one of the five ancient metropolitan sees in Christian hands. It began to use the metropolitan title in documents, but received no official recognition of its claim. Its first bishop, Pedro (1070–1093), was appointed by Sancho II, and therefore enjoyed little favour with Alfonso VI.

But Alfonso VI, through his marriage to a Burgundian princess, was responsible for the introduction of the Cluniac reform into the Peninsular church. The reformers were devoted to the principle of Papal supremacy which was widely accepted after the election of Hildebrand as Pope in 1073: in their zeal for a Roman restoration, they had little enthusiasm for the pretensions of Santiago. In 1078 Alfonso VI invited the Pope to establish the Roman liturgy throughout his domains, an innovation which was opposed by the traditionalists of the Spanish church. In 1085 Alfonso was able to recover Toledo, the ancient capital of the Goths and headquarters of the Hispanic church. He promptly granted it to a French monk named Bernard, and shortly afterwards the Papacy recognized Bernard as Primate. The church of Santiago had difficulty in accepting either the Cluniac reform or the elevation of Toledo. Alfonso VI suddenly arrested the bishop of Santiago on a charge of treason and forced him to resign. But although Santiago was under a cloud, Braga's claim was still unrecognized. Bernard of Toledo consecrated the restored cathedral at Braga, but he ignored the question of the metropolitanate. Bishop Pedro was not a Cluniac, and he finally went to Italy and obtained a schismatic autonomy from the anti-pope, Gilbert of Ravenna.

But in 1096 another Cluniac, Gerald, a monk of St Pierre de Moissac, was appointed bishop of Braga, and he at last succeeded in obtaining recognition of the metropolitan title (1099–1100). The authority of Braga was accepted until the death of St Gerald in 1108, by which time the nobles and people of Portugal had also their own count. Meanwhile, the bishop of Santiago had taken the precaution of obtaining a bull of exemption for his diocese, so that the Apostle's shrine should remain independent of Braga. On his death no successor was appointed, and the see of Santiago was placed under an administrator, Diego Gelmírez. Such was the determination of Gelmírez not to give way to Braga that in 1102 he descended on the city and carried off by force the relics of St Victor and St Fructuosus. Gerald had recourse to Rome, and he obtained a reproof for his rival and confirmation of his own supremacy over all the sees of the west as far south as Coimbra, with the sole exception of Santiago. Thus Rome admitted the ecclesiastical unity of the area as in the time of St Martin of Dume, and the authority of Braga was accepted until the death of St Gerald in 1108.

But now events had led to the restoration of the dormant county of Portugal. After his conquest of Toledo Alfonso vi had extorted tribute from the Muslim *taifas* to the south with such effect that they were driven to appeal for help from North Africa. There a new movement, the Almoravids (*al-murabitin*, 'fighters in *rabita*, castle-monasteries, for the Holy War') had just achieved power. These Berbers had been driven out beyond the desert, where they converted the Negroes to Islam. With their black guards armed with shields of hippopotamus hide, their desert-drums and their baggage-camels, they swept over Morocco imposing a strict and puritanical reform. Their armies now crossed into the Peninsula and advanced on the *taifa* of Badajoz (which had replaced Mérida). The rulers of Badajoz had been forced to pay tribute to Alfonso, but the Muslim victory of Zallaka or Sagralias (near Badajoz) ended this submission. The Almoravids returned to Africa. But the rulers of Badajoz were soon faced with demands by their faqihs to recall them. The Muslim princes were as much intimidated by their strange allies as by the Christians, and decided to seek the protection of Alfonso vi, offering him the towns of Santarém, Lisbon and Sintra. Thus at a single stroke the western frontier of Portugal was advanced from the Mondego to the Tagus.

During the crisis that followed Zallaka, Alfonso had appealed to his Burgundian relatives, and a number of knights rallied to him. They included his queen's nephew, Duke Eudes, and a cousin, Raimund. The departure of the Almoravids made their services unnecessary, but they visited Alfonso's court, and Raimund remained in Spain, becoming the husband of Alfonso's legitimate daughter and heiress Urraca. The cession of Santarém, Lisbon and Sintra made it urgently necessary to strengthen the western frontiers. In Coimbra Sisenand had died in 1092. He had been a negotiator rather than a warrior. But now the resources of Coimbra alone were insufficient for the emergency. By April 1093 Alfonso had placed his son-in-law Raimund in Coimbra, and he had sent Sueiro Mendes to garrison the three newly acquired cities. Soon Raimund's jurisdiction was extended to include Galicia. In 1094 he was 'Count of Galicia' and 'Lord of Coimbra and all Galicia'.

But an Almoravid army now fell on the allied Muslim taifa of Badajoz and put its rulers to death before the Christians could intervene. By November 1094 Raimund had assembled the barons and knights of Galicia and Portugal. But he failed to hold the new frontier. Lisbon was soon lost. In August 1095 Raimund still called himself 'Lord of Galicia and Santarém', but the Muslims soon recovered the latter place.

The Almoravid invasions obliged the dilated pseudo-empire of Leon and Castile to face the social realities of its situation. In the west the county of Portugal was the most densely populated region of the Atlantic seaboard, and it alone could withstand new attacks. It was entrusted to Raimund's cousin Henry of Burgundy. By December 1095 he was count of Coimbra. In 1097 he was styled 'Count of Portugal', with authority from the Minho to the Muslim frontier. This was at first called 'Portugal and Coimbra', but as the Portuguese took over its defence their name was applied to the whole.

The new defender, like his cousin, entered the imperial family by marriage to a daughter of Alfonso VI. This was Teresa, a bastard, whose mother, Ximena Nunes, held a castle in the Bierzo. The county of Portugal was bestowed on the couple, and their son Afonso Henriques, born in 1106, was to make himself its first king. In his documents, Afonso Henriques frequently refers to himself as the Emperor's grandson and to his mother as queen. His father is usually called count of Portugal, but occasionally 'consul'.

The relations between Henry and Raimund are illustrated by a 'pact of succession', by which Henry promised to help his cousin against all rivals and in return Raimund would grant Henry Toledo, or, if he could not, Galicia. The pact is undated, but was negotiated by one Dalmatius Gevet representing Abbot Hugo of Cluny, perhaps the Cluniac Dalmatius who became bishop of Santiago in 1095. Its context may have been the fourth marriage of Alfonso VI to the daughter of the deposed Muslim king of Seville, who became the mother of his only son Sancho, born in 1097. Count Raimund's reputation as a soldier was tarnished, but he was the husband of the heiress to the throne, and he was resolved that she and their son Alfonso Raimúndez should succeed: for this he needed the active support of Henry of Portugal.

The birth of the boy Sancho threatened this arrangement, and in 1098 Henry and Teresa visited Raimund and Urraca at

Santiago. But the pact lapsed with the death of Raimund in 1107. Soon after, the little prince Sancho was killed in a fight with the Almoravids, and the old Emperor formally recognized Urraca and her son Alfonso Raimúndez as his heirs. Henry's ambitions were dashed, and although he visited the old Emperor, he was given no satisfaction and left in anger. When Alfonso vi died (July 1109), Urraca was declared heiress. It was arranged that she should marry Alfonso the Battler, king of Aragon. But this solution displeased the barons of the west, who proclaimed the little Alfonso Raimúndez. There followed a long series of incidents in which Urraca quarrelled with her new husband and was reconciled with him, only to be finally separated. Henry of Portugal unashamedly changed sides in a desperate bid to further his own interests. He was given the territory of Astorga by the Battler, but he rejoined Urraca, visiting Santiago in 1112. He then returned to Astorga, where he suddenly died (30 April 1112).

The county of Portugal now passed to Henry's young widow Teresa. Their son Afonso Henriques was a child of about six, and had been entrusted to the care of the greatest magnate of the Douro valley, Egas Moniz. The seat of the count's court was at Guimarãis. In 1095–6 Henry had bestowed a charter of privileges on the burghers. In Guimarãis no one might be arrested for debt. No knight might enter a house unless invited by the owner. No *sagio*, the count's agent, might enter the house of a resident. There were severe penalties against acts of violence: a weapon drawn in wrath out of doors brought a fine of 60 *solidi*; a wound that drew blood cost $7\frac{1}{2}$ *solidi*; a blow with the fist 12 *denarii*. Each house paid a tax of 12*d.*; so did 'the benches where meat is sold'. No tax was paid on sales of less than 12*d.*, but the sale of a horse cost 12*d.*, an ass 6*d.*, on cattle 2*d.*, a sheep, goat or pig 1*d.*; a rabbit-skin 3*d.*, a blanket or cloak 2*d.*, and a cowhide or length of linen 1*d.* Henry had attracted some foreign merchants who had their street and bought ground for a chapel.

The chief figures of the count's court were the magnates of the district, who were appointed as *tenentes* to hold territories and administer them. The head of the civil administration was a *maiordomus palatii de ille comes, de illa regina*. The forces were led by a standard-bearer, sometimes called *armiger* or *vexillifer*, sometimes by the Arabic term *alferes*. Few documents (in all about thirty-one) survive from Henry's time. They were drawn by a notary, often a canon of Guimarãis or subdeacon of Braga. If the count was away, he had recourse to the scriptorium of a monastery or church. On Henry's death Teresa governed the county (1112–1128). While St Gerald had lived, the ecclesiastical unity of the country was respected. He had died in 1108, and the metropolitanate of Braga passed to another French priest, Maurice Bourdin, formerly bishop of Coimbra. To his annoyance, the see of Toledo appointed a successor to Coimbra. He therefore sought an alliance with Diego Gelmírez of Santiago, and appointed Gelmírez's archdeacon, Hugo, to be bishop of Oporto. Teresa granted Hugo full jurisdiction over the city of Oporto. Even worse, Bishop Maurice went to Italy and became anti-pope, crowning the Emperor Henry v in March 1117, and being excommunicated and disgraced. This tempted the ambitious Gelmírez to try to wrest the metropolitanate from Braga. He sent a mission to Rome with a large gift of gold; but fortunately for Braga, the envoys were arrested in Aragon and the treasure seized. In 1118 the Pope confirmed the metropolitanate of Braga, but upheld the exemption of Santiago and promised Gelmírez the metropolitanate of Lusitania when Mérida should be retaken from the Muslims.

Meanwhile in 1116 the Almoravids had attacked Coimbra and occupied two castles that covered its approaches, Santa Eulália and Miranda. Coimbra itself was surrounded, with Teresa in its keep (1117). She appealed to Galicia for help, and the leader of the Galician magnates, Pedro Froilaz, sent his son Fernando Peres of Trava to direct the defence for her. The Galician warrior became lord of Oporto and Coimbra in 1121. He also abandoned his family in the north for an association with Teresa.

The magnates of Portugal witnessed with disapproval the influence of the Galician favourite on their countess and of the Galician prelate in their church. Their only course was to await the majority of her son, Afonso Henriques. In 1125 he armed himself knight in the church of Zamora. His cousin, Alfonso Raimúndez, had done the same at Santiago a year earlier, and in 1126 began to rule the Leonese empire as Alfonso vii. He confirmed Teresa in possession of Portugal, but under the influence of Gelmírez he soon invaded her and compelled her to do homage

and surrender land she held north of the Minho. Followers
of Afonso Henriques in Guimarãis held out as long as they could,
but finally did homage in the name of their prince. Then
Guimarãis and other places began to repudiate Teresa. In March
1128 documents still appear subscribed by both mother and son,
but in April he confirmed the charter of privileges his father had
given to Guimarãis, and on 26 May he appointed the archbishop of Braga, Paio Mendes, to be his chaplain. His cousin
Alfonso vii had given Gelmírez the right to appoint the staff of
his chancery, and Afonso Henriques was to grant a modified
form of the same privilege to Braga. Thus the two powers,
secular and ecclesiastical, were drawn together in defence of
Portuguese independence. By July 1128 Afonso Henriques was
recognized in Bragança. On 24 July Teresa and Fernando Peres
approached Braga and fought the young count's supporters at
São Mamede, near Guimarãis. They were defeated, captured and
expelled to Galicia. All Portugal, including the southern county
of Coimbra, adhered to Afonso Henriques.

More than a decade elapsed before he assumed the title of
king. He sent no homage to his cousin Alfonso vii, and when in
1130 the Emperor bade the other rulers of the Peninsula to a
great assembly in Leon, he was conspicuously absent. The Emperor appeared on the southern frontier of Galicia to force
Afonso Henriques to accept a pact of homage which was to be
ratified by one hundred and fifty of the count's vassals. But these
bickerings were a luxury which Christian princes could afford
only in time of peace. The Emperor might be reluctant to make
concessions to his cousin, but he could not ignore the responsibility of the ruler of Portugal for the defence of the southern
frontier.

The Almoravids had been driven off from Coimbra, and in
1128 the Templars were installed at Soure to guard access to it.
The Christians attempted to advance to Leiria, but this outpost
was sacked in 1137 and 1140. Then a crisis in Africa opened the
way for fresh advances. The Almoravids were challenged by a
new reformist movement, that of the Almohads, or 'uniters',
inspired by the mystic ibn Tumart. In the face of the threat the
Almoravid ruler recalled his son from Spain in 1138. In the
following year Afonso Henriques won a victory over the Muslims of Santarém, and probably collected tribute from at least

part of the old taifa of Badajoz. This was the legendary battle of Ourique, perhaps fought at Chão de Ourique near Santarém. Afonso Henriques seemed to have brought back the great days of Alfonso VI when tribute had been laid on the Muslim taifas near and far. In 1139 or 1140 he ceased to style himself *comes* or *princeps*, but became '*rex Alphonsus*'. He was already sure of the support of his barons and his church. When the see of Coimbra fell vacant, Archbishop Paio Mendes promptly consecrated his archdeacon Bernard, and won the goodwill of Rome by admitting the Cluniac reformers, who founded the monastery of Santa Cruz in Coimbra, the first Portuguese house 'of the protection of St Peter', subordinated directly to the Holy See. Afonso Henriques endowed it generously and heeded the advice of its priors. The arrangement was concluded by a priest named John Peculiar. When in 1136 the bishop of Oporto, Gelmírez's nominee, died, John was appointed in his place. Two years later John Peculiar became archbishop of Braga: his reign lasted thirty-seven years and he proved the staunchest of the king's collaborators.

Afonso Henriques took five of his chancellors from the see of Braga. However, few of his scribes or other officials came from the archdiocese. He dwelt little in his father's town of Guimarãis, and established his court at Coimbra, drawing on Santa Cruz for the staff of his scriptorium. Coimbra was both a Roman city and a fortress a day's ride from the frontier. The charter conferred on it in 1111 shows a military society. Its habitants were *maiores* or *minores*; the former, being knights or *milites*, paid no tribute. If a *miles* married a tribute-payer, her property was exempted. If a tribute-payer became qualified to be a knight by owning a horse and property, he obtained the privileges of a knight (*morem militum*). When a *miles* became too old to fight, he retained his honour for the rest of his life: on his death, his widow kept his rank. No one might marry her or her daughter against their will. If a *miles* lost his horse and could not afford another, the count would buy him one: in any case he kept his rank until he could get one. The clergy of Coimbra had the privileges of knights. None of the lower nobility (*infanção*) might have a dwelling in Coimbra unless he agreed to serve with the *milites*. When the inhabitants made a raid against the Muslims, they paid the count one-fifth of the booty, no more. The inhabitants were self-governing through their *consilium*. The governor and judge must be natives of the city. The count's *sagio* was not to place his seal on houses: if anyone did anything illicit, he was to be taken before the council and judged.

The charter of Guimarãis makes no reference to an autonomous council: presumably the count had traditionally done justice in his burgh. But in the frontier capital the *milites* managed their own affairs. This class was open to all who could afford knightly standing. The *minores*, or tribute-paying class, included merchants, artisans, Jews and Muslims, captive or free: most were perhaps farmers or labourers who dwelt within the walls, but devoted themselves to tilling the neighbouring fields.

The majority of the Portuguese population—even the residents of the capitals—was essentially agrarian. The wealthiest nobles, the magnates or *ricos-homens*, controlled large areas. The king delegated the administration and jurisdiction of territories to them. The county of Portugal itself had been such a territory. Now there were many, especially between the Douro and Mondego: surviving documents of the twelfth century mention some thirty-seven, greatly varying in extent. The nobles also owned large estates. Since the organization of the Portuguese territory, *presores* had seized vacant stretches of land or *villae*. This process still existed, but in the twelfth century the count or king usually assumed control of newly annexed land and granted it to his followers. In addition, churches and monasteries received extensive grants of land from the king, or as donations from pious and wealthy magnates, or increased their domains by purchase. The king conferred a special status on these lands, issuing a privilege which defined their limits and made them *coutos* (from *cavere*), from which the officials of nobles and even of the crown were excluded.

It was also usual to grant charters to groups of settlers who formed more or less self-governing communities. Teresa had conferred such a *foral* on the inhabitants of Zalatane (Sátão) in 1111. They were tribute-payers, and paid the most general levy, that of the yoke or *jugada*: each man with a yoke of oxen paid two *modii* or measures, a third in wheat and two-thirds in a second crop, together with a sixth of the wine, flax and beans he produced: men who ploughed with only one ox paid one measure. The settlers included horsemen (*caballerios*), the *cavaleiros-vilãos* or villein-knights. These, if their horse died, kept their rank for three years so that they might find another— an indication of the high cost of horses. If they died, their widow and sons kept their rank. Others, the *pedones*, who served on foot, could dispose of their property at their will with no seigniorial restraints. This document is subscribed by the countess and by seven of the magnates who are described as holding (*continens*) the territories of Lamego, Anaia, Penafiel, Brião, Santa Cruz, S. Martim and S. Cristóvão.

This charter illustrates the existence of two classes of free but tax-paying cultivators, the villein-knights, who kept horses and were not usually expected to pay the *jugada*, and the peasant who occupied his dwelling (*casal*) with his family and tilled his plot of land. Those who owned a yoke of oxen paid a fixed quantity of their main crop. If they had more than one yoke, they paid only once; if only one ox, they paid half. The main crop is usually wheat, but the *jugada* is paid partly in this and partly in a secondary crop, which indicates the existence of biennial or triennial rotations. The quantities of wheat, wine or other produce were delivered to the local *mordomo*, who disposed of them according to the directions of the *mordomo-mór* in the comital or royal household.

But the customs of the territory of Portugal were by no means uniform. The north, the oldest part of the country, was also the most servile, in the sense that more of the humbler folk were attached to the land and burdened by seigniorial obligations. Some of these dated back to forms of serfdom that had existed in late Roman times or under the Suevic kings or to ancient practices on ecclesiastical lands. The southward expansion brought greater freedom (except for Muslim captives and slaves). The tendency was towards the payment of rent, either as a fixed sum or as a proportion of the product. But many surviving practices referred back to Roman precarious tenure or to Suevic personal serfdom. Among the former was *manaria*, *maninhadego*, by which the lord recovered the lands of a peasant who died without descent: the latter may include payments at the time of marriages (*gaiosa*) to compensate the lord when the peasant's sons set up house for themselves, or the *lutuosa* paid by the tenant family when its head died, a vestige of the right lords had once had to inherit all their serfs' possessions. Personal services existed in many forms, but were much commoner in the north than in the south: they included transport with carts, taking messages, repairs, domestic tasks, the obligation to go hunting with the lord or to fish for him. The commonest obligation was the provision of labour, the *jeira* or corvée, frequent between Minho and Douro, but less common in Trás-os-Montes and south of the Douro. It was usual on monastic land, where the tenant was required to dig or to dress vines. It seldom exceeded one day a week, the equivalent of a tax of one-sixth. But the movement of population to the south contributed to liberalize these practices. It was now usual for the lord to occupy his own part of his estate (the *quinta* and the harvest-fields, *searas*), claiming only such services as were needed to work it. The rest of the land was let out to the occupants of the *casais*.

Until the reign of Alfonso vi no coin had been minted in the Christian north: monetary transactions, when they occurred, were carried out with Roman or Frankish coins, though the usual means of exchange was the *modius* of wheat or its equivalent, the sheep. With the collapse of Córdoba and the opportunity to lay tribute on the Muslim *taifas*, great changes had occurred. Ferdinand i had used Sisenand of Coimbra to negotiate with the Muslim counts, and Alfonso vi sent leaders such as the Cid to exact payment. It had been in part Alfonso's cupidity that drove the Muslims to appeal to the Almoravids. These last had Islamized the Negro peoples beyond the Sahara, whence they obtained gold and produced the fine coins known as *morabitinos*. But their defence of Muslim Spain began to falter after 1130, and the Peninsular Muslims again had to pay tribute to the Christians. From this time, the *morabitinos* became the usual means of payment in Portugal. Thus the documents that have survived from Guimarãis, many of them deeds of sale, are at first sometimes expressed in *modii* of wheat or lengths of linen, but this practice quickly disappears and all values are given in *morabitinos*. In a few early documents Afonso Henriques made grants in return for wheat or cloth; but once the Muslims of Santarém began to pay tribute, he disposed of ample gold. It was because of this that he was able to make himself king: the actual conquest of Santarém and Lisbon and the expansion of Portugal to the Tagus came later.

Coimbra had been defended by a screen of castles to its south, but attempts to occupy Leiria met with stiff Muslim opposition: during the struggles much of the countryside was probably abandoned, leaving a void. Once Afonso Henriques had extracted tribute from Santarém, he turned his attention to Lisbon. He used the services of some English and other crusaders who chanced to appear in Portuguese waters. The campaign led to a settlement under which he probably received tribute, to the disappointment of the English adventurers, who hoped for booty (1142–3). In the spring of 1147 he denounced the treaty with Santarém and sent forward an expedition which took it by surprise. Some weeks later a large expedition of crusaders from England, the Low Countries, France and Germany put in at the Douro, and the bishop of Oporto persuaded them to join in a new assault on Lisbon. Afonso Henriques and his army met them outside the city. The siege is fully described by an English crusader. Lisbon surrendered in October 1147, and Sintra at once capitulated. Thus Afonso Henriques regained the places entrusted to Raimund and Henry of Burgundy, and Portuguese territory was carried to the Tagus and beyond. Almada and Palmela were abandoned by the Muslims, whose frontier fortresses now became al-Qaṣr Abi Dānis (Alcácer do Sal) and Évora. As the declining Almoravid empire capitulated to the new power of the Almohads in North Africa, the Peninsular Muslims were again left to fend for themselves. The leading family of the frontier was that of ibn Wazir of Évora, who was disposed to pay tribute. But in 1143 a mystic named ibn Qasi of Silves began a religious revival at Mértola, and his supporters succeeded in annexing Beja and Évora. He was deposed by ibn Wazir, but fled to Africa, where he appealed to the Almohads to defend the Peninsular Muslims. Thus in 1146 the new masters of Africa intervened, and sent a detachment of troops to instal ibn Qasi as governor of the Algarve. They occupied Silves and Mértola, and ibn Wazir was obliged to submit to them with Beja and Badajoz. At this point the Almohads were distracted further east by Alfonso VII's advance into Murcia. Thus the Portuguese frontier, which had formerly been at the level of Leiria, moved down to the thinly populated *charnecas* or heaths of the Alentejo. The fields of Beja and Évora remained in Muslim hands.

Afonso Henriques' expansion embraced the western or Atlantic half of Portuguese territory. The eastern or landward frontier lagged behind. This was partly because Trás-os-Montes and eastern Beira were very thinly populated, and partly because the collapse of the *taifa* of Badajoz had disorganized the whole region. The Christian advances there were made by adventurers. After the death of the Emperor Alfonso VII, his son, Ferdinand II of Leon, founded the town of Ciudad Rodrigo (1160) to control these lands, and he laid claim to the tribute of Badajoz. In the previous year Afonso Henriques had obtained the submission of Évora and Badajoz, but he had held Badajoz only two months. Two years later the Almohads retook Évora. In 1166 a Portuguese frontiersman, Geraldo Sem Pavor, entered Évora by surprise, and a flock of adventurers rallied to him. He then occupied Cáceres and Montánchez, as well as Serpa and Juromenha. In the full flush of success, he laid siege to Badajoz and appealed to Afonso Henriques for help. Afonso Henriques came to him, but the people of Badajoz claimed the protection of Ferdinand II, who also arrived. Afonso was unhorsed and broke a leg, and was captured by Ferdinand. He then recognized the Leonese claim to Badajoz and was released, but the injury ended his military career.

The Almohads returned to the west in 1171. They now removed ibn Wazir from Beja, and his and other wealthy Muslim families who had been prepared to submit to the Christians withdrew to Seville. Afonso Henriques then made a truce for five years (1172–7). In 1179 the Almohads restored the fortifications of Beja, sending teams of labourers from Silves to rebuild the keep and walls: it seems likely that the normal population of the place had dwindled and was insufficient to sustain the work.

The continuity of the Portuguese monarchy was now assured by the Papacy. Afonso Henriques had married Mafalda, daughter of the count of Savoy, and had a son, Sancho, and two daughters, named Urraca and Teresa (like those of his grandfather, the Emperor Alfonso VI). Sancho was armed knight at Coimbra in 1170, and received his own household and command. In 1179 the Papacy finally recognized Afonso's title as king, and in return for this Afonso promised to pay an annual tribute of two marks of gold—four times as much as before. There was thus no question of Sancho's rights: indeed, the English chroniclers thought that he was already king, adding that Afonso still survived, though very old. He died in 1185, and was buried with

Mafalda at Santa Cruz in Coimbra, the Papal monastery on which he had bestowed such generous donations, and where a considerable part of his treasure was stored.

Coimbra had now supplanted Guimarãis as the usual seat of the count and the royal family, the holders of the principal offices, and certain of the *ricos-homens*, prelates and priors. The highest office, that of *mordomo-mór*, was held successively by Ermígio Moniz, Egas Moniz, Fernando Petres de Castro and Gonçalo Mendes de Sousa, each apparently appointed for life. Egas Moniz was Afonso Henriques' tutor and held a great territory, the *honra* of Rèsende, on both banks of the Douro. Gonçalo Mendes de Sousa was a baron from the Minho who became *tenens* of Estremadura (comprising a great part of the new conquests), his son being governor of Lisbon. No doubt many other northern families acquired great possessions and influence in the drive to the south.

The office of chancellor or notary, almost sporadic under Count Henry, was now of great importance. It was long exercised by Magister Albertus (1142–1169), a member of the monastery of Santa Cruz and archdeacon of the cathedral of Coimbra: his successor, Pedro Feijão (1169–1181) was a canon of Braga. In both these offices the executive work was now done by subordinates, members of the *palatium* and *scriptorium*.

The third of the high offices was the headship of the armed forces, called *alferes* or *signifer*. It was held by Lourenço Viegas, Fernando Peres Cativo, Mendo de Bragança (briefly in 1147; he left for Leon, where he held the same office), Pedro Pais (who commanded for 22 years and was also governor of Lisbon), and finally Pedro Afonso, a bastard of the king.

Within the *palatium* others served for many years, but did not attain the highest offices. During the long tenure of Egas Moniz, the duties of the *mordomo-mór* were often performed by the *comes* Rodrigo Peres and sometimes by another *comes,* Mendo Afonso. When the king's son was given his household, there were two *mordomo-móres* and two *alferes* (1169–71). Vasco Sanches, the son of the king's nephew, appears as *mordomo* to both king and prince, but passed to Sancho in 1172. By 1179 Sancho was in effect regent.

Some prominent figures at court owned estates or governed castles in the vicinity of Coimbra, but as the frontier shifted southward, professional military organizations defended it. The Templars had been entrusted with the defence of Soure since 1128, and they were prominent in the conquest of Santarém. They were granted the revenues of the churches of Leiria and later those of Santarém. When the see of Lisbon was restored, it claimed jurisdiction over Santarém, and the Templars were compensated by a grant of land at Tomar, where their Master, Gualdim Pais, built their headquarters. In Spain new military orders were created for the defence of the frontier, those of Santiago, Alcântara and Calatrava. These bodies were soon introduced into Portuguese territory, the Order of Santiago undertaking the defence of Lisbon from its headquarters at Palmela. Most of the Alentejo, the middle course of the Tagus and Beira Baixa was defended and colonized by one or other of the Orders, which thus dominated great tracts of land in this region.

The problem of repopulating the new conquests was a pressing one. Barons from north of the Douro and their retainers sufficed to hold Coimbra and its region. But beyond Leiria the country was virtually depopulated. A large grant of land was made to the Cistercian monks who built the great abbey of Alcobaça and gradually made a new landscape and a new economy there. In addition to this intensively cultivated region, Alcobaça acquired considerable territories beyond the Tagus, where its granges accumulated stocks of wheat. Its territories came to cover 40,000 hectares.

In eastern Portugal the problem of resettlement was more difficult. Trás-os-Montes was itself thinly populated. It was isolated from the Minho by the mass of the Marão. Its soil was poor, and its people, thrown on their own resources, had developed a system of agriculture based on open fields, long fallows and grazing. Their society was marked by political autonomy, social equality and a preference for communal exploitation. Its natural zone of expansion, Beira Baixa and the Alentejo, was also thinly populated, but the needs of defence demanded a society subordinated to powerful authorities, whether individuals or the military Orders. The result was a region of great estates, cultivated from large villages and preserving the communal practices and combination of cereals and cattle found in the north-east.

The creation of large estates for common defence did not necessarily lead to large-scale operations. The owners often pre-

ferred to lease their land to cultivators by emphyteusis, or copy-
hold, a method used by the nobles, the military orders and the
abbey of Alcobaça. It required no investment on the part of the
owner, but ensured the breaking in of uncultivated land and
encouraged intensified development.

Attempts were made to attract settlers from outside. After
the conquest of Lisbon, some of the foreign crusaders decided to
remain. The most prominent of these was an Englishman, Gilbert of Hastings, who became first bishop of the restored see.
He returned to England to preach the crusade and attract settlers,
but nothing is known of the measure of his success. Other
leaders of foreign contingents, William des Cornes and Allard,
were granted land at Atouguia and Vila Franca, where they
were permitted to govern themselves according to their own
customs. It is impossible to say what proportion of the former
population departed for Muslim territory, but many remained,
and in 1170 the 'free Moors' of Lisbon, Almada, Palmela and
Alcácer received a charter by which they were entitled to elect
their own governor and judge, and were protected from abuses
by Christians or Jews. They paid Afonso Henriques a tribute of
one *morabitino* a head, and cultivated the king's vineyards and
disposed of the figs and oil produced on royal lands. The crown
had seized considerable territories in the Lisbon area, and it was
anxious that Christian immigrants should not disturb the Muslim
cultivators from whom it derived its revenues.

Afonso Henriques' charter granted in 1154 to the settlers of
Sintra throws light on life in the new conquests. Most of the
Christian inhabitants lived in the castle: they would get first
choice if the king decided to permit dwellings in the suburb
(*arravalde*). They had thirty houses in Lisbon to provide them
with income, and were required to give military service in the
event of attack as far as Lisbon but not beyond, unless called by
an *apelido*. They kept all the booty they took. They comprised
milites and *pedites*. A *miles* who lost his horse kept his rank for
five years, and *pedes* who had a horse became a *miles*. The widow
of a *miles* kept his rank. If he left several sons and one qualified
for his rank, then all did. The *milites* and *pedites* of Sintra were
equal to any *milites* or *pedites* in the land. They might not be required to work on the royal lands. They served under the
governor (*alcaide*), who rewarded them with a good gift. Their

clergy, judge and *sagio* were drawn from the inhabitants. The clergy could not be removed unless for a crime. The people of Sintra were judged by their *iudex* and council, the judge taking a quarter of the fines paid and the *sagio* a tenth of his share. Fines were prescribed for crimes of violence, homicide, rape, breaking down of houses, aggression with sword or spear: the crown took half of these monies.

Such were the benefits for those who threw themselves into the conquest. But it was the king's function to confer or renew charters on communities throughout Portugal. For Herculano, the apostle of Portuguese liberalism, the great merit of these *forais* lay in the gradual emergence of electoral institutions, and he arranged the *forais* in groups—rudimentary, incomplete and perfect—according to whether councils were present or not. He also supposed that these councils could be traced back to the Roman *municipia*. It now seems rather that the attachment of the rural population to the land had its origins in the estates, laic or ecclesiastic, of late Roman times, in which the Germanic landowners had acquiesced, and that free institutions resulted from the survival of pockets of Germanic or tribal tradition which extended their influence during the long struggle against the Muslims. The Roman *municipium* died before the Muslim conquest, and the code of Recceswinth provides for no popular councils, though this does not prove that they did not exist. Recceswinth's code survived as a kind of constitution for the Christian states. But in the Castilian area in particular it was subordinated to customary law: with the succession of the Navarro-Castilian dynasty formal consent was given to local councils. One of the earliest Castilian charters, that of Castrogeriz (i.e. Castrum Sigerici) dated 974, admits the right of the inhabitants to band together against exactions or abuses. Ferdinand I sanctioned such privileges in Portuguese territory, and Alfonso VI and Henry and Teresa renewed or extended them. Thus while the tenth century produced a territory administered by a count and divided into *villae* held by lords or monasteries, the eleventh saw the magnates holding, not single *villae*, but large *territórios*, on or among which free societies existed, and the twelfth witnessed the elevation of the count to kingship and the winning of large but thinly populated new territories which he might grant to barons to administer, but to which he was obliged to attract settlers by the concession of extensive privileges. These privileges often claimed to be the equal of the best prevailing, but they did not always provide for representative institutions. About forty *forais* of Afonso Henriques have survived. He renewed the privileges his parents had granted to Guimarãis (1126), confirmed those of Ansiães, first given by Ferdinand I (1137–1139), and confirmed charters for Seia (1130), Penela (1137), Germanelo (1142–4) and Leiria (1142), all castles defending Coimbra. In 1157 he conferred the privileges already granted by the rulers of Leon to Salamanca on places in eastern Beira, Trancoso, Marialva, Aguiar, Celorico and Moreira do Rei. Similarly the charter given to Avila was the model for that of Évora (1166), itself imitated for Abrantes (1179), Coruche (1182) and Palmela (1189). His most important charters were the new *foral* of Coimbra (1179) and those of Santarém and Lisbon of the same year, which was also that in which the Papacy recognized his monarchy.

The *foral* of Coimbra is directed especially to the class of *milites*. The king might appoint one of his nobles to be governor (*pretor*) of the city, but the governorship of the castle (*alcaidaria*) should only be granted to a man of Coimbra. The rank of *milites* in Coimbra is extended to nobles, members of the Military Orders, priors of monasteries and other clergy. The commander (*alcaide*) of the ships in Coimbra and five of his men are also *milites*. The *milites* of Coimbra testify in court in the fashion of the *infanções*, the second rank of nobility, elsewhere. Their houses are not entered by royal officials without a written warrant of the *pretor*. On campaign they obey only the royal call. If more than sixty *milites* go out, the king shares the booty among them. They are not to be given the rear to guard. Crossbowmen have the rank of *milites*.

Coimbra had its council, but the charter says little of its operations. It and the *alcaide* appointed the inspector of the markets (called by the Arabic name of *almotacé*). Shops, ovens and potters' stalls were free. Smiths, shoemakers and furriers paid nothing if they had a house, nor did householders who kept a Muslim shoemaker or furrier. But smiths or shoemakers who were not householders must pay dues. There were tolls on some articles, including bringing in fish. There were also sales taxes:

a *morabitino* on a horse worth ten, on a mare or ox 2 *solidi*, on a cow or ass 1*s.*; on a pig or sheep 2 *denarii*; on a goat 1*d.* On the sale of a Moor, half a *morabitino* was paid. There were also taxes on skins dyed red or white, on cloth, linen and wooden vessels. Many of the inhabitants owned land outside the town or worked the land of others. The *cavaleiros* paid no *jugada*, but others who owned a yoke of oxen paid a *modius* of wheat or millet. Partners of *cavaleiros* with no yoke of their own paid nothing. Men who had no ox but hoed their own plots (*cavão*, 'delver') paid a bag of wheat or millet. Wine from outside paid a tax, and the king reserved the right to sell his first: those who broke his priority paid a fine of 5 *solidi* for the first two offences; on the third, their vats were broken.

There were stiff penalties for violence, homicide, rape or armed violation of domicile. Outside the city-limits, the *cautum*, the penalties were less. On lands belonging to the inhabitants of Coimbra fines were paid for homicide, rape and theft, half going to the king and half to the lord. Articles found were taken to the *maiordomus* of the city, who had the crier announce them once a month for three months: if unclaimed, he kept them.

In Afonso's capital the buildings of the royal palace stood on top of the hill on ground now occupied by the University. The cathedral, the Sé Velha, survives with little alteration. Between the walls and the river lay the quarter of the Jews, the *vicus judaeorum*, with its fountain and cemetery: here the monastery of Santa Cruz was built. There were several other monasteries and churches in which the *ricos-homens* and their followers lodged when they came to court.

The war against the Muslims had greatly enriched the king and his nobles and *milites*. Afonso's descendant Dinis noted in 1306 that 'D. Afonso, the first king of Portugal, who took Santarém and Lisbon . . . took them expressly for himself, as he took all the other royal lands (*reguengos*) and everything else . . .' In 1179 Afonso drew up a testament disposing of 22,000 *morabitinos* kept at Santa Cruz. He left 500 *m.* to each of the dioceses, Braga, Oporto, Lamego, Viseu, Coimbra, Lisbon and Évora, and to the abbey of Alcobaça, as well as alms for the poor. He gave 1,000 Almoravid and 1,000 Almohad *morabitinos* to Santa Cruz, with his Muslim captives and his horses and mules. He set aside 3,210 *m.* for 'the monasteries to which I am accustomed to give' and 3,000 for St John at Tarouca. He also remembered the Hospitallers and gave the Master of Évora 10,000 m. for the defence of the city. The process of expansion and accumulation was continued, with interruptions, during the reign of Sancho I (1185-1211). The Almohads who had taken over the defence of the Muslim part of the Peninsula reached the peak of their power with the victory of Alarcos over the king of Castile in 1195, and went down in defeat at Las Navas in 1212. A decade later the Almohad dynasty was rent with internal strife, and Ferdinand III, reuniting Leon and Castile, was able to conquer Córdoba (1236) and Seville (1248). For the Portuguese, Sancho held Santarém during the Almohad offensive of 1184. In 1189 the Almohad ruler arrived in the Peninsula and began to prepare great armies. But in the same year a large party of Frisian and Danish crusaders put in at Galicia. Memories of Norse incursions of the ninth century were revived, and it was feared that they intended to steal the Apostle's head, and they were beaten off. But on reaching Lisbon they agreed to participate with the Portuguese fleet in an attack on Alvor, a new fort built to defend Silves. It was successful, and the crusaders went on their way to Palestine. They were soon followed by ships from Flanders and Germany which had also picked up English crusaders at Dartmouth. It was decided to organize an attack on Silves, and in July 1189 a force of thirty-six ships and 3,500 men sailed from the Tagus to the Algarve, landed at Portimão, and took Silves after a lengthy siege. The city, by far the largest in the Algarve, was said to have 20,000-30,000 inhabitants. Sancho wished to pay the crusaders 10,000 *morabitinos* in lieu of the booty they expected. He even doubled the offer, but the crusaders would not wait for the money to be brought from Évora and Coimbra, and the place was sacked.

The Muslims now again appealed to Africa, and the Almohads marched against Santarém, where Sancho was, and Tomar, with its garrison of Templars. Richard Lion-heart's fleet arrived in Lisbon at this time, and contributed a force to relieve Santarém, sending another shipload to reinforce Silves. The Almohads withdrew from Santarém, but in the following year they took Alcácer do Sal, razed Palmela and entered the Tagus. Silves fell, and of all the Portuguese conquests beyond the Tagus only Évora was left.

For Sancho it was necessary not only to do battle with the Muslims but to man the eastern frontier, where much of what is now eastern Beira was unoccupied. In 1199 he founded Guarda as the centre of a military district, to replace the ancient see of Egitania which had been destroyed. The knights of Évora settled Benavente in 1200, and the Templars held much of the land to the east of the Zêzere. To the west of this river an estate was made for Sancho's half-brother, Pedro Afonso, who established the *concelhos* of Arega (1201), Figueiró (1204) and Pedrógão (1206). The knights of Santiago held Palmela and Alcácer, now overrun. Throughout all this area the population was sparse. After the Muslim reconquest of Silves, one William, its former dean, went to Flanders and returned with a colony of Flemings who were placed between Santarém and Alenquer: their leader Raulino was still *pretor* of Azambuja in 1221. Sesimbra, also partly settled by 'Franks', received its *foral* in 1207, and the foreign colony at Lourinhã settled Pontevel.

There was now no longer any prospect of restoring the ancient Roman provinces, as the church had once intended. Mérida, the ancient capital of Lusitania, had sunk into insignificance, and Braga had annexed all the sees to Lisbon and Évora. By the middle of the twelfth century the rulers of the Peninsular states were planning the projection of their frontiers to the south. The church duly acquiesced in the drawing of new national frontiers, accepting the modifications to its dioceses that had become inevitable. It participated in the task of repopulation, and it sought to co-ordinate the defence of the frontier through its patronage of the Military Orders, which were, at least in theory, international institutions.

When Sancho I died in 1211, the crown enjoyed abundant resources, and the second king disposed of a fortune of nearly one million *morabitinos*. He himself had begun to strike money, and much of his wealth was in gold coin. To his heir, Afonso II, a youth of twenty-five, he bequeathed his kingdom with all its 'rents and granaries'. The bequest included 200,000 m. at Coimbra and 6,000 at Évora, cloths at Guimarãis, arms and horses. But Sancho was survived by seven children by Queen Dulce to each of whom he left 40,000 m. and a quantity of silver, as well as gifts to other relatives. He had also two illegitimate families, that of Maria Pais, to whom he had given Vila do Conde and other places, and that of Maria Aires, of Vila Nova and Colares: their three sons each received 8,000 m. and three daughters 7,000 m.

Little is known about the management of these considerable sums, or about the inauguration of the royal mint. The old royal household had been predominantly engaged in collecting and storing tributes and rents in kind. The change to a monetary economy is suggested by the first references to books of accounts 'de recabedo regni', dating from a regulation of the royal household of July 1216. Accounts were then issued in five copies, of which the fourth was for a register—such seems to be the sense of 'to him who has the fourth book of the royal revenue'. It is likely that these records were kept at Coimbra.*

The importance of the flood of Muslim gold in altering the traditional economy of northern Portugal is enhanced by the relatively low value of property. We have seen that under Afonso Henriques gold replaced wheat, cloth and sheep as a means of exchange. A series of documents from Guimarãis (1133–1255) suggests that rural property might be worth as little as one morabitino or as much as seventy. An estate at Tagilde was sold for forty-three in 1133, and a vineyard with its cottages fetched fifty in 1151. The estate of one D. Sesnando at Sande was worth $15\frac{1}{2}$ m. in 1202. In 1229 at Gonça, two fields and an apple-orchard were worth $3\frac{2}{3}$ m. The right to two-fifths of the water of a stream, the Nespereira, for irrigating an estate was worth $3\frac{1}{4}$ m. After 1200 a larger proportion of the documents refers to sales of property in Guimarãis itself, and there are indications both of the superior worth of town property and of rising values. In addition to its castle and monastery, the town had several streets, but the best residences were suburban estates known by the Arabic name of almunia. One of these was sold for 100 m. in 1215: it may have been the one 'under the castle' that fetched 18 m. in 1183. A house in the Rua Sapateira was sold in 1167 for 23 m., evidently a shoemaker's, since the deal was clinched with some shoes of godomeci. Two houses in the same

---

* Afonso Henriques rarely left Coimbra in his later years. All his documents that are marked with the place of issue are from Coimbra, except for visits to Lisbon (1160), Lafões (1169) and Leiria (1172).

street were worth 18 and 20 *m*. in 1201, though one sold for only 6 *m*. in 1211. An eighth share in the ovens of Guimarãis was worth 16 *m*. in 1215 and in 1247 two shops in the butchers' quarter were worth 150 *m*. The only larger, and the only really large, transaction was one involving the king, Afonso II, and the church, in which eight properties were transferred for 701 *m*. in 1211.

Afonso II celebrated at Coimbra a full meeting of the nobility and prelates who composed the royal *curia* and reached an accord with his subjects, which, if not a 'great charter', served as a sort of constitution. The crown, which had long granted privileges, began to make laws. It now acknowledged the priority of ecclesiastical law as lately elaborated by the Papacy. The clergy were to be amenable only to their bishops in criminal cases, though questions of property were dealt with by civil courts. All royal officials were bidden to protect churches and monasteries, and the clergy was exempted from *colheita*, *anúclowa* and other obligations. In return, a timid step was taken towards limiting the passage of land to the church. It would not in future purchase property unless to celebrate the king's birthday. As churches and monasteries gained most of their wealth by donations and individual members of the clergy were still free to buy and sell, this measure can have had little effect.

In secular matters, the crown undertook not to execute sentence of death until twenty days had elapsed after sentence. In cases of treason or perjury, the crown could not confiscate the possessions of the guilty party unless he had premeditated the murder of the king or a member of the royal family. The king could not force anyone to marry, since 'marriage should be free'. He constituted himself a court of appeal from the decisions of his nobles. An appellant against the sentence of a judge might have recourse to him, but if the judge's sentence were upheld, he must pay 10 *m*. if a knight or prelate, or 5 *m*. if a member of the lower clergy or a *pedes*. The king and his *ricoshomens* would not on their travels demand to be supplied with food at a third less than the proper price. All free men living on their own land might choose anyone as their lord or patron, but if they lived on another's land, he was their patron. All free men might sell or pledge their property, giving preference to their kinsfolk.

This first Portuguese code was probably the work of Master Julian, who had been Sancho's chief adviser and was now the mind behind the young ruler. In spite of it, the court was soon divided by the first of a series of bitter conflicts. It seems to have arisen when Afonso II (or Julian) insisted on appointing the governors of the castles bequeathed to his sisters. Of Afonso's brothers one, Pedro, went to Leon and urged its king Alfonso IX to intervene on his sisters' account: the other, Ferdinand, sought a career in France. Gonçalo Mendes de Sousa, son of Mendo Sousão, the leading figure in Estremadura, ceased to be *mordomo-mór* and took up the cause of the princesses. The two great offices of *mordomo* and *alferes* were bestowed on two brothers, Pedro and Martim Anes. The Leonese began an invasion. Finally Pope Innocent III appointed judges. Although Alfonso's grandfather had undertaken to pay tribute to Rome his father had never complied. But when Alfonso sent fifty-six gold marks (1213), representing the arrears for Sancho's reign, he received in return confirmation of his succession and of his contention that his father had no right to alienate the royal patrimony: his sisters were to receive only the usufruct of the disputed castles. The principle was thus accepted that the crown retained inherent rights when it made grants or donations.

In 1220 the crown instituted royal commissions of inquiry to investigate the ownership of land in the north. In this part of the country, the occupation was older than the nation. Much of the land had been appropriated by noble or ecclesiastical *presores*, whose families had extended their original holdings by various methods. The crown now claimed that they had usurped royal lands (*reguengos*). The commission interrogated the oldest 'good men' in each parish. Where the occupants could not prove possession, it recommended that land be opened to royal officials. The archbishop of Braga excommunicated the court and laid an interdict on the kingdom, but this did not prevent the commission from singling out its lands for special attention. The archbishop fled the country and his properties were seized. The Pope deprived Afonso of his patronage of the churches, ordered the bishop of Coimbra to leave the court and released the Portuguese from their allegiance. When the king fell ill and died (March 1223), the church refused to grant him funeral rites until the royal chancery capitulated. By June 1223 undertakings had been given that the *inquirições* would be revised and ecclesiastical law respected.

But the harmony between crown and church which had marked the twelfth century was lost, and the thirteenth was characterized by bitter struggles. The eldest of Afonso II's four children, Sancho II (1223–1246), succeeded as a boy of about eleven. His reign is obscure, but he seems neither to have asserted himself over his barons nor to have placated the church: he was finally deposed by the Papacy. In 1228 a papal legate, John of Abbeville, arrived at Coimbra to hold a council, but he did not achieve a permanent settlement. The family of Mendes de Sousa, prominent in Afonso Henriques' day, held power for a time, but were displaced by the *alferes* Martim Anes and the chancellor Master Vicente, who had served under Afonso II. The Pope consecrated a new archbishop of Braga, Godinho, who attempted to rally the bishops in defence of ecclesiastical privileges. His colleague of Oporto bitterly denounced the encroachments of the crown and the misdeeds of the king's uncle, Rodrigo Sanches, who was governing the north.

Sancho II passed under the influence of Martim Gil of Soverosa, son of Gil Vasques and Maria Aires, the mistress of Sancho I. In 1241 this favourite arranged his marriage to Mécia López de Haro. The prelates of Braga, Oporto and Lisbon were now in Rome seeking remedies against the court. In 1245 Pope Innocent IV took refuge in France, where he summoned the Council of Lyons. At it the marriage of Sancho II was denounced as uncanonical and steps were taken to enable his younger brother to supplant him. This prince, Afonso, had left Portugal to acquire by marriage the title of Count of Boulogne. The Papacy delivered a lengthy accusation against Sancho, and the bishops returned to Portugal to prepare for his removal. The pretender took an oath in Paris to restore good customs and punish crimes. He arrived in Lisbon in 1246, and at once received the support of the Military Orders, which owed allegiance to the Papacy. The city of Lisbon declared for him. He took the title of 'Defender and Visitor of the Kingdom for the Supreme Pontiff'. Sancho II remained in Coimbra, whence a brother of the archbishop carried off his wife. Although her brother and the prince of Castile, Alfonso (x), entered Portugal to help him, he left the country and died soon after in Toledo.

Many believed that the demonstration of papal supremacy in Portugal was principally intended to impress those European princes who were flouting it. Despite the Pope's enthusiastic commendation of the pretender, and the latter's oaths to protect the church in Portugal, the reign of Afonso III (1246–1279) did not secure the triumph of the ecclesiastical cause. He had little difficulty in taking over the reins of power. He now ruled the whole of Portugal, for during the crisis of the previous reign the reconquest of the Algarve had been begun by the efforts of the Military Orders. That of Santiago which held Alcácer do Sal had advanced on Aljustrel and Mértola under the command of Pero Pais Correia. Tavira and Cacela soon fell. In 1249 Afonso III occupied Faro. This followed the Castilian conquest of Seville in the previous year. A Muslim leader, ibn Mahfud, who had seized Niebla and Silves, made submission to Castile, thus casting doubt on the Portuguese claim to the Algarve. However, a truce was concluded, and Afonso III (whose wife, the Countess of Boulogne, still lived) married a daughter of Alfonso X, Beatriz Guillén: the sovereignty of the Algarve was restored to their son Dinis. Thus Portugal attained its modern limits by the middle of the thirteenth century.

In 1251 Afonso III called an assembly of the Portuguese barons and in February 1253 he celebrated a gathering of all three estates at Leiria, the first *cortes* at which the commoners were represented. This new institution, which served as the Portuguese parliament until the end of the seventeenth century, had its roots in Leon, where the commoners were first summoned in 1188. In each case, the cause was probably fiscal. The flow of Muslim tribute was now at an end. The crown, short of gold, called in the coin and debased it, deriving a substantial profit from the transaction. The confusion caused to daily life was deeply resented, and in Leon the summoning of the third estate was originally to agree a currency and a system of payments. The Portuguese cortes of 1253 also met in the wake of reports of a debasement, and Afonso agreed to cancel this in return for a special tribute, the *monetágio*. After seven years, *cortes* were summoned to Coimbra to discuss the content and value of new coin. Afonso then undertook not to 'break' the coin for the rest of his reign, receiving in compensation a new tax on income.

If Afonso III came to Portugal as the Pope's choice, he won

the support of much of the nobility, the clergy, the Military Orders and the *concelhos*, to whom he gave order after the anarchy of his brother's reign. But he also launched new *inquirições* (1258). The church reacted as before, and only one of the nine bishops, that of Lisbon, supported the king. In 1267 the archbishop and four bishops left their dioceses under an interdict and went to Rome. Afonso showed no haste in coming to terms. The ecclesiastical penalties were pronounced against him, including that of deposition. It was only when he fell ill that he promised obedience and received absolution before his death in 1279.

Thus his young son Dinis (1279–1325) was excommunicate when he began his reign. The fulminations of Rome now had little effect. He married Isabel of Aragon, the saintly queen—a Rainha Santa—in 1282, launched a new series of *inquirições* in 1284, celebrated *cortes* at Lisbon in 1285 and obtained approval for laws which forbade religious corporations to buy land and required that land newly bought be sold. Yet it was only in 1289 that a settlement with the church was reached. By then the concept of kingdoms as departments of a universal church had failed. Monarchs exercised autonomy. Even the Military Orders, which had been the outward evidence of universal power, were nationalized. Calatrava, founded in Castile, defended Évora in Portugal and was therefore first known as the Knights of Évora: Afonso II had given them Avis, and they were now renamed the Order of Avis. The Order of Santiago, which had played a prominent part in the reconquest of the Algarve, was given a separate Master in Portugal in 1288. When the Popes of Avignon suppressed the Templars, it was proposed to transfer their possessions to the Hospitallers; but Dinis wanted a specifically Portuguese Order, and in 1319 John XXII authorized the creation of the Order of Christ with its headquarters at Castro Marim near the mouth of the Guadiana. It received Tomar, Castelo Branco and other properties of the Templars: Dinis himself took over Pombal and Soure.

It was now too that a national culture may be said to have emerged. The language of the Portuguese closely resembled that of the Galicians. It was highly evolved from Latin in the twelfth century, but no convention existed for writing it down, and only snatches of the vernacular appear in Latin deeds. The

5. Trás-os-Montes: threshing rye
6. Beira Baixa: a street in Monsanto

primitive culture of Portugal and Leon was essentially Latin. There is no evidence of the revival of Germanic epics such as those which commemorate the legendary history of Castile and the feats of the Cid. Popular tales and songs have gone unrecorded, or at least unpreserved. The art of writing seems to have been almost confined to ecclesiastical purposes, legal documents and fragmentary annals: the ecclesiastical reform of the twelfth century is undoubtedly reflected in an improvement of written Latin. The earliest surviving literature in the vernacular is the courtly lyric—specifically poems attributed to Sancho I and addressed to his mistress Maria Ribeira. These songs show that the Portuguese of the court was written down at least by the opening of the thirteenth century. The Galaico-Portuguese language became the usual vehicle for lyric poetry not only in its own territory, but at the court of Castile, where Alfonso X composed his devotional poems, the *Cantigas de Santa Maria*, in it.

In prose, the general replacement of Latin by Portuguese occurred in the course of the thirteenth century. At court King Dinis ordered the translation of the legal works of his grandfather, Alfonso X of Castile, and of a historical chronicle of Spain, which was intended to be read by, or at least to, his nobles. The transition from Latin to Portuguese is clearly seen in the documents of Guimarãis of the same reign. The decline in the use of Latin may not have been entirely without influence in causing the Portuguese clergy to press for a Portuguese centre of learning. They addressed an appeal to the Pope, in 1288, and in August 1290 he authorized the creation of General Studies in Lisbon. They were transferred to Coimbra in 1310. Provision was made for the study of grammar, logic, law and medicine.

The main objects of the founder and his followers, the conquest of land and wealth and the overthrow of the Muslims, had been achieved with the complete subjection of the Algarve, and Portuguese society must now adjust itself to new times. The Algarve, once regarded as one of the most prosperous parts of the Peninsula, had been seriously depopulated and recovered only slowly from the conquest. The flow of tribute from the Muslims was at an end.

As the supply of gold dwindled, its place was taken by the northern medium of silver. Thus Afonso III calculated his revenues by the European system of *librae*, *solidi* and *denarii*, though

7. King John I, portrait in the Museu de Arte Antiga, Lisbon, formerly at Vienna

he continued to strike *morabitinos*. Dinis made *libras* of silver, though he still followed the practice of debasing the coin: silver was not produced in Portugal, and it could only be obtained by trade.

Shipping and fishing were well established in the ports and estuaries of northern Portugal. The geographer Idrisī, writing in Sicily, refers to the use made of the rivers for transport and to coastal communications. Even the Mondego was navigable as far as Coimbra. The organization of the crusades to the Holy Land brought large fleets of northerners into the Douro, and they were turned to account in the conquest of Lisbon and the Algarve. After the conquest of Lisbon, Afonso Henriques' own ships were able to raid the Muslims of Ceuta. Now Portuguese merchantmen from the ports between the Minho and the Douro sailed to the northern countries. They brought in metals and arms, as well as textiles, and they took out cargoes of oil, wine, hides, wax and honey. During the century after its conquest Lisbon was also drawn into the orbit of this northern trade.

For centuries the Muslims had controlled the Straits of Gibraltar, thus dividing the ports of the Mediterranean from those of the Christian north. The armed fleets of the crusaders had gone through on their way to Palestine; but until the Castilian reconquest of Seville in 1248, Christian merchant ships could not pass safely. Within a few years of that event the Genoese had strengthened their trading contingent in Seville and begun to frequent the northern ports of England, the Low Countries and France. The great port of Lisbon was thus opened to an important international traffic. Its own shipbuilding industry began to expand, probably accounting for Dinis' decision to plant the pine-forests of Leiria. By 1293 the Portuguese had a merchant-fleet of ships of over 100 tons, whose owners paid 20 *solidi* a vessel into a general fund, which permitted them to maintain a deposit of 100 marks of silver in Flanders.

The general penetration of commerce outside the ports is illustrated by the growth of fairs. It had long been the practice for rulers to establish fairs by charter, guaranteeing the safe passage of fairgoers and offering privileges to stimulate trade. But before 1250 only a handful of places had received such charters. Afonso III granted sixteen, and Dinis no fewer than forty-three. In two generations the practice of holding fairs spread the length and breadth of the country. They were particularly numerous in Trás-os-Montes and north-eastern Beira, where there were few towns of consequence and it was desired to stimulate settlement. In the more urban centre and south, they were much less numerous and often coincided with the existing cities. It would perhaps be erroneous to suppose that the fairs gave rise to any large new urban centres, or that any of them attained vast proportions: they indicate rather a general spread of commerce even in the most remote areas of the agrarian monarchy. The fairs themselves did not necessarily give rise to new classes, but they stimulated the growth of the towns and the development of craftsmen and merchants, who by the middle of the fourteenth century had acquired an important place in Portuguese society.

The main activity of the countryside was the production of cereals, wine and oil. Wheat was the noble cereal, and most royal and other dues were paid in it. It was also generally produced, the poorer grains on which the peasants lived tending to have a regional predominance, millet in the north, rye in the east and barley in the south. The accumulations of wheat in royal and other granaries were used to supply the towns, particularly Lisbon, and were exported. These transfers—not without opposition—gradually diminished the localism of the economy and assisted in the accretion of new resources. The *lei de almotaceria* of 1252–3 may be regarded as establishing a national economy: it proclaims the free sale of produce, and fixes the wages of agricultural workers and servants, usually part in money and part in food and clothing. Nevertheless, the change to a monetary economy was gradual: as late as the fifteenth century, the crown was still paying its grants (*tenças*) to the nobles largely in wheat and barley.

The military expansion of the twelfth century had greatly increased the numbers and influence of the nobility. The first rank of nobles, the *ricos-homens*, gave their protection to the lower levels, the *infanções* and *cavaleiros*. The crown had found it necessary to settle donations or grants on the *ricos-homens*, and in 1261 Afonso III required that they must come to court if summoned or given duties in the palace. Those with 5,000 *maravedis* should be accompanied by not more than five knights, those with 6,000 six knights, and those with 7,000 to 10,000 seven knights, who put up at their patron's lodging. If the king invited the *rico-homem* to dine, his company ate elsewhere. The lower nobility, the *infanções*, must not bring more than one knight and five beasts to court, and no *cavaleiro* might bring more than three beasts. But the wealthy nobles were few: many of those who claimed nobility—and were now often known by the term *fidalgo*, recently borrowed from the Castilian *hidalgo*— were rural gentry with slender resources. In Bragança in 1290, twenty-three *fidalgos* owned two and a half villages with two hundred houses. In 1311 Dinis forbade descendants of *fidalgos* to be smiths or shoemakers or tailors. However, most of the lesser nobles were owners of estates, which by virtue of their rank were free of tribute and not to be entered by the royal *mordomos* or other officials. The *inquirições* suggest that it was common for nobles to erect markers on royal land. They also gave out their offspring to be nursed by village-women, whose homes were thus ennobled (as *honras*), an abuse forbidden in 1290. It evidently continued, for in 1307 Dinis ordered all *honras* so created to be suppressed. In the north, which had been formed before the expansion, the estates were small, and nobles often owned scattered houses or fields from which they drew rents. It was common to find single houses or groups of houses, some belonging to the crown, others to nobles and yet others to the church. The northern countryside was dotted with these mixed settlements with here and there the fortified house (*torre*) of a nobleman or the buildings of monasteries. In the district of Braga, dominated by the church, there were no royal lands, while in that of Guimarãis royal lands (*reguengos*) predominated.

If the donations of the century of expansion were unevenly spread among the nobles, the other privileged class, the clergy, had also been requited on a very irregular scale. By 1320 the church comprised an archbishop and ten bishops, with a total income of 222,804 *libras*, an average of 20,254. There were also one hundred and two monasteries with a total income of 134,858 *libras*, an average of 1,322. The number of parish churches and chaplaincies was 2,478, with an income of 270,465 *libras*, an average of one hundred and nine. Thus the average bishop was as wealthy as fourteen monasteries or nearly two hundred parishes. The main reason for the accumulation of this wealth was a perhaps excessive devotion. Large donations were made to the institution which could intercede for salvation. In this sense the church was an insurance company, and a company with exemptions from secular taxation. However, donors often reserved such benefits as the right for themselves and their heirs to be lodged and fed in monasteries, which increased as their descendants multiplied, and might impoverish the institution they had sought to benefit. Within the church itself the lower clergy paid a third of their annual income to the higher, and the bishops and their retinues received food and lodgings on their visitations and collected a series of conventional dues: if a living were vacant, half its income went to the bishop. In extreme cases, the higher clergy used the parish priest to supervise the tilling of ecclesiastical land. Ecclesiastical control of urban population was apt to produce unrest. In particular, Teresa had granted the jurisdiction of the city of Oporto to its bishop, whose successors were constantly in conflict with the crown and the burghers. The crown founded the settlement of Vila Nova da Gaia on the south bank of the Douro to share in the revenues of the port. When the new mendicant orders entered Oporto, it was supposed that they would strengthen the church, but they sided with the populace. It was only under John I that the episcopal jurisdiction over the city was ended.

Among the remaining population, the conquest had given special advantages to the villein-knights (cavaleiros-vilãos) who tilled the land and possessed horses on which they went to war. In return for their services, they were in specific places granted the same legal standing as the minor nobility: they could also serve the greater nobles. But most of them formed an agricultural land-holding middle-class, sometimes described, perhaps loosely, as an 'agricultural bourgeoisie'. In return for maintaining a horse and arms—a horse alone now cost 25 to 50 *libras* —they were exempt from the general tribute of the *jugada*. They also enjoyed certain jurisdictional privileges, and they participated actively in the life of the *concelhos*. They were most numerous in the north, where some royal lands were inhabited solely by *cavaleiros-vilãos*, though this was exceptional. In Terra de Prado (1258) they numbered seventy in some twenty parishes. On the lands of the nobles and the church they were fewer. In Beira Baixa and the south, the Roman pattern of large estates prevailed and peasant labour was relatively scarce: here the Portuguese yeoman often lacked the resources to project himself. In the thirteenth and fourteenth centuries they were able to use paid labour on their own farms and to buy the land of peasants who paid them rent. Not only did they extend their own economic activities, but they were essentially the *homens-bons*, the 'good men', who governed the *concelhos*, and so managed local administrative and juridical activities. In this capacity, they went to *cortes* as representatives of the commoners, becoming thus the only part of the non-privileged population with means of political expression.

For the rest of the rural population the terms of existence were set by the proprietors of the land, the crown, nobles and church. Formal attachment to the land, usual in Roman, barbarian and early medieval times, had disappeared with the great expansion, though its influence persisted in many rural practices which inhibited freedom of movement and of employment. In places it was possible to fine the peasant who abandoned his cottage or land, and monasteries in particular might fine or dismiss peasants for failure to cultivate. Complex forms of compulsion were numerous. But some charters, notably those of the cities of Coimbra, Santarém and Lisbon, clearly express the right of the inhabitants to leave, taking their possessions with them. In the countryside, the delicate balance between freedom and security of tenure was expressed in leases for one, two or three lives, or in contracts based on the annual cycle of cultivation. Similarly the change from personal service to the payment of tributes or rent had also produced a multiplicity of conditions. Personal service still existed. The *jeira* or *corvée* consisted of digging, wine-dressing or other agricultural tasks, and varied from place to place: it seems to have remained rather common on ecclesiastical land.

But it was much more usual for the dependent classes to pay their tribute or rent in kind. These took the form of a fixed payment or a proportion of the yield, or a combination of both. In addition, the produce of non-ecclesiastical land paid tithes and first-fruits to the church. The most usual payment was the *jugada*, the Roman tribute in respect of the land tilled by a yoke of oxen: indeed, the word *jugadeiro* was applied in a broad sense to the tributary rural class.

King Dinis died in 1325, and was succeeded by his legitimate son Afonso IV. He also left six or seven illegitimate children, who included D. Pedro, Count of Barcelos, compiler of the *Livro das Linhagens*, one of the earliest monuments of Portuguese prose, and Afonso Sanches, whom he made *mordomo-mór*. Dinis was disposed to legitimize Afonso Sanches, and during the last years of the reign his heir rebelled in the north and seized Coimbra and Leiria. The saintly Queen Isabel intervened to make peace. On the succession of Afonso IV (1325–1357), Afonso Sanches left Portugal and set himself up on the Spanish side of the frontier, where he married the daughter of the lord of Albuquerque. Afonso IV had been married to a Castilian princess, and he married his heir Pedro to another, Constanza, daughter of the regent and writer, D. Juan Manuel: she reached Portugal in 1340. But Pedro fell in love with one of her ladies, the Galician Inês de Castro, who for a time was expelled and lived at Albuquerque. She then returned and lived with Pedro at Coimbra until Afonso IV, fearful of foreign influences over his son, gave his consent to her murder. The story of Inês de Castro, woven by Camões into the *Lusiads* and dramatized by the first Portuguese tragedist, António Ferreira, is one of the most famous national legends. It serves to emphasize the conflict between the ruler as an individual and as the symbol of the society at whose head he was placed. A generation later the personal drama of Pedro and Inês would be played out again and the survival of Portugal would indeed be at stake.

The ruler had ceased to be a military figure, as the founder had been. In 1340 a new dynasty in the Magrib, that of the Marinids, attempted to invade the Peninsula, and Afonso IV joined with Alfonso XI of Castile to defeat it in the battle of the Salado, fought near the scene of the first Muslim victory over the Goths. It was the last serious Muslim threat to Portugal, and the end of the long crusade of the Reconquest. The Military Orders, on which the defences of southern Portugal had been made to rest, lost their original reason for existing.

The kings of Portugal were now primarily givers of justice to their subjects. It had long been recognized that appeals from the jurisdiction of the nobles went to the palace, and the pressure of both church and commoners tended to limit the powers of the *ricos-homens* to military command and to the governorship of castles. The crown extended its authority by appointing functionaries to execute its own justice. By about 1268 Portugal was divided into five or six regions or *comarcas*, each under a royal official, the *meirinho*. In each town or district, the crown might appoint its own judge, the *corregedor*. In the time of Afonso IV, but perhaps owing to the influence of his son Pedro, codes of instructions or *regimentos* were drawn up for the *corregedores*. The *regimento* was to remain a prominent feature of Portuguese administration. It derives from St Thomas Aquinas, and in particular from the 'Regiment of Princes' of Egidio Colonna (1247–1316), a work cherished by John I and Duarte.

Similarly, the crown had control of the finances of the state. The old network of *mordomos* collected and stored payments in kind, especially in cereals and wine delivered to them by farmers and peasants. But in the south a parallel function was performed by an official known by the Arabic name of *almoxarife*. This word now came into general use and the whole country was divided into *almoxarifados*, each with its chief-collector, the *almoxarife-maior*, and his subordinate collectors in the *concelhos* or groups of parishes (*almoxarifes menores*).* The word is also applied to the collectors of special revenues and to the stewards of nobles or of the Orders. In some places similar functions were performed by *recenseadores* or other officials. In the south the practice of tax-farming was commoner, and when revenues were farmed to *rendeiros*, these collected the revenues and delivered the sum stipulated to the *almoxarife*. The accounts were submitted to the court, and at least as early as 1347 Afonso IV had a general record of receipts in the 'book of many places'. The keeping of these accounts was done with the aid of Jewish advisers: thus Dinis made the chief rabbi Judas administrator of his treasury: and Pedro employed Moisés Navarro as *almoxarife-mór*.

---

* The *comarcas* with their *almoxarifados* came to be divided as follows in the sixteenth century: (i) Entre-Douro-e-Minho (Ponte do Lima, Viana, Guimarãis, Oporto); (ii) Trás-os-Montes (Torre do Moncorvo, Vila Real, Miranda); (iii) Beira (Lamego, Viseu, Pinhel, Guarda, Coimbra, Aveiro, Leiria, Castelo Branco); (iv) Estremadura (Lisbon, Sintra, Alenquer, Santarém, Abrantes, Tomar); (v) Entre-Tejo-e-Guadiana (Setúbal, Évora, Elvas, Estremós, Portalegre, Beja, Ourique); (vi) Algarve.

For the reign of Pedro I (1357–1367) we have the first of the works of Fernão Lopes, whom Southey thought the 'greatest chronicler of any age or nation'. It gives a graphic account of the restless ruler's travels to do justice in all parts of his kingdom and leaves no doubt of the popularity of his summary procedures. His father, Afonso IV, had also been a peripatetic monarch, and documents show that in the period 1325–42 he was thirty-six times in Lisbon, twenty-four in Santarém and eighteen in Coimbra. This was the main circuit of the court. But Afonso also travelled to the Alentejo on nine occasions and visited Oporto on three. He only once reached the extreme north and south.

The opening of administrative lines of communication contributed to enhance the wealth and population of the towns, and Fernão Lopes gives a vivid picture of the activity of Lisbon, which now had substantial colonies of foreign merchants. Many were Italians—Genoese, Piacentines and Florentines—but there were also southern French, Flemings and English. The Portuguese merchants were also active, and in 1353 those of Lisbon and Oporto were organized in corporations and made a convention with Edward III of England in their own interests and apparently without the intervention of the Portuguese crown. Fernão Lopes tells us that when Pedro died and was succeeded by his son Ferdinand, he was the richest king yet to rule in Portugal, with 800,000 pieces of gold and 400,000 silver marks in the castle of Lisbon alone. The royal revenues reached 200,000 *dobras*; and the customs-dues of Lisbon alone were worth 35,000 or 40,000 a year. The chronicler thought that as many as four hundred and fifty trading ships might lie in the Tagus at once, and that they took out 12,000 tuns of wine in a year.

Fernão Lopes is writing in the following century, when Portugal had passed through a political and social ordeal which seemed to threaten her very existence: its effect was to debase the currency on an unprecedented scale, so that by contrast the reign of Pedro I must have appeared one of great prosperity. In fact, the tendency of the crown to take over the jurisdiction of the nobles had produced a concentration of resources in Lisbon and obliged the crown to recompense the nobles with a regular scale of pensions. At the beginning of the fourteenth century the revenues of the crown may have been a million *libras*. But probably at least a quarter and perhaps as much as half of this was absorbed in pensions for the nobles, who drew about as much again from their *honras*. As the coin was devalued, there must have been pressure on the crown to increase its subsidies or to supplement them. Under Ferdinand this was done by making donations of royal lands to the nobles, a process which may be traced back to the considerable rewards bestowed by Afonso IV on his favourite João de Alpoïm. The alienation of royal land on behalf of the nobles was unpopular, and goes far to explain the rift between the nobles and the rest of Portuguese society in 1385.

But this dissatisfaction was intensified for other reasons. The Black Death reached the Peninsula in 1348. It is usually supposed to have devastated the Portuguese countryside. But it was perhaps most serious in the towns, or where there were large concourses (as in the Spanish army investing Gibraltar in 1350, where King Alfonso XI died of it). Its effect was to raise wages and salaries in the towns and to bring about a migration of the rural population, which forsook the poorer countryside to acquire crafts and swell the throng of guildsfolk. By 1361 there were complaints of lack of labour on the land. The cortes of Évora urged that *corregedores* oblige young men to give service. In 1363 farmers complained that fidalgos, ladies and abbots took labourers from the land to Guimarãis, and the king ordered preference to be given to agricultural requirements. In 1364 Pedro ordered all *serviçais* in Santarém to be listed in a book, with their daily wage for the various tasks they performed and which no one was to exceed. Subsequently cortes repeatedly refer to the same subject, reflecting evidently the needs of the yeoman-farmer. For the rest of the century there are constant efforts to compel the rural population to work for wages.

The crisis of the fourteenth century was a political conflict with strong social and economic overtones. In Castile King Pedro was threatened by the rebellion of his bastard half-brother, Henry of Trastámara, who finally defeated and murdered him. The towns of Galicia, as well as Zamora and Ciudad Rodrigo, which had adhered to Pedro, now offered to recognize the young king of Portugal rather than submit to Henry, who entered Galicia, invaded Portugal and burned Braga. Ferdinand sent his favourite, Count João Afonso Telo, to seek an alliance in Aragon, but finally accepted the peace of Alcoutim with Castile

(1371). The favourite Telo then arranged for the king to marry his niece, Leonor Teles: her husband, unwilling for a divorce, was obliged to flee to Castile. The people of Lisbon protested against this unfortunate match, led by a tailor named Fernão Vasques, who later paid for his rashness with his life. But now Ferdinand made an alliance with John of Gaunt, who had married the daughter of Pedro and claimed the Castilian crown. Henry replied by invading Beira and reaching Viseu. He then turned southward and laid siege to Lisbon (February 1373), burning the Rua Nova and Jewry. Ferdinand was forced to accept a peace by which he renounced John of Gaunt, became the ally of Henry 11 and promised Castile ships for use against the English.

However, Ferdinand used the peace to rebuild the walls of Lisbon and Oporto and to train men. The building of ships was encouraged by free permits to cut timber in the royal forests, and the *lei das sesmarias* (1375) sought to promote agriculture, making the ownership of land contingent on cultivation and appointing two good men in every village to ensure that the soil was tilled and to make a register of unused land. All who had once worked on the land were required to return to it, and the poor and idle were ordered to leave the towns. Fernão Lopes notes that these measures were necessary because of the lack of wheat and barley and the high prices that prevailed.

On the death of the ferocious Henry 11 of Castile his son Juan proposed a marriage with the infant heiress of Portugal, Beatriz, the only child of Ferdinand and Leonor Teles. But Ferdinand at once began to revive the English alliance, and in May 1381 he declared war on Castile. The Earl of Cambridge and a small army arrived in the Tagus, but in 1382 when the Castilians again invaded, Ferdinand made peace, and promised to marry Beatriz to Juan 1 of Castile, now a widower. On Ferdinand's death Juan would thus become king of Portugal. Ferdinand died in October 1383, and Juan asked Leonor Teles to have him proclaimed. A group of nobles approached a son of Pedro 1, John, Master of the Order of Avis, urging him to remove Leonor's Galician favourite. The Master was persuaded by Álvaro Pais, a burgher of Lisbon. John stabbed the favourite, and Álvaro Pais roused the people of Lisbon on his behalf. Leonor fled, and he assumed the title of Defender and Governor of Kingdom.

John of Avis had relatively few supporters among the aristocracy, and of the prelates, only Braga rallied to him. His champion was Nun'Álvares Pereira, one of the many sons of the Prior of the Hospitallers, and a soldier of genius at the age of twenty-three. John's chancellor was a jurist, João das Regras, who had studied law in Italy. His strongest support came from the people of Lisbon, where he created a new body, the House of Twenty-four, to which each of the twelve major guilds elected two representatives. Its delegates, the *juiz do povo*, or judge of the people, and four deputies, were given the right to attend the council of Lisbon and to make representations to the crown. The *juiz do povo* continued to express the views of the citizens, especially of the guilds, until the nineteenth century.

The popular nature of the national revolution of 1383 is emphasized by Fernão Lopes, who quotes the words of Leonor Teles' brother: 'such a folly as two cobblers and two tailors have got up'. Followers of John of Avis, 'small folk, ill-armed and uncaptained, with their bellies in the sun', reduced the castles of Hispanophile nobles. But early in 1384 Castilian troops had begun to move on Lisbon: they besieged it until September, when an outbreak of pestilence forced them to withdraw.

In March 1385 cortes were held at Coimbra. Some favoured the case of the sons of Pedro I by Inês de Castro, who were supposed to have been legitimized. But João das Regras produced evidence that Rome had refused Pedro's request for legitimization, and advocated John of Avis, who was thus proclaimed king on 6 April 1385. He appointed Nun'Álvares his constable and confirmed the privileges of Lisbon. By June Juan I of Castile had prepared a full-scale invasion. John of Avis and Nun'-Álvares awaited them at Aljubarrota on 14 August, and the Castilians were completely defeated. The victory guaranteed the independence of Portugal for two centuries. John commemorated it by building the splendid church of Santa Maria da Vitória at Batalha, a few miles to the north of the scene of his triumph.

3

THE AGE OF THE DISCOVERIES

The House of Avis has always been regarded as instituting a new chapter in the history of Portugal, although its founder was the bastard son of Pedro I, the penultimate ruler of the 'Burgundian' house of Afonso Henriques. What was new was that he owed his rise, not to the principle of legitimacy, but to the support of the Portuguese nation, as expressed by the people of Lisbon and confirmed in the cortes of Coimbra. During the reconquest against the Muslims the Christian states had rarely seriously molested one another, but now the long series of Castilian invasions under Henry II and Juan I had shattered relations between Portugal and Castile. Even after Aljubarrota peace was not restored on the frontier: a generation passed before an understanding was reached. The new dynasty, which had been aided in its victory by a contingent of English archers, promptly renewed negotiations with England. The Anglo-Portuguese Alliance was inaugurated by the Treaty of Windsor of May 9, 1386, which laid down that 'there shall be between the two abovementioned kings now reigning, their heirs and successors, and between the subjects of both kingdoms an inviolable, eternal, solid, perpetual and true league of friendship, alliance and union', so that 'each of them shall have the obligation to assist and give aid to the other against all people now born or who shall come to be born, or who shall seek to violate the peace of others'. These undertakings, renewed in the seventeenth and nineteenth centuries, served to produce the most enduring alliance in western history. Although John of Gaunt's visit to Portugal in quest of the Castilian crown was unsuccessful, the alliance was sealed by the marriage of John I to his daughter, Philippa of Lancaster. Their children, the '*inclita geração*', were famous figures, and to one of them, Prince Henry, belongs the glory of the Discoveries. The new house gave Portugal a foreign policy and a national programme.

But the wars had been ruinous. Even under Ferdinand it had been necessary to devalue the currency and to seize supplies of wheat. Under John I the gold coinage disappeared completely and the silver mark, which had made 25 *libras* under Ferdinand, made 29,000, according to the chronicler. By 1386 tributes and debts were paid in old coin, or in new coin of five times its face value, and the ratio later grew to ten and fifteen times. During the long crisis from Aljubarrota to the conquest of Ceuta, the public revenues, including the custom-duties, probably dropped by as much as a third.

It had long been understood that the crown paid annual grants to the nobility in return for their supposed contribution to its defence. By 1350 all nobles and their *contias* were inscribed in a register at court: on the birth of a noble's son the king made provision for him. Many of the old nobles had sided with Castile and forfeited their estates and pensions, but both the wars and the long period of insecurity that followed forced John to raise and reward a new class of defenders. The leading figure of the new nobility was Nun'Álvares Pereira, whose daughter married John's bastard son and thus gave rise to the powerful house of Bragança. John himself laid hands on the masterships of the Military Orders to establish his sons. But he so compromised the resources of the crown with hereditary grants that his successor was forced to assert the right to revise the grants of previous reigns. This was King Duarte's *Lei mental*, or 'mental law', so called because it was supposed to have been John's intention, though he had not published it. By it all grants made by the crown were rendered inalienable and indivisible, and reverted to it in default of a legitimate male heir. This was the origin of the system of *morgados* or entailed estates which maintained the smaller nobility and gentry until its abolition in 1832 and 1863.

The influence of the clergy, the other traditionally privileged class, had also been rendered more national. Its secular arm, the Military Orders, passed under the control of the king. In the shadow of the Great Schism, the crown, not the church, decided which Pope to support, and the decision obeyed political interests. It was at this time that the crown began to exercise the right of beneplacet, that is, of authorizing the transmission and publication of papal letters. When John seized power, the bishop of Lisbon, a Castilian, was killed by the mob. The lower clergy supported the national cause.

The class that most benefited by the new regime was that of the merchants and artisans of the towns. The tailor Fernão Vasques had defied Leonor Teles: the cooper Penedo brought the people of Lisbon behind John of Avis. In return, the twelve major guilds were given their house and their elected judge. The first *cortes* of John I asked him to make guild examinations and the inheritance of crafts compulsory. The ceremony of admission was modelled on that of knighthood. A strong sense of hierarchy prevailed. The Portuguese guild-system was less developed than in the more industrialized north, but it was more coherent than in neighbouring Castile, where many of the crafts were still in the hands of Muslims.

Muslim quarters existed in the cities of southern Portugal— such as the *mouraria* of Lisbon—and they were still governed by their own officials, but they seem not to have predominated in the trades. There were also Jewries in many cities and towns of the south and centre, and Jews did participate strongly in some of the Lisbon guilds. Each Jewish community paid tribute on a collective assessment either to the crown or to the lord of the place. Probably the majority of the Jews exercised such callings as tailoring and shoemaking. Some were prominent as doctors or astrologers, and a handful of families had acquired wealth as tax-farmers, entering the royal service. The Portuguese Jews, hitherto not numerous, were probably increased by refugees after the persecutions of Seville and other Spanish cities from 1391.

The fourteenth century had seen the consolidation of the influence of the commoners as expressed in cortes, which dealt with crucial matters of national policy at Coimbra. The cortes of 1385 recognized four classes, clergy, nobles, clerks (*letrados*) and citizens. In time of crisis, at least, a permanent body was required, and John was requested to appoint a council of fourteen advisers: he chose one churchman, two nobles, three clerks and four citizens—in Castile the defeated King Juan was blamed for having taken national decisions upon himself and required to make a similar choice.

The court was now firmly established at Lisbon, and attended

by the renovated nobility, and the new class of clerks. The leading functionaries were the *vêdor* and *contadores* of the royal
treasury. They now directed a cluster of institutions in or near
the capital — the treasury itself, the custom-house, the mint, the
tolls, supplies for the court, deposits of arms and public works
in the capital. They received taxes and debts, paid ambassadors
going abroad, inspected the accounts of royal ships and shipyards,
and of hospitals and chapels and royal lands. Provincial accounts
were submitted to the *contadores*, who verified them and issued
alvarás or quittances. Procedures in the provinces were adjusted
to those of Lisbon, where an archive was assembled in the tower
known as the Torre do Tombo. As late as 1378 the *vêdor* controlled the records, but by 1403 the Tombo had its own guard.
In 1418 the chronicler Fernão Lopes was appointed to keep the
archive, whose papers he used in writing his histories of the
reigns of Pedro I, Ferdinand and John. Later the archive remained in the castle, while the *contadores* functioned in the
custom-house. John I maintained the traditional post of
mordomo-mór as head of his household and appointed two *vêdores*
to inspect the accounts. He also created the new post of
contador-mór (1404) within the royal household, whose staff
received the accounts of the *almoxarifes* of the provinces. With
the emergence of this royal service, the *contadores* of Lisbon
confined themselves mainly to local affairs, which evidently
constituted an important part of the whole.

Peace with Castile was made in 1411. The king of Castile was
now the infant Juan II, and his regent and uncle Ferdinand
wished to accept the vacant throne of Aragon. Thus relieved
from any threat from his neighbour, John I decided to embark
on the conquest of Ceuta in North Africa. The chroniclers emphasize the desire of a new generation to emulate the deeds of
their fathers. John had been obliged to keep his kingdom on a
war-footing for a generation, and he hoped by renewing the
ancient crusade to gain the sympathy and support of the Papacy
and of Europe. He may also have expected to tap the supply of
gold brought to Ceuta by merchants who crossed the Sahara to
the legendary diggings of the Negro south. He was further presented with a unique opportunity. The Muslim king of Granada,
Muhammad V, had made himself strong by dividing and controlling the Magrib, but after his death this power failed. The

8. Lisbon: the Castle of St George

9. Barcelos: 15th c. noble house, the Solar dos Pinheiros

Castilian regent Ferdinand gained his fame by wresting Antequera from the Granadines, and the Magrib fell into anarchy. The famous fleet of Ceuta was temporarily dispersed. Thus in 1415 John mounted an enterprise which conquered Ceuta in a day, and made it the first Portuguese fortress beyond the sea. But he did not bring about the fall of the Magrib or draw on the trade of the Sahara. On the contrary, Ceuta required to be manned with a force of about 2,500 and supplied with wheat and other foodstuffs. Its conquest gave a new stimulus to the society and economy of the Algarve, but it was not until twenty years later that trade with southern Morocco and beyond began to bring in gold.

It was soon followed by the discovery and occupation of islands in the Atlantic, the Madeira group, first visited by João Gonçalves Zarco and Tristão Vaz Teixeira in 1418, and the isles of the Azores, reached in 1427. Both groups had been uninhabited by man since the beginning of time. Accounts of Atlantic explorations from Lisbon in Muslim times are probably legendary, but after the opening of the Straits of Gibraltar to Christian shipping, the Italians reached the Canaries (1336–41), and henceforth maps show various islands in the Atlantic. A Genoese had been given the title of admiral of Castile, and a similar title was created in Portugal for an Italian, Emmanuele Pezzagno, in 1317. Thus the seamanship and nautical lore of the Mediterranean and Atlantic navigators were brought together at Lisbon.

Madeira was divided into two captaincies, which were bestowed on its explorers: the neighbouring Porto Santo group was granted to the Italian Perestrelo, whose daughter was to marry Columbus. The first colonists on Madeira cut the timber from which the island takes its name and planted wheat, which was soon exported to Lisbon. Shortly afterwards began the settlement of the nearer islands of the Azores, which also contributed to relieve the shortage of cereals endemic in the capital. The Portuguese claim to the Canaries was opposed by the Castilian crown, which asserted that it had already disposed of the group, thus giving rise to a lengthy dispute, finally settled in favour of Spain.

The sons of John of Avis and Philippa were notable patrons of learning, and particularly of applied knowledge, whether scientific or moral. The tradition of courtly amatory verse was in eclipse. If it survived it was under the moralizing influence of John Gower, whose *Confessio* was introduced by one of Philippa's followers. John I composed a treatise on hunting. His successor, Duarte (1433–1438), was the author of a philosophical treatise, the *Loyal Counsellor*. His second son, Pedro, afterwards regent, travelled the courts of Europe in search of experience and information, much of it geographical. The austere Henry, Master of the Order of Christ, was essentially a crusader intent on the conquest of Islam in Africa, but also the resolute organizer of explorations for new wealth and of the conquest of knowledge. The resources of his Order were thus turned to account—while in Castile the Orders fell into the hands of adventurers and were used as private armies. Henry had brought the Majorcan cartographer Cresques to Portugal as early as 1421, but it was only in 1434, the year after the death of John I, that his captain Gil Eanes passed Cape Bojador. Eanes's successors passed the land of the Moors, and reached that of the Negroes. In 1442 they brought back specimens of gold-dust. D. Pedro, now regent of Portugal, gave his brother a monopoly of trade with the newly discovered coasts, and Henry established himself near the promontory of Sagres, sending forth his ships from the port of Lagos. It seems likely that the trade of Africa was seen not simply as a substitute for the disappointing lack of commerce at Ceuta, but as a means of fortifying the economy of the Algarve which must support the Portuguese garrison of Ceuta. In 1437 Prince Henry attempted to annex Tangier: the cortes of Évora had opposed the plan, but King Duarte gave his consent. The expedition was a failure, and their younger brother, Ferdinand, was captured by the Muslims, dying in captivity. The conscience-stricken King Duarte died in 1438, and the crown passed to his six-year-old son, Afonso v (1438–1481).

The regency was exercised by John's second son, D. Pedro, who favoured Prince Henry's ambitions. The first European trading-post in West Africa was established at Arguim in 1438–9. It was let to private operators for a ten-year lease. Caravels—the new type of shipping that was now coming into general use among the Portuguese—brought in corn, cloth and horses, and took out gold and slaves; the latter, numbering seven hundred or eight hundred a year, were sold at Lagos and remedied the shortage of labour in southern Portugal. Meanwhile, by 1445, some eight hundred Portuguese had established four settlements in Madeira, and produced wheat, honey and wax. The sugar-cane was introduced and spread rapidly, bringing a considerable income to the Order of Christ and rendering what had formerly been a luxury an article of widespread, if not yet general, consumption. In the Azores, Portuguese settlers were supplemented by groups of Flemings and others: cattle and sheep multiplied on the island pastures, and provided Lisbon with meat, hides, wool and cheese.

The regent D. Pedro attempted to perpetuate his authority by marrying the young king to his daughter, Isabel. But although Nun'Álvares Pereira, the great Constable, who had launched the new dynasty, had retired from worldly life to die as a humble lay-brother in a Lisbon monastery, his heir, the Count of Barcelos, was not only the wealthiest nobleman in the land, but also the most ambitious. His son claimed that the title of Constable was hereditary in his family, but the regent bestowed it on his own son. The house of Barcelos was granted the mastership of Santiago, but remained dissatisfied. Even the title of Duke of Bragança was not enough. When Afonso v came of age, the duke won his favour, manoeuvred the regent into a rebellion and attacked and killed him at Alfarrobeira (1449).

For the rest of his reign, Afonso v could rarely resist the ambitions of the Braganças, or of other powerful nobles. The title of duke had been introduced for the princes by John of Avis: its only other holder was Bragança. The title of marquis, hitherto unknown, was created for his eldest son. The family also held three counties and the duke's brother was Afonso's chancellor. As if in emulation, D. Jorge da Costa, Cardinal of Alpedrinha, accumulated the three archbishoprics of Braga, Lisbon and Évora and the bishopric of Coimbra, and also bought out the Abbot of Alcobaça, the greatest monastery in the kingdom. The cortes of Lisbon of 1460 urged the king to rule with a firm hand and not to alienate his possessions, but in vain.

Nevertheless, from the middle of the century the enterprise of the overseas expansion began to take on a new importance. In these years, the advance of the Turks, culminating in the conquest of Constantinople and the final fall of the Byzantine empire in 1453, posed a new threat of Islam against Christendom. The Papacy again urged the need to crusade on the Christian princes, reviving the sale of bulls and indulgences. In 1455 the bull *Romanus Pontifex* referred to Prince Henry and his aspirations to circumnavigate Africa and make contact with the Indian Christians, and confirmed the monopoly exercised by the Portuguese: the document was publicly proclaimed in Lisbon. In the following year, another bull, *Inter Caetera*, expressly ratified the role of the Order of Christ in the enterprise. In 1454 the Portuguese crown contributed to Prince Henry's work with a massive subsidy of 16 *contos*: he also received loans from the House of Bragança, the abbey of Alcobaça and the Jews. The economy had already begun to benefit from the African trade, so that it was possible to restore the long-abandoned gold currency in 1435: in 1457 a new gold coin, significantly christened the *cruzado* or 'crusader', was introduced: it was maintained at its original fineness until 1536.

When Prince Henry died in 1460, his caravels had reached Sierra Leone, still short of the equator: he had just made over the spiritual dominion of the five newly discovered Cape Verde Islands to the Order of Christ and the temporal to the Portuguese crown. His work was carried on by his nephew D. Fernando and others. In 1469 Afonso v leased the trading monopoly of the Gulf of Guinea to a Lisbon merchant Fernão Gomes, on condition that he explore a hundred leagues of coast a year.

After the failure at Tangier, the Moroccan enterprise lapsed for twenty years. Only with the fall of Constantinople did the Papacy press for a renewal of the war against Islam, and in 1458 Afonso v crossed to Africa and captured al-Qaṣr as-Saghīr (Alcácer Seguir), which was garrisoned and held. In 1463 he made a new and unsuccessful attempt against Tangier; but in 1471 the Marinid dynasty having collapsed, he led a force against Arzila: it was taken, and the Muslims then abandoned Tangier. By virtue of his possession of this string of coastal fortresses in the Magrib, Afonso v became 'King of Portugal and of the Algarves on this side and beyond the sea in Africa'. When chroniclers called him 'the African' they alluded to these exploits, not to the voyages of discovery to the West Coast. In the closing years of his reign, he thought he discerned the opportunity to become king of Spain. Some Spaniards, dissatisfied with the accession of Ferdinand and Isabella, offered him their allegiance, and he occupied Zamora and Toro. The war ran against him, and he departed for

France to seek the help of Louis XI, entrusting his kingdom to his strong and competent son, John (II). Disappointed, he thought for a moment to abdicate and become a pilgrim, but he returned to Portugal to conclude a disadvantageous peace with Spain before dying in 1481.

His son, John II (1481–1495), lost no time in restoring the authority of the crown, exacting a new and rigorous oath of submission from the higher nobility. His first task was to abrogate his father's treaty with Castile by which his son would marry the eldest of the Castilian princesses and be educated in a mixed court at Moura near the frontier, almost as a hostage. Even as he negotiated, he prepared to arrest Bragança. He prepared an elaborate array of charges and condemned him to death after a trial lasting three weeks. Bragança was beheaded in Évora (June 1484). His brothers, the Marquis of Montemór and Count of Faro, fled to Castile. His brother-in-law, the Duke of Viseu, John stabbed with his own hand at a meeting at Alcácer. The power of Bragança, with its many titles, its fifty cities, towns and castles, and its private army, was temporarily broken. Royal judges were then appointed to territories from which they had hitherto been excluded by the jurisdiction of the great nobles. For writers of the next century, John II was the 'Perfect Prince'.

John II did little to multiply the garrisons his father had established in the Magrib, but like his grandfather, the regent D. Pedro, gave his support to the policy of exploration. In 1482 he ordered the construction of the fortified trading-post at Mina, built by Diogo de Azambuja as the chief factory for the gold-trade. The flow of gold entered Portugal by a special trading-house, the Casa da Mina, whose income rose in the same decade to 133,000 of the new *cruzados* a year, thus doubling the revenues of the crown. Also in 1482 Diogo Cão visited the mouth of the Congo river and sailed on down the coast of Angola. The king of the Congo proved friendly and desired to be converted and to adopt the laws and ways of the Portuguese. The arrival of missionaries and advisers launched the attempt to create an assimilated but independent negro monarchy in the heart of Africa. Long before, Abyssinians had reached Europe, and their country was confused with the legendary land of Prester John. Reports were now received at Benin of an African potentate far to the East. In 1487 John II sent Pero da Covilhã and Afonso de Paiva to Alexandria, whence Pero reached India and crossed to East Africa. At Cairo he met two Jews whom John had sent after him. He learned that Paiva had died, and himself reached Abyssinia, where he settled down and was found by the Portuguese embassy of D. Rodrigo de Lima in 1526.

Meanwhile, John had sent an expedition of two caravels, commanded by Bartolomeu Dias, to find how far south the continent of Africa extended. It passed the furthest point reached by Cão and continued beyond. For some weeks it was out of sight of land, but on February 3 it put in at Mossel Bay. Dias had rounded the Cape without having seen it, and having thus entered the Indian Ocean, he turned back, arriving in Lisbon in December 1488. It only remained to organize the expedition that should cross the Ocean to India itself. But this was to remain for John's successor.

In the century that had elapsed since Aljubarrota the royal household had become a complex organization. In 1478 Afonso v's income, the *fazenda d'El-Rei*, amounted to 43 *contos* or millions of *reis*. Of this his household consumed 13·8 *contos*. The eleven members of the royal council were modestly remunerated (4,276 *reis* to 8,572). A considerable part of the revenues provided the allowances (*moradias*) to the *fidalgos*. These were now classified as *cavaleiros-fidalgos* (numbering 107), *escudeiros-fidalgos* (38), and *moços-fidalgos* (51). Young nobles entered the court as *moços*, drawing 1,000 *reis* a month, in the hope of promotion to the other two classes. Senior *fidalgos* drew 3,900 *reis* a month. The king also maintained twenty-four attendants (*moços de câmara*), thirty-five grooms, twenty huntsmen and a bodyguard. In 1471 Prince John had married his cousin D. Leonor, and soon after received a household at Beja with thirty *fidalgos* of the first class, fifty *escudeiros* and fifteen *moços*, as well as twelve attendants, twelve grooms, twelve huntsmen and his bodyguard. In addition, the king gave considerable grants (*assentamentos*) to the great nobles, together with rewards for services and lavish gifts on weddings and other occasions. The prince was already Master of Santiago and Avis, the revenues of the former being reckoned at 865,198 *reis*, and those of the latter rather more. In 1470 the king gave him the revenues of the customs of Lisbon, worth 4 *contos*.

The number of nobles and servitors attached to the court does not appear to be very large—it greatly increased in the reign of King Manuel. But the sums distributed by the crown were vast in proportion to the low prices of land and the cost of everyday wares, and the concentration of economic power in the hands of the court and its adherents was great. Even the house of Bragança, which was organized on similar lines, if on a smaller scale, was thought able to maintain 3,000 horse and 10,000 foot. The concentration of resources heralds the situation of the sixteenth century, after the discovery of India, when there were in effect two economies, one related to the expansion and its commerce, and the other based on the relatively modest values of the land and its produce. In the absence of accurate demographic information, we may suppose some growth of the official and urban classes who shared in the advantages of the new situation, but a much larger growth of the rural poor who did not. Oliveira Martins thought the population of Portugal in the twelfth century no more than half a million, which now seems low: three centuries later it was probably more than a million but under a million and a half. In 1472 the cortes of Coimbra noted the need for more judges to deal with more suits owing to the increase of population. The north, the Minho and Trás-os-Montes was exempt from military service at Ceuta, and the male population paid a fee of 10 *reais* instead: the cortes of Évora of 1490 showed that the sum received in this way had grown from 300,000 to 500,000. In Santarém the production of wheat doubled in the second half of the fifteenth century: Cartaxo, which had been a hamlet of six hearths, had over ninety in 1458, when it sought its autonomy.

But there was now no question of the predominance of Lisbon. The city itself had been rewalled by Ferdinand, and possessed seventy-seven towers, with sixteen gates on the landward side and twenty-two towards the sea. However, the walled space contained unoccupied land and orchards. Even in 1527 there were only 13,000 householders, giving a population of some 52,000. The king dwelt in the Castle of St George, still known by the Arabic name of Alcáçova. Below it was the Cathedral, or Sé, and near that the council-house, the palace of the *concelho*. The bishop lived near the church of Santa Cruz. The Rossio was still a common for grazing cattle. The streets of the lower town were narrow. The chief of them was the Rua Nova d'el-Rei.

Most houses consisted of a ground floor, the *loja* or 'shop', and one storey above, though some had three storeys. It was common to build balconies to project over the streets, and some houses had gardens with orange-trees, vines and pools. There was only one drainage channel, and much dirt was left to rot. There were some twenty parish-churches and several large monasteries. The busiest part of the city was the port, the custom-house and the shipyards on the site of the present Terreiro do Paço. The Mouraria contained the largest single Muslim community left in Portugal. It had its *faqihs*, but they were a diminishing minority, for many former Muslims had intermarried with the Christian population.

The Portuguese wore leather jerkins or long cloaks, often black. When going abroad they would put on a white woollen wrap and a broad hat. They wore beards and long locks down to their shoulders. *Fidalgos* began to shave in the time of John II, who is said to have disliked the innovation. The women wore low-cut dresses and heavy skirts. Popplau, who was there in 1484, noted that the Portuguese did not like to take in guests for money, that they were moderate in eating and drinking, many living on bread and water, and that they were more loyal to one another and to their king than the English, 'except the nobles'. He thought them ignorant and 'presumptuous of being very wise, like the English who admit no world equal to theirs. . . . There are Portuguese who are witty, but I met none to compare with myself'.

The second city of Portugal was now Évora in the Alentejo, which by the end of the century had 4,500 hearths, giving a population of about 25,000. Duarte had built a palace there and his successors added to it. Although the Alentejo nearer the capital was often poor heath and thinly settled, its eastern sector was dotted with small towns, in which the nobles built palaces or country-houses in the *mudéjar* style. Beja, though small, was in the midst of a wheat-belt which made it the richest *almoxarifado* in the Alentejo : it was strongly walled. There were some two dozen other places with castles in the region, which was also famous for its horses. While Lisbon had tended to draw the nobility from the rest of the country, it was still possible for the nobles of the Alentejo to travel between their estates and the court. Another city favoured by the court and nobles was Santarém, which could be reached from Lisbon by barge. A favourite occupation of the court was hunting, which could be practised in the Alentejo, also accessible from Santarém. With the growth of Lisbon, Coimbra had stagnated. It was now dominated by its bishop, who for his services in the campaign of Arzila and Tangier in 1472 had been granted the title of Count of Arganil. The see was engaged in a bitter quarrel with the prior of Santa Cruz, said to have originated in a dispute between their respective servants sent to buy provisions in the market: it became necessary for the king to send troops to pacify the warring clerics. Since the provincial *fidalgos* were not allowed to stay in Oporto, they frequently solaced themselves in Coimbra where, if on royal service, they could obtain a month's free board. With the exception of Estremadura, which included Lisbon, central Portugal or Beira was the most populous part of the country with nearly a quarter of the total population.

However, the northern province of the Minho, the cradle of Portugal, was the most thickly populated, not in virtue of its cities, most of which were very small, but because of its teeming countryside. Oporto was the third city of Portugal, and was soon to overtake Évora. Until the crisis of 1371–83, much of the interior of Trás-os-Montes and north-eastern Beira had traded across the frontier with Castile. But this area was now drawn into the hinterland of Oporto, which also benefited from the Portuguese expansion in the Atlantic. John I had finally bought the jurisdiction of the city back from the bishops whose rule had often led to riots. The city had only one parish, and there was only one monastery within the walls.

The relations of Portugal with the Low Countries had been intensified since the marriage of John I's daughter Isabel to Duke Philip the Good. This led to the installation of a Portuguese factor at Bruges: Pedro Eanes, *feitor* in 1441–3, was later treasurer for the duchess in Lisbon. Afonso V appointed two *escudeiros* of his household to be *feitores* in Bruges, and a Portuguese merchant named João Esteves held the position between 1466 and 1471. Later the Archduke and Emperor Maximilian gave foreign merchants privileges to reside in Antwerp, and although Bruges offered the Portuguese inducements to stay in 1493, the shift was made in the following year. If at first this northern trade was European, and the Portuguese sent such commodities as oil, wine, dried fruits and cork, it was not long before the products of West Africa found their way to Bruges. The produce of Arguim and Mina was not limited to slaves and gold, but included ivory, cotton, civet, parrots, feathers and skins. The first of the spices to be included was Malagueta pepper, known as 'grain of Paradise'. It was first sold in Flanders in 1472. With the foundation of Mina (1482) the trade was solidly established. The Negroes preferred to exchange it for copper, being at first willing to give an *arroba* or bushel of pepper for a copper *manilha*, though by 1505 they were demanding five or six for the same quantity of pepper.

It was perhaps inevitable that the Portuguese crown should direct the economy into a form of centralized capitalism. It controlled the only really considerable accumulation of resources, supported the nobility and maintained the garrisons in the Magrib. It also licensed and in part financed the voyages of discovery, and its *feitor* controlled the distribution of exports in Bruges. Under Afonso v, other members of the royal family had undertaken the organization of the voyages, and the king had both sold monopolies of trade and transferred the responsibility of new discoveries to private persons. But John ii had built the new fort of Mina and organized the exploration of the Cape route. There was now no reversing the crown's commitment. John ii himself did not live to launch the discovery of India. He died in 1495, and had been predeceased by his only legitimate son. He thought for a moment of legitimizing his other son, D. Jorge, but finally bequeathed his throne to D. Manuel, Duke of Beja, the brother of his wife and of the Duke of Viseu whom he had put to death.

Manuel i (1495–1521), was the Fortunate, both to rule, being the youngest of nine children, and to reap the final reward of the great venture of Prince Henry. John ii had appointed his admiral to organize the fleet for India, but the admiral was now dead, and Manuel entrusted the command to his son Vasco da Gama, who left Lisbon on July 8, 1497, with three vessels and a store-ship. He reached Moçambique in March and was well received by the sultan of Melinde, who found him a pilot for Calicut. Having obtained quantities of Oriental spices, not without friction, he set sail for home, reaching Lisbon in September 1499. Only two ships and about half the crew survived the journey of two years and two months.

Six months later, Manuel assembled the largest fleet yet gathered for a voyage of discovery, thirteen ships, and placed it under a young nobleman, Pedro Álvares Cabral, who was to act as ambassador to the Indian princes. The fleet sailed far to the west, and in April 1500 sighted what was at first thought to be a large island, the 'land of the True Cross'. It was later shown to be a great continent, the mainland of South America, and named Brazil from the quantities of dye-wood found on its shores. A ship was sent back to report the discovery, and Cabral continued on his way to open up the trade of the East. Although he lost half of his ships, those that returned brought enough spices amply to cover the cost of the undertaking and to show a handsome profit.

Until this time the Portuguese expansion had consisted of the defence of the fortresses in the Magrib, the colonization of the uninhabited Atlantic isles and the exploration of the African coast. Three Papal bulls had granted a monopoly of trade in the South Atlantic. When Columbus reached what he thought to be the Indies, the Papacy promptly granted a monopoly of navigation to the rulers of Spain. John II opened negotiations, and by the Treaty of Tordesillas a theoretical line was drawn across the Atlantic, which had the effect of reserving Brazil, as yet undiscovered, for Portugal. Portugal also kept her monopoly of the African Atlantic, with the sole exception of the Canaries, now occupied by Spain. Brazil had no great indigenous civilizations, and it at first offered little interest except the export of its red dye-wood, then much esteemed. But the opening of the Cape sea-route gave Portugal the key to the new world of the Orient, with its fabulous wealth, legendary in the West since the time of Marco Polo. The Portuguese crown had no hesitation in plunging into the adventure. It was fortunate in finding the Indian Ocean almost free of armed shipping, though the trade was virtually monopolized by Muslim merchants. The ruler of Calicut, after first receiving the Portuguese, decided to adhere to the Muslims, but the Portuguese were able to trade at Cochin and Cannanore. In 1505 King Manuel sent D. Francisco de Almeida with the title of viceroy to organize commercial posts and wrest control of the spice-trade from the Muslims. Egyptian warships emerging from the Red Sea attempted to protect the Muslims, but Almeida worsted them. Meanwhile, Afonso de

Albuquerque had been sent to seal off the Red Sea and explore the approaches to Abyssinia, the still mysterious land of Prester John. Albuquerque was convinced that the Indian Ocean and its trade could be controlled with four fortresses and 3,000 Portuguese troops, and when he succeeded Almeida as governor, he conquered Goa from its Muslim ruler, harnessed Malacca, the focus of the spiceries, and occupied Ormuz, thus tapping the trade of Persia and controlling the point from which Persian horses were distributed to the Indian princes. Although Albuquerque's more ambitious schemes, such as capturing Mecca, could not be realized, and the Negus was reached only after his death in 1515, he established Portuguese power in the East for a century.

In Portugal, the organization, manning and financing of expeditions, the accumulation of supplies, the storing of the commodities and their distribution were overwhelmingly a royal enterprise. The crown supervised the preparation of fleets which were concentrated in Lisbon, and decided when they should depart. It held the stocks of spices in the cellars of its palaces on the Lisbon waterfront, and it endeavoured to stipulate the prices at which they should be sold. The nature of the trade, in goods much sought after and once rare, but now arriving in increasing volume, forced the crown to exercise control. Manuel was at once 'Lord of the Navigation, Conquest and Commerce of Ethiopia, Arabia, Persia and India', and the 'Grocer-King'.

The economy of rural Portugal was still distantly based on the medieval doctrine of the just price: it preserved memories of the age when a *modius* of wheat or a sheep were the measures of value. The new economy was entirely speculative. Already the cultivation of sugar on Madeira had brought down the prices throughout western Europe. In 1425 Madeira was a wilderness: by 1433 sugar was in cultivation for export. In 1455 the yield was 400 *cântaros*. It appeared at Bristol in 1466, and in Flanders in 1468. By 1494 the official register put the crop at 80,451 *arrobas*. In the previous year it was noted in Nuremberg that 'there is so much produced that all Europe has more sugar than formerly'. In 1498 the crown limited exports from Madeira to 120,000 *arrobas*. In 1469 the price of sugar was 650–800 *reais* an *arroba*: by 1496 it was 350–600 *reais*.

The sugar-industry of Madeira was the model enterprise of modern colonization. It had begun with small cultivations near Funchal. Most of the colonists did their own labour, but as the industry grew and moved farther from the capital the farms tended to become bigger. The 'engines' (*engenhos*) with their crushing-machinery required considerable capital. Most of the growers were Portuguese, though there were a small number of foreigners, mainly Italians. But the export-trade was largely in the hands of Jews and Italians. The Jews perhaps arrived to manage the affairs of nobles with interests in the island. As early as 1472 there were protests in cortes against the predominance of Italians in the Madeira sugar-trade, and these were repeated in 1481–2. Foreigners were thought not only to take gold and silver out of the country, but to 'seek the secrets of the discovery of Mina and the isles'.

Italian merchants had long been established in Portugal, and they had intermarried with the Portuguese and often identified themselves with the land of their adoption. The crown had not hesitated to allow Italian navigators to visit West Africa. But the sudden contact with the fabled economies of the Orient made it impossible for the Portuguese crown to disengage itself from the main trading and financial centres of Europe. The discovery of the sea-way to India led to a dislocation of the European finances towards the west, a movement soon to be sealed by the flow of precious metals from America to Spain.

Almost since the reopening of the Straits of Gibraltar, it had been the practice of the Portuguese crown to grant privileges to foreigners trading in Lisbon. At first these were devised especially to speed visiting merchants on their way. But very soon resident communities existed in Portugal. There were English merchants in the time of John I and Philippa. The Flemish marriage (1430) brought settlers for the Azores. In 1456 a merchant of Bruges obtained the monopoly of the export of cork for ten years, and in 1468 duties on Flemish cloth entering Lisbon were reduced. In 1472 the Flemish merchants formed a brotherhood, paying a levy on exports of oil, honey, soap, wine, wax, cork, sardines and Malagueta pepper to support a chapel.

In 1494 the Portuguese factory was shifted from Bruges to Antwerp, and it was here that the royal factors began to dispose of the spices brought by Vasco da Gama. Soon the Spaniards,

Germans and Italians also transferred their interests to Antwerp, which at the beginning of the sixteenth century became the most important market in Europe. There were at first doubts about the quality of the spices brought by the Portuguese, for Europeans were used to paying the high prices exacted by Arab and Venetian middlemen. But Nicholas von Rechtergem, a German living in Antwerp, undertook the distribution of Portuguese pepper and made a fortune for himself: his business passed to Erasmus Schets, the friend of Erasmus, who married his daughter.*

Meanwhile, the Venetians sent one Pisani to Lisbon in March 1501 to obtain the distribution of the goods brought by Cabral—indeed Pisani was dining with King Manuel when Cabral arrived, and records that Portugal had pepper at less than a ducat a *quintal* and other spices at prices he was afraid to mention. The transfer of great commercial interests from Venice to Lisbon soon followed. In 1503 the Germans moved their trade from the Rialto to Lisbon. One Simon Seitz obtained privileges for fifteen years. It was the year of Gama's return from his second voyage, and the Germans obtained permission to send representatives to India. Seitz represented a company launched by Anton Welser and others in 1498. The Welsers of Augsburg had earlier joined with the Vohlins to control the production of metals in eastern Europe. Their rivals, the Fuggers, who owned even greater resources, the copper and silver of the Tyrol and merchant and banking interests, also had an agent in Lisbon in 1503, obtaining similar privileges. Portugal had no metals of her own, and her African clients sought especially copper, and her Oriental suppliers silver. The Germans seemed capable therefore of building very strong interests at Lisbon. However, the crowning of Maximilian's grandson, Charles of Ghent, as king of Spain and Emperor diverted the great capitalists to Spain, and the conquest of Mexico and Peru deprived the German control of European silver of its significance. The flood of American treasure attracted both German and Italian bankers to Spain. While Charles v struggled with an ever-rising mountain of debts, born of the silver of Potosí, the son of the Grocer-King, John III (1521–1557), strove rather with rising costs and falling prices.

---

*Rechtergem received Portuguese pepper in 1502, but it is not certain whether this was African or Indian.

Manuel's reign was a period of unparalleled courtly magnificence. The king himself built the new palace-monastery of the Jerónimos at Belem. The style that bears his name is rather an elaborate system of decoration of doors and windows which gives a national cast to the florid Gothic. It is luxuriant in Lisbon, the Alentejo and Tomar and enhances the great church of Batalha. Its effect is less in the north and little in the north-east, suggesting limits to the radiant effect of the new prosperity. The court, already famous for its banquets and receptions (*saraus*), saw the inception of the drama, with the plays composed by Gil Vicente for royal occasions and festivities. The chronicler Garcia de Rèsende collected the works of the court versifiers. A greater poet, Sá de Miranda, who had visited Italy, composed sonnets and classical comedies: at length, depressed by the rivalries and intrigues of the court, he retired to a rural estate in the Minho. The art of printing had entered Portugal in about 1487: three of the earliest printers were Jews, and all the first eleven Portuguese incunabula are in Hebrew. The chief Portuguese presses were in Lisbon.

King Manuel had been married three times, to Spanish princesses. His son John III, who succeeded in 1521 at the age of nineteen, married Catarina, the sister of the Emperor Charles V: the Emperor married his sister Isabel, and their son, Philip II, would make himself king of Portugal in 1580. Many factors conspired to align the two Peninsular nations together. They stood side by side as the pioneers of expansion, and the other European monarchies were their rivals. Their conflict in the Atlantic had been resolved by drawing the line conceived at Tordesillas: competition on the other side of the world, the Spice Islands, which the Portuguese reached from the Indies and the Spaniards from the Philippines, was finally resolved by the treaty of Saragossa of 1529, after which no important overseas conflict divided the two countries. Repeated marriages between the two royal houses diminished the resistance to Spain: most of the Portuguese writers of the sixteenth century did not hesitate to use both languages. The religious crisis that now sundered Europe drew the Catholic courts together: the Anglo-Portuguese Alliance, which had been confirmed by successive rulers of both countries, ceased to be observed after the Reformation.

4

PENINSULAR INTEGRATION

Although John III, who had been educated by prominent humanists, had at first been looked on as likely to protect the new learning, he is now often portrayed as a repressive and reactionary figure—the consequence of the long struggle of his court to introduce the Inquisition against the opposition of the Papacy. The Inquisition had been established in Spain in 1478 to repress heresy, especially among the many Jews who had ostensibly embraced Catholicism since the pogroms of 1391. In 1492, after completing the conquest of Muslim Granada, the Spanish crown had ordered the expulsion of the Jewish population. Its object was to secure conformity by intimidation, but many Spanish Jews sought a refuge in Portugal. The Portuguese cortes were reluctant to admit them, but John II proposed to collect a tax of eight *cruzados* a head at the frontier. Metal-workers and armourers would pay half. Officials were appointed to collect the tax at five points, issuing receipts which served as passports to enter Portugal. After eight months, the Portuguese crown would provide transport elsewhere. Six hundred wealthy families made a special contract to remain in Portugal, and were settled in the larger cities. The rest may have numbered 60,000. There were, of course, already communities of Jews attached to most of the towns—at least forty—where the tri-communal system of Muslim times still endured. Most of these communities paid a tribute or poll-tax to the crown or nobles. John II probably regarded the newcomers as potential taxpayers, and failed to provide them with shipping, except to Tangier and the African fortresses, which had no attraction for them. Some were enslaved for not having left the kingdom as required. When Manuel acceded, and married a daughter of the Spanish rulers, he was pressed to align his policy with theirs. In December 1496 all Jews and Muslims who refused to be baptized were to be ex-

10. Alentejo: a 16th c. house in Serpa
11. Alentejo: Palace of the Braganças at Vila Viçosa

Esperanza   *Dutch Consuls Quinta*   *St Catharine*   *St Francisco*   *La Moira*   *St V*

pelled. But soon after, orders were issued to remove their children, who were to be educated as Christians. It was then announced the recusants must embark at Lisbon. When they arrived in the capital, attempts were made to induce or coerce them to be converted. A few prominent figures resisted and were allowed to depart, but most accepted a nominal conversion on the understanding that no inquiry would be made into their beliefs for twenty years. Those who remained were then forbidden to leave the country.

Several incidents of hostility to the New Christians are recorded. But in 1506 there occurred a massacre in Lisbon. Two Dominicans raised the cry of heresy, and the mob murdered five hundred persons. The scene was repeated on the following days. The king was at Avis, and he ordered rigorous punishments. Some fifty persons, including the two Dominicans, were condemned to death, and the monastery of São Domingos was closed. The house of the guilds, the Casa dos Vinte e Quatro, was suppressed (but reopened in 1508). The crown raised the ban on New Christians leaving the kingdom, but sought to induce them to stay by confirming the period during which they were to be free of investigation. This was again confirmed by John III in 1524. It is possible that a slow absorption of the New Christians would have occurred, had not John III asked the Papacy for permission to instal the Inquisition (1531). The Papacy now regretted the authority it had granted to the Spanish crown, distrusted Peninsular fanaticism and suspected that the confiscation of property was a dominant motive of inquisitors. It resisted the royal request for a quarter of a century, seeking at first to keep inquisitorial powers in the hands of the bishops, and appointing its own inquisitors. This was not what John wanted, and he put forward his brother Henry, whom he made Archbishop of Évora: Rome then suspended the Inquisition and ordered a general pardon. It was only in 1547 that the Pope accepted Cardinal Henry, on condition that there should be no confiscation for ten years.

This struggle, in which the New Christians intervened by sending representatives to Rome, was doubtless prolonged by John's obstinate desire to imitate the Spaniards and to have his own way. It owed much to the Spanish doctrine of 'purity of blood' which had developed in the church of Toledo. By the time

12. Lisbon: the India House (Casa da India) drawn by D. Vieira Serrão, 1622
13. Lisbon: before the earthquake of 1755

the struggle was over it was generally believed that the New Christians were a separate people, and the mistrust the lower clergy and urban populace had felt for the Jews had been firmly attached to them. Accusations of Judaism branded whole families whatever their racial origin: there is therefore some reason for regarding the palace of the Inquisition as a 'factory of Jews'. Although tribunals of the Inquisition functioned in six Portuguese cities, that of Oporto celebrated only one auto-da-fé (1543) before its suppression. After 1547 three tribunals remained, at Lisbon, Évora and Coimbra.

By now it could no longer be held that heresy was the monopoly of a given race, but lately converted. Few Portuguese were perhaps directly influenced by the great rift that occurred in the north, but as conservative opinion hardened, the levity with which a Gil Vicente had treated the clergy seemed suspect to some. Although Erasmus, who had heard of John III's attachment to culture, dedicated a work to him, he did not gain the hoped-for reward, though perhaps for rather unexpected reasons.* The Portuguese historian, Damião de Gois, who met both Erasmus and Melanchthon while *feitor* to John III in the north, was in his later years molested on that account. Yet the profound excitement caused by the rediscovery of antiquity and intense curiosity to learn more, heightened by the circulation of knowledge in printed books, stirred men as never before. Some went to Italy to study, others to Paris. John II had brought Cataldo Siculo to educate his son: his chancellor, João Teixeira, sent his sons to Italy to study with Poliziano. In 1516 Estêvão Cavaleiro proclaimed that the Roman Empire was wherever Latin was spoken. André Rèsende held that the darkness cast by the Goths had been ended and all Europe was reborn. In 1537 John III decided to shut down the University of Lisbon with its medieval tradition of scholasticism, and transfer it to Coimbra where a modern style of education would prevail. It opened with classes in theology, law, medicine and arts. Most of the two hundred and thirty students were registered in civil or common law, but forty-four entered the programme of arts. How stale and barren

---

* His dedication contained a reference to Portuguese economic policy, which he thought had raised the price of sugar in the Low Countries.

the law and its equivocations must have seemed to the young devotees of the Muses! If Camões, probably born in 1524, was not of them (and there is no record that he was, though his uncle was head of the college of Santa Cruz), his spirit was theirs. Pains had been taken to find eminent teachers, and the academic world buzzed with rumours of John's munificence. In 1547 a new college was established 'in which all the arts shall be read'. Its principal was Dr André de Gouveia, and one of its teachers the Scottish humanist George Buchanan. It enrolled 1,200 students in the first year. But the foundation was followed by bitter quarrels and intrigues and accusations against the opinions and morals of the staff. The Inquisition was drawn in, and it was shut down. Its heritage was handed over to the Jesuits, who thus became dominant at Coimbra.

The Basque soldier who founded the Society of Jesus had known the University of Paris and found it lacking in devotion and discipline. His objects included missionary work, and John III, on hearing of this, thought that the Jesuits might tackle the problems of Portuguese India. Not all the Portuguese clergy was anxious to receive the Jesuits in Portugal. The king's brother, Henry, now a cardinal, thought they should go overseas. But John finally resolved to give them a college in Coimbra and selected Simão Rodrigues as tutor to his son, also John. Cardinal Henry's doubts were resolved by an inquiry in 1544, after which he took a Jesuit as his confessor. He later asked John to found a Jesuit University at Évora: Coimbra was at first opposed to this, but after John's death his Spanish queen appealed to the Pope, and the Jesuit University of Évora was established in 1559.

As John's reign proceeded, the cost of maintaining his possessions outdistanced the revenues he drew from them, and his debts steeply increased. He had paid Spain 350,000 *cruzados* to resolve the dispute over the Spice Islands. The Emperor had insisted on an enormous dowry on marrying John's sister. Thus in the years 1526–9 Portugal turned over to the Castilian treasury 1,250,000 *cruzados*. These were, of course, non-recurring payments. But the crown had to bear the cost of holding the outposts in Morocco and its fortresses and wars in the East, to buy cereals and other commodities to meet domestic deficiencies, and to withstand the heavy losses of its ships from Mina and the Cape at the hands of corsairs: in 1531 António de Ataide,

Count of Castanheira, John III's minister, estimated that over 300 ships had been taken by the French. In the period 1523–43 John's deficits were 3,160,000 *cruzados*. He was forced to take loans in Flanders and elsewhere at rates of 16–20 per cent: in 1544 the *feitor* in Flanders reported rates of 25 per cent. Interest cost a further 2,200,000 *cruzados*, giving a total deficit of 5,360,000. By contrast the subsidies paid by cortes were insignificant—100,000 *cruzados* in 1525, 150,000 in 1535, and 200,000 in 1544. Thus the Oriental enterprise passed over the the head of the traditional Portuguese economy, perhaps scarcely benefiting it. A substantial part of the revenues went to bankers in Flanders and some to suppliers in southern Spain. At Lisbon German interests declined during the course of the reign, and Italian merchants and bankers recovered their ascendancy.

During the years from 1533 John III and his council spent much of their time at Évora, sending Castanheira to Lisbon to prepare the fleets for India. Castanheira would report almost daily on arrangements he made as regards the ships and those who were to command them and on negotiations for the sale of spices. He might recommend the size of fleets or the number of men, seek the advice of nobles who had been in India and discuss the *regimentos* given to all captains. He also received information about the demand for spices in Flanders and Spain and endeavoured to link sales of commodities in demand with those of which stocks were large. He interviewed the leading merchants and bankers, such as the Italians Affaitati and Geraldi and directed the affairs of the Casas da Mina and da Índia, which handled the details of the enterprises of West Africa and the East respectively. The merchants could see the stocks of goods for sale in the warehouses, but it was perhaps important to conceal the quantities. One merchant, a Jew, was to leave Lisbon as soon as his business was done. John had given orders that no New Christian should go to India.

It was only slowly that Brazil was drawn into the system. The voyages of Amerigo Vespucci in 1501–2 demonstrated that it was not an island but a continent. But its Indians were small groups who still lived in the Stone Age: no high civilizations and no traces of precious metals were found. In 1502, Fernão de Noronha, a New Christian, was granted the monopoly of dyewood, but French interlopers also cut wood and carried it off.

By 1530, John III was obliged to occupy the territory or lose it. In view of his own commitments elsewhere, he decided to divide the coast into strips, which were offered to donatories, noblemen who received extensive privileges in return for putting down colonists and cultivating the soil. Of the dozen donatories only two or three succeeded in implanting thriving colonies. Martim Afonso de Sousa established the colony of São Vicente near the present port of Santos and a village in the interior called Piratininga, the present São Paulo. But it was farther north, at Bahia and Pernambuco, that Brazil began to contribute substantially to the Portuguese economy. The cultivation of the sugar-cane was introduced from Madeira as early as 1516. In 1549 the problem of defence made it necessary to appoint a governor of Brazil, and Tomé de Sousa established a capital at Bahia. The rich *recôncavo* was planted with sugar and Negro slaves were introduced from Africa to perform the field-work. This method of cultivation had already been evolved on São Tomé. By about 1560 Brazil had overtaken Madeira as the great source of sugar. In 1570 it had sixty mills, and in 1585 one hundred and twenty-two. As in Madeira, a substantial part of the export-trade was in the hands of New Christians, who were numerous in Bahia and Pernambuco. Exports were directed mainly to Lisbon and the other Portuguese ports, but there was a growing participation of Dutch hulks in transport.

The few townships of Brazil were modest replicas of those of Portugal, but the countryside consisted of plantations of moderate size in which the owner directed his African labourers. If there was an equivalent of the Portuguese village it was to be found rather in the Indian settlements, now converted to Christianity and to Lusitanian ways, largely through the ministrations of the Jesuits. Members of the Society of Jesus arrived in Brazil with the first governor in 1549. One of them, Manuel de Nóbrega, undertook the evangelization of the north and centre, while José de Anchieta taught the Indians at São Paulo. Miscegenation between Portuguese and Indians dated from the earliest times. Thus the characteristic framework of Brazilian society was already being established: Portuguese towns, Indian villages, Negro plantations, living in loose interdependence.

The organization of this society was no longer that traditional in Portugal. There were Portuguese nobles in Brazil, but there was not a Brazilian nobility. Even the Brazilian church rested on the Jesuits and the Orders rather than the parish priest. There was no question of the transfer of the cortes to Brazil. These and other differences emphasize the extent to which Portugal itself had been reordered. Not only the humanists, the revivers of classical learning, but also the lawyers were impregnated with a yearning to restore the Roman state, rejecting the Middle Ages as barbarian. The scattered legislation of the land was drawn together in imitation of the great codes of the later Roman Empire: the *Ordenações*, named *Afonsinas* after Afonso v, were published by his son John II, to be revised and republished as the *Ordenações Manuelinas*. The authority of the monarch was held to be absolute. The jurisdictions of the nobility had long been whittled away (though they were transplanted to the Atlantic Islands and to Brazil). The nobles were converted into a company of administrators directly dependent on the court. The medieval titles of duke and marquis were out of favour: Manuel and John preferred to grant that of count, with its Constantinian overtones. The court itself resembled the establishment of the later Roman Empire. No less than 4,937 persons drew allowances from the crown. They included seventy *cavaleiros* of the council, and 1,297 other *cavaleiros*. The *fidalgos* of the lower ranks were almost as numerous, six hundred and forty-nine *escudeiros* and five hundred and nine *moços*. It was among these that John chose his governors, commanders and captains. The rest of his household had increased in similar proportions. The ecclesiastical establishment numbered five bishops, one hundred and forty-five chaplains and one hundred and twenty-four choirboys. John's attendants included nine hundred and eleven *moços da câmara*, one hundred and nineteen stewards, eighty-eight grooms and twenty-nine cooks. John himself was a retiring figure, known only to his family, council and secretaries. Small wonder that to many the court seemed a network of interests and intrigues and the world itself a state of confusion quite unlike the idealized realms of the humanists. The medieval concept of a society of nobles, clerics and commoners had no representative force. The cortes continued to meet and to present grievances, but no longer made any claim to be able to execute their own proposals and their contribution to royal revenues was a relatively minor one. The cortes drew their popu-

lar representation from the *concelhos*. Although these had originally been both urban and rural, only the more important places
had acquired *câmaras*, and representation was in effect confined
to the towns. This indeed was in accord with classical doctrine:
Romanists appreciated the supremacy of cities. But the new
administration thought less in terms of a free league of townships gathered in cortes than of the capital city as an exemplar
for the rest. Thus the *câmara* of Lisbon made use of the title of
Senate. In the overseas territories Bahia in Brazil, Gôa in India
and even Macau in China were constituted on similar lines. In
each place, the *câmara* addressed itself to the crown on problems
of policy and local government and expressed the aspirations of
the population in public works and institutions, such as the
Misericórdias, which now spread over the whole Portuguese
world. It was a Roman reconstruction, though perhaps of an
Empire that had scarcely existed, for it combined reminiscences
of the first century with those of the Christian fourth.

The Misericórdias are the typical social institutions of the
renascence monarchy. That of Évora dates from 1499, and
others followed throughout the century with the aid of queens,
administrators, the clergy, the *câmaras* and the guilds. In some
cases the Misericórdia established its own hospital or orphanage,
and in others it took over existing institutions. It cared for the
sick and for waifs and widows, provided free meals for the poor,
and contributed to ransom captives in the Magrib.

The exuberance of the early Portuguese renascence had expressed itself in the florid style known as Manueline. The introduction of purely classical forms obeying the 'measures of the
Roman' does not much antecede 1530 and becomes general only
after 1540. Thus the artist Francisco de Olanda, who spent the
years 1538–47 in Italy, could observe that 'when I returned
from Rome I did not know this country'. The return to religious
discipline may be counted from the introduction of the Inquisition and of the Jesuits, though the principles of the counter-
reformation were formulated only by the Council of Trent. The
censorship of books, though it existed in theory from 1517,
passed to the Inquisition, and from 1539 books were licensed.
Cardinal Henry, now chief Inquisitor, produced a list of forbidden works in 1551 and another in 1561. It was only in 1576
that the ecclesiastical licence was supplemented by a royal

censorship. At the end of John's reign the crown was less anxious to support humanistic culture than to control it. He died in 1557. His heir had predeceased him, but left a posthumous son, Sebastian, born in 1554, who thus succeeded. The Spanish queen Catarina acted as regent for her grandchild: she was closely attached to her homeland and to her brother the Emperor, who now abdicated his various realms and retired to the monastery of Yuste. Some feared her influence, and inclined towards her only possible rival, John's brother, Cardinal Henry, but he himself was Inquisitor-general and a protector of the Jesuits, both Spanish institutions. Catarina placed him in her debt by satisfying his desire to instal the Jesuit University at Évora. The queen wished the Spanish Dominican, Fr. Luis de Granada, to be Sebastian's tutor, but Henry succeeded in appointing a Portuguese Jesuit. At the end of 1560 the regency was again in question, and Catarina, rather than summon cortes, consulted those eligible to attend by letter, the majority of the replies being favourable to her. But early in 1562 the fortress of Mazagão was subjected to a long siege by the Muslims, and Catarina was blamed for delays in sending relief. At the end of the year cortes were summoned and she resigned. Henry became regent, but Catarina remained in charge of her grandson's education: he was to attain his majority at fourteen.

The cortes of 1562 urged that Sebastian should be brought up according to Portuguese customs: 'let him dress Portuguese, eat Portuguese, ride Portuguese, speak Portuguese, all his acts be Portuguese'. Henry rejected the recommendation that he should appoint a council of twelve, and ignored all four persons suggested by cortes in creating a Council of State. But in 1568 Sebastian came of age and the cardinal's regency ended. The young prince had been brought up in the Jesuit image of a crusader. He divided his time between his devotions and knightly exercises against the day when he should be able to fight the infidel. He had suffered a disease believed to portend impotence, and violent exercise seemed to produce new attacks: in 1569 he was thought unfit to marry for four years. At that time he suddenly cut himself off from his grandmother and changed his advisers. He then visited Sintra and Alcobaça, where he had the tombs of his ancestors opened to contemplate their bones. His chief mentors were two Portuguese Jesuits, Fr. Luis da Câmara and his brother Martim Gonçalves da Câmara, who occupied the office of private secretary (*escrivão da poridade*) and held the reins of state until his fall in 1576. During this time Sebastian showed himself bored with the tasks of government, and intent solely on his military exercises. He crossed to Ceuta in 1574, without having made any plans, and without accomplishing anything: worse was to follow. The new favourite, D. Alvaro de Castro, a member of the Council of State and *vèdor* of the treasury, won Sebastian's favour by supporting his dreams of Africa, and brought back the former royal secretary Pedro de Alcáçova Carneiro, a loyal follower of Queen Catarina and a vehicle for Spanish influence. From this time the Council was dominated by young nobles who kept the favour of the hallucinated king by flattering him. In December 1576 Sebastian met Philip II at Guadalupe to persuade him to join in an expedition against Larache. The prudent king of Spain disengaged himself without disabusing his nephew: Sebastian now devoted himself to his crusade, seeking loans, mortgaging revenues and raising troops abroad. Cardinal Henry had no influence, and Queen Catarina died. In June 1578 Sebastian and his army embarked. On 4 August his forces were routed in the Battle of the Three Kings at al-Qaṣr al-kabir (Alcazar Quivir). He himself disappeared in the fray: some 8,000 men fell with him, and 15,000 were taken captive.

Sebastian's nearest legitimate relative was his great-uncle, Cardinal Henry, who was duly crowned. He was old and in failing health. The only other members of the royal house were a bastard nephew, António, prior of Crato, and a niece, the wife of the Duke of Bragança. But Philip II was already determined to inherit the Portuguese crown. His ambassador laid his claim before the Lisbon municipality and scotched the wild plan to marry the elderly cardinal-king. Cortes met in Lisbon on 1 April 1579 and chose candidates from whom Henry would appoint governors to take charge on his death and judges to assess the claims of the candidates. Philip II engaged lawyers to support his case, and sought to win friends with bribes. New cortes met on 11 January 1580 at Almeirim and Santarém. The clergy favoured a settlement with Philip. The nobles were intimidated by Philip's envoys. The commoners, led by Febo Moniz, sought wider consultation. Henry died on 31 January leaving Portugal in the hands of five governors, three of whom had been suborned by Spanish agents. They gathered troops to preserve order. They decided to close the cortes, though the commoners insisted on setting up a standing committee. In May Philip announced that he rejected the right of judges to pronounce on his case and gave the governors a month in which to obey him. The commoners asked for new cortes. But Philip's armies entered Portugal on 18 June. On the 19th António, prior of Crato, was proclaimed king at Santarém and was welcomed in Lisbon, while the governors fled. Alba's armies marched across the Alentejo and appeared outside Lisbon. António's improvised force was easily defeated in the Battle of Alcântara fought outside the city. He escaped to Coimbra, roused the students and occupied Aveiro, but when Spanish troops approached he went into hiding, escaping to France in May 1581. Philip himself had entered Portugal in the previous December.

The Spanish conquest was bitterly unpopular, but there was now no prospect of a second Aljubarrota. The Spain of 1580 was immeasurably more powerful than the Castile of 1383. Portugal had recently suffered the disastrous defeat at al-Qaṣr al-Kabir, and the prisoners, or most of them, had been released for an enormous ransom. Both the machinery of administration and the art of war had become far more professional, and resistance could no longer be improvised. Queen Elizabeth had sent an envoy to survey the situation, but he had quickly decided that there was nothing to be done : the religious rift had paralysed the old Alliance. Moreover, Philip was not without friends. His mother, the Empress, had been a Portuguese. He soon summoned cortes at Tomar. He had now a reliable council and offered pardon for those who had sided with António, though with numerous exceptions. He published a document in which he gave extensive guarantees. He would wear the crown of Portugal, but the country would retain its autonomy. He would be represented in Portugal by a member of his family, or failing that by a Portuguese. He would have with him a Council of Portugal of six members, through which he would dispatch the country's business. All rights and privileges should be respected. All offices, civil, military and ecclesiastical, would be held by Portuguese. Cortes would meet only in Portugal. The language, coinage, justice and garrisons would be Portuguese. There was nothing to do but accept. The nobility at Tomar asked for an extension of the pardon, and the commoners for the withdrawal of the Spanish garrisons, which was refused. So too was a request that taxes be lowered. Pleas that Philip marry a Portuguese and have his son educated in Portugal, and that New Christians be refused office were passed over. In February 1583 Philip ended his long stay in his new conquest and departed for Spain, leaving his nephew, the Cardinal-Archduke Albert, as his governor.

Only one corner of Portuguese territory had maintained the resistance to Philip—the Azores, where seven of the islands had proclaimed António, under the leadership of Dr Ciprião de Figueiredo, a magistrate at Angra on Terceira. A fleet sent from Lisbon attempted a landing, but the Spanish troops were rebuffed when a herd of bulls was driven into them. But the Azoreans became dissatisfied with Figueiredo and asked António to send another governor, whom they detested. António himself had gone to England, but found Elizabeth unready for war with Philip. In France, he obtained the support of Catherine of Medici, promising to cede Brazil. She sent a detachment to hold Terceira and disposed a fleet under Philippe Strozzi to eject the Spaniards from the islands of São Miguel and Santa Maria. It left Belle Isle in June 1582. The following month Santa Cruz arrived and routed the French fleet, killing Strozzi. António was on Terceira, but left for France to raise 1,500 men, returning in June 1583. Santa Cruz had also strengthened his forces and had little difficulty in taking Terceira. António's leading supporters were executed, and he himself fled to France. He again approached Elizabeth, and after the failure of the Spanish Armada she sent Drake with a force of thirty ships to attempt to place the pretender in Lisbon (1589). The capital showed little disposition to rise on his behalf, and the expedition was a failure. António died in Paris in 1595.

He had never been generally accepted as the symbol of Portuguese independence. That part was played by none other than the lost king Sebastian. His body had been ransomed from the Muslims, but an incident after the battle had convinced some Portuguese that he had survived. It was said that when Philip entered Lisbon, a street-vendor greeted him as king 'until Sebastian should return'. Popular fancy fed on the legend, and Sebastianism took a firm hold, nourished perhaps by the

Messianic beliefs of New Christians, which had found expression in the mystical verses of Gonçalo Anes Bandarra, a cobbler of Trancoso, brought to the notice of the Inquisition in 1541. Not only did the Portuguese people believe in the return of Sebastian, but in the course of the next twenty years no fewer than four false Sebastians incarnated these beliefs. The first appeared as a hermit at Penamacor, speaking gibberish which he pretended to be Arabic and claiming to be doing penance. He formed a little court; when news of his doings reached the authorities, a troop of horse was sent to arrest him and he was condemned to the galleys. Two years later, King Sebastian appeared in the guise of a hermit at Ericeira: he described the battle, uttering groans and sighs for the downfall of Portugal, and later formed a rural army and conferred titles on his followers. They resisted the royal troops, and some two hundred were executed. The third and fourth pretenders appeared outside Portugal, one the 'pastry-cook of Madrigal' deceived an illegitimate daughter of John of Austria, a nun in that small Castilian town; the other was a political creation by a colony of Portuguese loyalists in Italy: he was an Italian who bore no resemblance to Sebastian, and was condemned to the galleys and finally executed.

The mythology of Sebastianism illustrates the pathetic anxiety of an ignorant society to recover its own personality. The more conscious classes of society were neither deceived in this way nor rebelled against their new situation. The guarantees given by Philip were respected. A court at which Spanish was spoken was no novelty, and Portuguese writers had often used the better-known language in the past. Camões, who had dedicated his *Lusiads* to Sebastian with the hope that the young king would lead his people to new heights, had died at the time of the invasion, but Philip had asked to see his work and pensioned his mother: the conquest thus enhanced the fame of the national poet and led to his diffusion in Spanish. Portuguese historians had devoted themselves to the story of the national epic in India, and their work continued. A work on Lisbon, published in 1608, though doubtless composed earlier, attempted to show that the capital was more suited to be the head of a great empire than any other city in Europe. This boast was based on the breadth of its commercial interests, unparalleled in any age.

If the cardinal-king had not declared against Philip, it was because he had seen no other way of defending Portugal's far-flung possessions or of preventing civil strife. The cortes of Tomar appeared to assure her internal autonomy. Yet it was inevitable that she should surrender any independent foreign policy. Spain's enemies became hers. The great fleet of the Spanish Armada was prepared in Lisbon: its failure was followed by Elizabeth's unsuccessful expedition to restore António and by the closure of Portuguese ports to English shipping. As Philip pursued his campaigns in the Low Countries, the Dutch were forbidden to trade in Portugal, and in 1594 fifty Dutch ships were seized in the Tagus. A Dutch resident in Lisbon who had sailed to the East in Portuguese ships offered to show the way to his compatriots, and in 1595 sailed for Java. In 1598 eight Dutch ships left for the Spiceries, and in 1600 forty. In 1602 the Dutch East India Company was founded, and it created a network of interests throughout the East. The jealously-guarded Portuguese monopoly was broken, and the twelve-year truce between Spaniards and Dutch concluded in 1609 did nothing to restore it.

There was now no question of the pre-eminence of Brazil among the Portuguese possessions. The number of sugar-mills continued to grow, and a large proportion of the exported sugar proceeded direct to Amsterdam, which became the great distributing centre for the commodity. A law of 1559 had forbidden refining in Lisbon and thus facilitated the exclusion of the Portuguese metropolis. By contrast the production of Madeira was in decline, and the contribution of São Tomé relatively small. The main source of royal revenue was the tithe on production. Under Philip ii even the religious paid this tax on their sugar. It was usually settled in kind, for money was scarce in Brazil: indeed, sugar was often used as the means of exchange. This situation was somewhat alleviated by the circulation of Spanish silver from Peru, which entered Brazil through the new Spanish settlements on the River Plate.

The Portuguese economy had long been deficient in metals. Portugal herself had been drained of treasure to ransom the captives of al-Qaṣr al-kabir. The reduced supply of gold from Mina rarely sufficed to supply the mint. In the kingdom of Congo, the African currency of cowries was in use, and when Paulo Dias de Novais established Luanda in the new territory of Angola shell-fishing became a source of revenue. Elsewhere in Africa rolls of cloth were the usual medium of exchange. Evidently many of the transactions of the Lisbon commodity-market were conducted by bills of exchange, and the presence of foreign bankers had enabled a great economic development to occur without the conventional supply of gold and silver. Gold and silver coin were probably almost restricted to the court and the main centres of exchange. The artisans, the dwellers in small towns and the peasants used only copper or bronze coinage.

Attempts had been made to remedy the lack of metals. In Brazil traces of gold had been reported as early as 1560, but no significant quantities had appeared. The Spanish kings intensified the quest, and in 1608 the governor Francisco de Sousa was given a body of experts to develop mining, but there were no results until the end of the century. The absence of technicians in Portugal was a serious handicap. The mineral resources of Angola and Benguela, copper, iron and lead, were reported, and Philip II provided experts, yet development was slow. In East Africa, Almeida had built the fort of Sofala in 1505, hoping to tap the legendary gold of Ophir, but little was obtained. In 1558 Moçambique became the regular station for ships sailing between Portugal and India, and the captain of the fortress of St Sebastian was instructed to send captains into the interior to find the native potentate, the Monomotapa, thought to control great goldfields, but still nothing was found.

With the decline of the speculative empire and the swollen court of Manuel and John III, the more modest needs of Portugal were fairly easily met by imports from Spain. The constant debasements of the currency came to an end, and Portugal enjoyed a period of monetary stability. Philip II replaced the four vèdores of the treasury with a single vèdor, the head of a council of finance, the Conselho da Fazenda, after the Spanish model. Efforts were made to revive agriculture, and his laws, the Ordenações Filipinas, published in 1602, show that the corregedores were required to bring idle land into use and to protect farmers from the effects of lawsuits and seigniorial abuses. Writers of the period often complain of depopulation, though it is not easy to tell what emphasis should be placed on this. Nor are the social consequences of the Spanish conquest well known. The contraction of the Portuguese court and economy limited the prospects of the nobility, some of whom sought their fortune in the neighbouring country. There was Portuguese migration to Seville, the true capital of Spanish America, where the painter Velásquez was born of a Portuguese father in 1599: it was said that a quarter of the population of Seville was of Portuguese origin, but this is clearly an exaggeration. It is likely that the diminishing opportunities within Portugal explain the growing tendency of the lesser nobility to entail their estates. While the practice has its roots in the reign of Duarte, it is in the later sixteenth and early seventeenth century that the *morgado* becomes the pillar of Portuguese rural life. There is also an increase in the number of the clergy, and in the number of women destined for the conventual life, perhaps reflecting the straitening of opportunity in the secular world. The patronage of culture is increasingly ecclesiastic. The two Spanish institutions, the Jesuits and the Inquisition, lost nothing by the change. Francis Borja, the Spanish aristocrat, Jesuit and saint, bestowed his unrivalled collection of relics on the Jesuit church of São Roque in Lisbon: they were paraded in the streets to stir up enthusiasm for the Spanish Armada. The classical style of architecture favoured by the Jesuits predominated, and the Jesuit hold over the University was now unchallenged. Meanwhile, the Inquisition carefully scrutinized foreign ships arriving in Lisbon for any manifestations of dissent. In 1590 it extended its attentions to northern Brazil, where numbers of New Christians had returned to Judaism.

The Spanish domination of Portugal lasted sixty years (1580–1640). If Philip II (I of Portugal) could be said to have observed his undertakings in general, the same was not true of his successors, Philip III and IV (II and III). The idle Philip III (1598–1621) failed to visit Portugal until 1619, nearly at the end of his reign, and appointed Spaniards to the Council of Portugal in Madrid and as inspectors of the treasury and the Casa da Índia in Lisbon. In 1615 he attempted to appoint a Spaniard to govern Portugal, but in the face of general protests, he gave way and appointed the Archbishop of Lisbon. Two years later, he again nominated the same Spaniard, on whom he had conferred a Portuguese title. The Spanish state was now faced with dwindling imports of treasure from America and mounting economic difficulties. Philip's minister, the Duke of Lerma, was therefore inclined to come to terms with the New Christians, who offered 170,000 *cruzados* for permission to leave Portugal. He then suggested that they might be allowed to remain and be admitted to offices for ten times this sum. The Portuguese were bitterly opposed to the scheme, not simply on grounds of religious prejudice, though this existed. Some saw the opening of offices as a device by which the Spaniards might appoint their own administration. The three archbishops went to Spain to oppose the plan, and offered 800,000 *cruzados* in lieu of it. The Portuguese towns refused to find the money, and the Spaniards then resumed negotiations with the New Christians on the basis of a payment of 1,700,000 *cruzados* for toleration without admission to office. But in 1610 all privileges granted to the New Christians were withdrawn, and the restrictions were steadily intensified: after 1604 they were excluded from the Military Orders, and after 1612 from the parish priesthood. From about 1621 'purity of blood' was demanded of University teachers, and in 1630 it was required for the holders of all canonries and benefices in the archdiocese of Lisbon. Finally in 1640 the Inquisition produced regulations which forbade the descendants of any person condemned by it from holding any public office, or from using the insignia of any civil or ecclesiastic dignity. These statutes were never applied systematically, but they made mystery and terror a weapon of authority.

It was under Philip iv that the Portuguese finally rejected Spanish rule. The truce between the Spaniards and the Dutch, which had permitted the revival of trade at Lisbon, lapsed in 1621, and the Spanish minister Olivares decided not to renew it. The Dutch, animated by the success of the Eastern enterprise, now founded a West Indian Company to prey on Peninsular shipping. In 1624 it seized Bahia and occupied the neighbouring sugar-estates. Olivares promptly responded by organizing a joint Spanish and Portuguese expedition which expelled the Dutch in the following year. The victory perhaps encouraged Olivares to think in terms of a unification of the Peninsula. His plan was accepted by Philip iv: it involved merging the Portuguese nobles with the Castilian by intermarriage, imposing new taxes on the Portuguese without the consent of their cortes, and general military service. In 1628 he demanded a forced loan for defence and revived the negotiations with the New Christians.

14. Manueline architecture. The Convent of Christ, Tomar

15. Portalegre: the Câmara Municipal, 1632

News of his designs had circulated widely and when in 1630 the Dutch West Indian Company again invaded Brazil, seizing the city of Pernambuco, the Portuguese were no longer prepared to collaborate with Olivares. Thus the Dutch gained possession of one hundred and twenty of the one hundred and sixty-six sugar-mills in the province, and later sent an expedition to Africa to capture Mina and part of Angola, the sources of the slaves who worked the plantations. Dutch Brazil flourished under the enlightened rule of Johan Maurits of Nassau, though most of the sugar continued to be produced by Brazilian Portuguese. The Dutch colony was essentially military; yet it could not annex neighbouring Bahia.

Spanish attempts to extract new taxation now met with a stubborn resistance. The *câmara* of Lisbon evaded the issue, and a special *junta* threw the responsibility on cortes; but in order not to summon cortes, it was decided to consult five nobles, five clergy and ten commoners. These last would be chosen by Lisbon and four other places; but in Lisbon the procurators of the guilds refused to vote without consulting the *juiz do povo* and the *Casa dos Vinte e Quatro*, who in turn refused. For months no quorum was possible, and the crown was reduced to temporary expedients to meet its needs. In Évora, similar procedures led to popular riots: troops were introduced and two ringleaders were executed (1638).

The grievances against Olivares were directed at the Spanish governor, an office Philip iv had bestowed on his cousin, Margaret, the widowed Duchess of Mantua. Her secretary, Miguel de Vasconcelos, though a Portuguese, was seen as the tool of Spanish policy. Spain was now engaged in a bitter struggle with France for hegemony in Europe, and Richelieu had sent agents to Lisbon to offer support in case of a revolt. The obvious Portuguese pretender was the Duke of Bragança, whose mother had been the niece of John iii and the nearest legitimate Portuguese claimant in 1580. The present duke, John, had his palace at Vila Viçosa, in the Alentejo, and he was the greatest landowner in Portugal, for the spoliation of the Braganças by John ii had been reversed by Manuel. He was married to a Spaniard, Leonor de Guzmán, daughter of the Duke of Medina Sidonia, and distantly related to Olivares. However, while John was cautious about losing his vast possessions, his wife was anxious to be a queen. In the middle of 1640 the Catalans, also aggrieved by Olivares' policies, rebelled and murdered Philip's viceroy. They offered their allegiance to Louis XIII. Olivares' need for men and money was thus sharpened. The Portuguese decided to respond by throwing off Spanish rule. Bragança's agent, Dr João Pinto Ribeiro, negotiated with a group of nobles and officials in Lisbon. The revolution was planned for 1 December at nine in the morning. The conspirators assembled in the Terreiro do Paço, forced their way into the palace and killed Vasconcelos. The duchess was arrested, and there was no further resistance. On 6 December John IV arrived in Lisbon to inaugurate the new dynasty.

5

THE RESTORATION

The Portuguese Restoration began without a government, an army or allies. The Spaniards were too busy in Catalonia to invade, and the small foreign garrisons defending the Tagus, and at Setúbal and Viana, quickly surrendered. A Council of War was created on 11 December. It decided to appoint a governor to each province, who would call up all able-bodied men except farmers and a few others, and provide for its defence. Cortes were convoked at Lisbon on 28 January 1641, to raise money. It was reckoned that a sum of 1,800,000 *cruzados* would cover 4,000 horse and 20,000 infantry. It could be met by a 10 per cent property-tax to be paid by all except the church, each diocese of which would contribute according to its resources. The sum proved insufficient, and the next cortes, meeting in September 1642, voted 2,400,000 *cruzados* a year.

The cortes of the Restoration proposed that in future rulers of Portugal should be Portuguese-born and obliged to reside in the country. Members of the royal house who married abroad should be debarred from the succession in their marriage-contracts. The nobility urged that no foreigner might succeed, however closely related to the royal family. It was even proposed that the three most illustrious houses in the land be designated to provide a successor if the royal line should fail. If the Braganças could be elevated, so evidently might others in case of need. However, not everyone supported the Restoration. The Archbishop of Braga believed that it was rash to provoke a Castilian invasion and so persuaded the Marquis of Vila Real and his son, the Duke of Caminha, who sought allies and were denounced. Ten of them were executed. The Archbishop died in prison: the Inquisitor-general, also involved, was later released. Some nobles who were serving abroad still adhered to Philip. Of the possessions overseas, only Ceuta remained in Spanish hands.

A month after his accession, John IV sent an embassy to offer his obedience to the Pope. The bishop of Lamego reached Rome in November 1641, but the influence of Spain was so strong that he made no progress. As he left the house of the French ambassador, a street battle broke out between French and Portuguese and the Spanish ambassador's lackeys and guard, in which a dozen persons were killed. The delays continued, and when in 1649 the Portuguese cortes appealed to Rome, the only surviving bishop in Portugal was that of Elvas: there were none at all in the islands, Brazil or Africa, and only two in the East. In 1655 a Portuguese ambassador was at last received by a Pope, but it was not until after 1668, when Spain at length recognized Portuguese independence, that the Papacy modified its stand.

Portugal, with its revived monarchy and necessarily national church, must look elsewhere for support. In February 1641 embassies were sent to Spain's chief opponents, France and Holland. That to France was to ask for men, ships and a formal league. At first negotiations went well, but when the French realized that the Portuguese could not retreat, and that a treaty would tie their own hands by impeding a peace with Spain, they refused the league. John IV had attempted to conciliate the Dutch by restoring their right to trade at Lisbon, but he could scarcely offer more, since they were in possession of Northern Brazil. The French feared to compromise their own alliance with the Dutch by a firm commitment to Portugal. Thus in the Franco-Portuguese treaty of July 1641 France simply offered help provided her allies did the same. A French fleet entered the Tagus in August 1641 with the object of attacking Cádiz and perhaps stimulating a revolution in Andalusia, where John IV's brother-in-law Medina Sidonia was thought to be disaffected. But he had been arrested, and Cádiz was strongly held.

On 2 February 1641 John sent a mission to England in pursuit of an alliance. It was well received, and the negotiations were only delayed by the English insistence on receiving the same privileges as had been granted to the Dutch, including the practice of the protestant religion by English merchants in their houses. In Lisbon an archbishop's committee decided that liberty of conscience could not be allowed, but that there could be no objection to extending the rights of other foreigners to the English. Thus on 29 January 1642 a treaty was signed, and the

Ancient Alliance was revived. However, it was nullified with the change of regime in England and the execution of Charles I.

The most problematic negotiation was obviously that with the Dutch, who regarded the Portuguese Restoration as portending the collapse of Spain, and not as a signal to evacuate Brazil—indeed, it was after the enthronement of John IV that the Dutch sent a force to annex Portuguese West Africa. The Portuguese mission to the Hague proposed a ten-year truce, with the return of Northern Brazil and West Africa, the Dutch being compensated at the expense of Spain. But the Dutch refused to include permanent restitution in a temporary truce, and would only accept a suspension of hostilities for ten years, during which the status quo would be maintained in America, Africa and the East. The Dutch would send twenty ships to collaborate with the French and Portuguese, and would allow men and arms to be raised for service in Portugal. In return, they demanded freedom of worship for Dutchmen in Portugal, a promise that only Dutch ships would be freighted by Portugal, and that other foreigners would be excluded from the Portuguese colonies. The twenty Dutch ships were duly sent, but arrived too late to accompany the French and Portuguese expedition against Cádiz. However, twelve other ships carried Dutch officers, arms and horses for the defence of Portugal.

The main object of John IV was to secure the Alentejo against possible Spanish attack. The fortifications of Elvas and other frontier towns were repaired, but there were only small engagements in 1641. In the following year, activities were extended to Beira, but they were still in a minor key. John IV informed the French that he now had 3,000 horse and 20,000 foot, and had taken steps to defend the colonies. But there was difficulty in finding new funds. John IV asked for 2,400,000 *cruzados*. The commoners proposed that this should be divided between the three estates, but neither of the privileged classes was willing. The Jesuit orator, António Vieira, delivered an eloquent sermon on the obligation of nobles and church to support the throne, but the crown was obliged to find 900,000 *cruzados* and the remaining 1,500,000 was saddled on the third estate.

The first notable success of the frontier war was at Montijo in May 1644 when Matias de Albuquerque with 7,000 men, including the small body of Dutch cavalry, drove a large Spanish force back beyond the Guadiana. The Spaniards then tried to reduce Elvas, without success. Philip IV had at last become disillusioned with Olivares and dismissed him, but the Spanish fortunes in Aragon did not improve and the Portuguese continued their defensive operations in the Alentejo, refusing to invade Spain unless guaranteed by the alliance the French were still unwilling to concede. Hopes of a settlement through the general negotiations were disappointed. In 1652 Mazarin offered the coveted league for a payment of 3 million *cruzados*, which John could not find. The Spaniards were then able to transfer troops to the Portuguese frontier, but their attack was broken in the battle of Arronches. The two sides were still stalemated when John died in 1656.

He had lived long enough to see the final reincorporation of Northern Brazil in his realms. The Dutch West India Company was in difficulties, and therefore unwilling to meet the princely expenditures of Johan Maurits, who left Brazil in 1644. In the following May the Brazilians revolted, Portuguese, free Negroes and mixed-bloods taking up arms against a domination which, if it tolerated the Jews, showed little sense of miscegenation. The revolt had taken John by surprise: he feared lest it should expose Portuguese shipping to reprisals. He sent Vieira to offer the Dutch 3 million *cruzados* to leave Brazil, but they refused (1646) and resumed their attacks on Portuguese ships—two hundred and twenty were lost to them in the next two years. But under the influence of a new governor, Salvador Correa de Sá, the patriotic cause gathered momentum, and with the two battles of Guararapes the Luso-Brazilian forces recovered Pernambuco in 1654, bringing the Dutch occupation to a close.

John IV had instituted in 1645 the title of Prince of Brazil in favour of his heir Teodósio, on whose death it passed to his brother, the future Afonso VI (1656–1668). The heir was also Duke of Bragança and enjoyed the very considerable revenues of the house, which was to remain permanently separated from the property of the crown. John's youngest son, Pedro, was given a separate establishment, known as the Casa do Infantado: it included the city and district of Beja and all the properties confiscated from the executed Marquis of Vila Real and his son, the Duke of Caminha. Afonso had suffered a disease in infancy which had left him partly paralysed and impaired his understanding. His tutor found him difficult to control and taught him very little. There was some doubt about his capacity, but it was thought that the critical times required that the throne be occupied. Queen Leonor was regent until 1661. The long negotiations were resumed. Leonor again applied to France for a league and a dynastic alliance, offering a dowry of 1 million *cruzados* and either Tangier or Mazagão. Mazarin asked double, and an annual subsidy for the war. His envoy soon discovered that little could be expected from a 'kingdom afflicted on all sides'. The court was now divided into factions, and it was decided to dismiss the commander D. João da Costa, whose policy was defensive, and to bring in the Count of São Lourenço, who advocated attack. He failed and was dismissed. All hopes of the French league vanished when Mazarin concluded the Peace of the Pyrenees with Spain. In a secret article France agreed to break off relations with Portugal, so that 'the affairs of Portugal might be placed in the state they were in before the revolution'.

The Portuguese were able to engage a notable general, the Count-Duke of Schomberg, who reformed the army, organized regiments of cavalry and built new fortifications. Yet in May 1662 a Spanish army took Borba, and a year later Évora. The invaders were a third of the way to Lisbon, and there were riots in the capital. But Schomberg gathered his forces near Estremós, and won the victory of Ameixial (8 June 1663). Évora was recovered, and the Spanish drive broken. Three years later, when Philip iv died, his widow made peace.

With the final failure of the French league, Queen Leonor had turned her attention to England. The treaty of 1642 had lapsed with the execution of Charles i. In 1649 Prince Rupert had sailed into the Tagus, and had been well received, but the Commonwealth sent Admiral Blake to Lisbon and forced him to leave. John iv then sought a settlement with the Commonwealth which resulted in the Treaty of 1654. For the Portuguese this did little more than put forward a possible alternative to the elusive French league, but the English merchants seized the opportunity to incorporate in it all the privileges they had ever enjoyed at Lisbon. They were never to pay more than 23 per cent in custom-duties, and were to have religious liberty and their own burial-ground. English warships were to be admitted to

Portuguese ports for supplies or repairs, and merchants of either country were to have access to the colonies of the other. In particular, the English were to have their own judge-conservator, a Portuguese official paid by them and empowered to settle all their cases. This was a resuscitation of a medieval practice by which foreign merchants, anxious not to be delayed, were entitled to have all disputes settled summarily by a designated official, usually the judge of the custom-house. The 'judge of the English' was now regarded as the protector of the English privileges, a situation which paved the way for the highly favourable trade of the eighteenth century.

When France made peace with Spain, Queen Luisa instructed her ambassador in London to negotiate for arms and men. In April 1660 permission was given to recruit, but with the English Restoration it was necessary to start again. The English government were willing to send aid, but reluctant to risk war with Spain. The Portuguese ambassadors therefore raised the question of a league and a marriage alliance. Charles II would wed Catherine of Bragança, and England would defend Portugal against Spain and Holland. Catherine would bring a dowry fixed at 2 million *cruzados* with the cession of Tangier and the right to trade in the Portuguese colonies. The addition of Bombay was the beginning of British interest in India. The treaty was confirmed on 6 June 1661, and it revived those of 1642 and 1654. The English were to defend Portugal 'as if it were England itself'. In April 1662 Catherine of Bragança sailed from Lisbon, and English forces arrived in Portugal in time to stem the Spanish advance and participate in the victory of Ameixial.

Queen Luisa had already been removed from the regency. The young Afonso VI had made a favourite of a street-vendor called António Conti, who was installed in the palace, to the scandal of the court. The Queen established her youngest son Pedro in the neighbouring Corte-Real palace. In June 1661 the Duke of Cadaval arrested Conti and put him on a ship for Brazil. Luisa then called nobles, officials and representatives of the guilds and admonished Afonso, who displayed little interest. However, one of his attendants, the Count of Castelo-Melhor, persuaded him that he was in danger and took him to Alcântara, where he announced that he had taken over the reins of government. The Queen's regency was terminated, and Castelo-Melhor became

escrivão da poridade or secret secretary. In effect, he wielded
supreme power and held it for five years: Luisa retired to a convent.

It thus fell to Castelo-Melhor to negotiate for peace with
Spain. Schomberg crowned his career with the victory of Montes
Claros in June 1665. Three months later Philip IV died, and it
seemed possible that the Spanish court would at last accept the
existence of a king of Portugal. Since 1663 negotiations had been
afoot to marry Afonso to a French princess, Marie-Françoise-
Isabelle of Savoy. She finally reached Lisbon in August 1666. She
found Afonso completely under the control of Castelo-Melhor,
and therefore aligned herself with his rivals. In September 1667
Afonso was finally persuaded to dismiss the all-powerful minister,
who fled to England to become adviser to Catherine of Bragança.

The incapacity of the king was manifest, and a substantial
party favoured his removal. The *câmara* of Lisbon asked for a
session of cortes to declare his brother regent. Finally in November the French queen left him and retired to a convent. The
Marquis of Cascais then persuaded Afonso to surrender power
to Pedro. In January 1668 cortes were convoked in Lisbon, and
Pedro was made Prince-Regent. The marriage of Afonso to
Marie-Françoise was annulled, and she married Pedro. Afonso
was kept in confinement at Angra in the Azores until 1674, when
he was brought to Sintra. There he lived in captivity until his
death in 1683.

Portugal had little to fear from Spain during the long reign
of Philip IV's pathetic son, Charles II. France now sought to
wrest away the last vestiges of Spanish power in the north, while
England and Holland grew alarmed at the growing might of
Louis XIV. Portugal, impoverished by her long struggle, had no
desire to be involved in these quarrels. Her first object was not
to risk a new conflict with Spain. In 1661 the Dutch had recognized her recovery of Brazil in return for an indemnity which had
soon fallen into arrears. For France she was a useful tool in the
long campaign to weaken Spain. Colbert offered to help her to
recover the Eastern trade from the Dutch (1669). In 1672 the
French supplemented the plan for joint action against the Dutch
with an offer of troops for the defence of Portugal in the event of
a war with Spain: but this was precisely the war the Portuguese
wished to avoid.

The French made peace with Spain in 1679 and sought to consolidate their influence in the Peninsula by marrying Charles II to a French princess and Pedro's little heiress to a prince of Savoy. Cortes consented to this marriage, but when in 1682 a fleet was sent to bring back the bridegroom, he failed to appear. This rebuff gave great offence at the Portuguese court, and when Marie-Françoise died in the following year, Pedro married Maria of Neuberg, outside the French orbit. It was to the eldest son of this marriage, the future John v, that the Portuguese succession passed. Meanwhile Louis xiv was intent on securing the succession to the Spanish crown by creating a party in Madrid and appeasing the other powers at Spain's expense. In 1700 Charles ii accepted the Bourbon succession and died, and Louis's grandson became Philip v of Spain. Portugal, faced with a Franco-Spanish bloc, joined in a treaty of alliance for twenty years: in case of war she would close her ports to enemies of the Bourbons, who would help her to regain her possessions in the East.

But the extension of Bourbon power in the Peninsula and in Italy now aroused the other powers; and England, Holland and Austria entered into the Grand Alliance (October 1701), designed to bring an Austrian Habsburg to the throne of Spain. Louis xiv retorted by recognizing the Stuart succession to the English throne. For Portugal the Bourbon treaty was incompatible with the Anglo-Portuguese Alliance. When in May 1702 the Grand Alliance declared war on the Bourbon courts, negotiations were opened to secure Portugal's adherence. This was achieved by the first of the Methuen treaties in May 1703. The Austrian pretender to the Spanish throne would be enabled to launch a campaign from Portuguese territory, and the allies would in part finance the Portuguese army. The Archduke would himself wage war, and would make territorial concessions to Portugal, which would receive guarantees from England and Holland.

In the war of the Spanish Succession, Portuguese armies under the Marquis of Minas entered Madrid in 1706. But in the following year the Anglo-Portuguese forces were defeated in Valencia, and Bourbon troops occupied the Portuguese towns of Serpa and Moura. It was clear that the Austrian pretender had little real support outside Barcelona, and his succession to the Austrian throne in 1711 made his allies reconsider. The peace treaties established a balance of power in Europe. Portugal made terms first with France, then with Spain. The Peninsular frontier was restored, but in South America Portugal's claim to the Sacramento colony on the northern bank of the river Plate was recognized.

Pedro II had died in the midst of the war, and his son John V (1706–1750) married the sister of the Habsburg pretender, now Emperor. Under the peace the threat of a single Bourbon state incorporating France and Spain was removed: the interests of the two Bourbon courts were divergent, though they might be reconciled by family pacts. Against these Portugal had three remedies, the political and economic Alliance with England, the dynastic association with the distant Empire, and a dazzling increase in her own resources, the consequence of the discovery of treasure in Brazil.

If the regime of the Restoration was a new monarchy, its justification lay not in the personality of John IV, a great landowner with a taste for musical composition (much less in that of his successor, the unfortunate Afonso VI), but in the need to represent Portuguese society through a monarch, who must be a Portuguese and must represent the national concept of legitimacy. It was believed that the monarchy itself was divinely ordained on behalf of Afonso Henriques and that it was constituted by the supposed cortes of Lamego of 1139. This was a sophistication by seventeenth-century antiquarians. Nevertheless, its very invention shows that cortes were recognized as expressing the will of the nation. John IV duly celebrated cortes in 1641, 1642, 1645–6 and 1653–4. Under Afonso VI cortes were held in 1668, 1674, 1677 and 1679–80: Pedro II held cortes in 1697–8, after which the institution disappeared. All the cortes of the seventeenth century were held at Lisbon.

For John IV the purpose of cortes was to secure national support for and legitimization of his kingship and to obtain money. Under Afonso VI the problem of the king's person and the need for his removal and for a successor affected the nation. But from the time of Pedro II there were no further problems about the succession, and the ruler no longer depended on votes for supply. John IV's attempt to obtain grants from the nobility and clergy through cortes had failed, and although new taxes were levied on all classes, they were achieved through a special board on which the three estates were represented. The cortes were thus of diminishing importance after the war of the Restoration.

The crown had always preserved the right to decide when to summon cortes and which places to summon to represent the third estate. In 1668 ninety-two towns were summoned. The procurators were designated by the *concelhos* or their *câmaras*, and might be either commoners, or clergy or nobles. Thus in Lisbon, whose procurators were the spokesmen for the whole assembly, one was a leading nobleman and the other a lawyer or *letrado* acceptable to the bishop. The Lisbon *câmara* itself was not an elected body. In 1572 Sebastian had reorganized it and appointed a president and three *vereadores* with specific responsibilities. The president was a nobleman and the *vereadores* lawyers. By 1591, there were six *vereadores*, all *letrados* and *desembargadores*, or judges of the royal court, and their salaries were paid in part by the city and in part by the royal treasury.

Elsewhere, the officials of the *câmara* were elected triennially by methods laid down in the *Ordenações Manuelinas* and *Filipinas* and modified in 1670. The *corregedor* of each *comarca* was required to select three senior and notable citizens and obtain from them the names of those thought suitable to exercise local authority, taking into account their own aptitude and the record of their families. The *corregedor* then called these, and others, if he saw fit, and asked them to choose six electors, who finally chose the *vereadores* and other officials. As the instructions of the *corregedores* imply, there was an increasing tendency to regard office as hereditary, or at least to restrict it to *fidalgos*.

The only representation of the lower orders was through the *juiz do povo*, the people's judge, and the procurators of the guilds. Those of Lisbon, which were taken to be representative of the interests and opinions of the artisans of the whole country, not only participated in the deliberations of the *câmara*, but were consulted in the seventeenth century on critical issues. Thus when the peace with Spain was hanging in the balance, the British minister, Southwell, informed the people's judge of what had been concluded with Spain, and the popular enthusiasm for the settlement was such that D. Pedro could not oppose it.

John IV's chief advisers formed his Council of State, a small body of noblemen which met at least once a week, on Monday afternoons. The king worked constantly with his ministers, and sometimes the queen attended meetings. If the king did not go, its business was transmitted in writing by the royal secretary. Under Queen Luisa, the Council had two factions led by the Count of Cantanhede, a descendant of the first Duke of Bragança, and the Count of Odemira, a collateral of a former queen and tutor to Afonso vi. Under Pedro ii the leading figures were the Duke of Cadaval, two of whose sons married the king's illegitimate daughter, and the Marquis of Alegrete, himself a soldier and writer and a relative by marriage of the Marquis of Minas and Count of Atalaia, the leading generals of the day.

John iv's secretaries, the Secretary of State and Secretary of the Wardrobe, belonged to neither of the parties. He had thought of reviving the old office of *escrivão da puridade* or secret secretary. The title was finally assumed by the Count of Castelo-Melhor, who was in fact universal minister or vizir to Afonso vi. Under Pedro ii the half-dozen members of the Council, the duke, two marquises and three counts, were the principal advisers, and the two secretaries were less prominent figures, one acting as secretary to the Council and the other handling foreign affairs. It was only in the eighteenth century that the secretaries became ministers in the modern sense.

The Spanish regime had led to the formation of the Junta for finance (*fazenda*) or treasury. The *vèdor da Fazenda* was a member of the Council of State, and under Pedro ii the Count of Ericeira held the office from 1675 until his death in 1690, pursuing a policy of protectionism and industrialization. On his death, there were two treasurers, Alegrete and Roque Monteiro, who was private secretary and confidential adviser to the king. Immediately after the restoration in 1643, John iv had instituted a body to deal with matters of military organization and to supervise the collection of new taxes: the second capacity proved the more lasting, and it was composed of representatives of the three orders of cortes, and therefore known as the Junta of the Three Estates. Of its seven members one was appointed by the crown, one chosen by the nobles, two by the church and two by the third estate: these last were *fidalgos*, not citizens. In the same year of 1643, John instituted a new board, the Conselho Ultramarino, to advise on the affairs of the overseas provinces.

The machinery of government was comprised in or about the royal household. With the exception of the traditional offices of

Mordomo-mór, Constable and Meirinho-mór, and of the one or two dukes, precedence was held by the principal juridical and fiscal officials, the Regedor of the Court of Appeal (Casa de Suplicação), the Chanceler-mór, the vèdores of the treasury, the desembargadores, or judges of appeal, and the corregedores. The six members of the Desembargo formed a privy council for judicial and administrative affairs. All these were fidalgos. There was a strong concentration of administrative authority at court. There had long been dissatisfaction that all appeals had to go to Lisbon, and Sebastian had set up the alçadas (assizes), one to the north of the Tagus and the other to the south. It was left to Philip II to decide, perhaps for political reasons, to establish a separate court of appeal, the Relação, at Oporto; its territory comprised the Minho, Trás-os-Montes and part of Beira. Thus the northern capital acquired a certain pre-eminence over the northern part of the country.

For the purposes of general administration Portugal was considered to consist of six provinces—Entre-Douro-e-Minho, Trás-os-Montes, Beira, Estremadura, Entre-Tejo-e-Guadiana (i.e. Alentejo) and Algarve. The word comarca was now applied to their subdivisions, in each of which the corregedor performed administrative, judicial and even military functions. It was his duty to see that the concelhos elected the câmaras and if they failed to do so to appoint vereadores himself. He was similarly expected to decide conflicts between concelhos.

In all the more important places, and indeed wherever it thought appropriate, the crown could appoint a qualified judge, who, coming from outside, was known as the juiz de fora. The practice of appointing these professional magistrates had been greatly extended in the sixteenth century. Elsewhere, in smaller places, the usual local magistrates were the juizes ordinários appointed by the concelhos, often two in number. They carried red wands and held court weekly in places with less than sixty households and twice weekly in places with more. They were elected for three years. It was perhaps not always easy to find suitable candidates: when in 1642 the corregedor of Alenquer discovered that one of the juizes was illiterate, he forbade the election of such persons. The fiscal affairs of the comarcas were controlled by provedores, who oversaw the collection of revenue and inspected the books of the concelhos.

By the end of the seventeenth century the royal revenues were estimated at about 10,000 *contos* of *reis* (or 10 million *milreis*). About half of this was disbursed in pensions and similar obligations. During the Spanish occupation the nobility had played a rather subdued role; a number of titles had lapsed and few had been created. With the Restoration, new honours had been granted, but these could not be on a lavish scale. The Braganças were wealthy in their own right, and they had devoted much of their resources to the pursuit of the war: when it was over, they were better off than their subjects.

The chief source of internal revenue was the *sisa*, or sales-tax, which Philip II described as the mainstay of the royal estate, defence and justice. It had been supplemented by the *real de água*, a tax on sales of wine and meat, so called because it was introduced first to pay for the Lisbon water-supply. Its generalization, together with an increase of 25 per cent in the *sisa*, had been a chief cause of discontent with the Spanish regime. This partly explains John IV's solicitude to consult *cortes* at the beginning of his reign, and his interest in finding new sources of taxation. The long struggle near the frontier had impoverished, and in part depopulated the eastern Alentejo.

John IV had seen the revival of trade as his best resource. The Braganças, although essentially landowners, themselves had industrial interests in Portugal and drew revenues from the overseas possessions. John had flung open the ports to the merchants of all countries and allowed them to take out their profits. British, Dutch and others had supplied him with arms, metals and wheat, and had exported Portuguese wines, salt, dried fruits and sugar. The customs-dues of 20 per cent on imports was a considerable item in the revenues, but with the decline in sugar prices it was increasingly difficult to match essential imports. After 1680 as the value of sugar fell, the duties on it were increased. Moreover, since the Restoration a large part of Portugal's trade had been in foreign hands. It was necessary to stimulate commerce among the Portuguese. In 1643 Vieira drew attention to the folly of persecuting the New Christians, who alone possessed the experience and, it was believed, the capital, to restore the economy. Six years passed before John ordered the Inquisition to return the property of New Christians to be used to found a Brazil Company, which was to have its own charter, fleet and means of defence. It proved that the New Christian families were less wealthy than had been supposed. Moreover, with the English acquisition of Jamaica the market for Brazilian sugar was narrowed and the continued increase in planting lowered prices and profits. In 1658 it was necessary to terminate the new company, which was taken over by the state.

The conclusion of the war with Spain, instead of giving relief, coincided with a period of restriction. It was thought that the period of enforced restraint was followed by a wave of extravagance and Ericeira attempted to curb display in clothes, adornments, coaches and servants, while also seeking to stimulate Portuguese production. Silk stockings were now in vogue, and Ericeira ordered the planting of mulberry-trees and the hiring of Spanish weavers to create a Portuguese silk-industry. He also decreed that only Portuguese hats, ribbons and lace should be used, and forbade the import of various woollens (1686). It would appear that the Restoration had put an end to the practice of transhumance of sheep between Spain and Portugal and obliged the Portuguese to import woollens. The sumptuary laws forbade the introduction of coloured cloths and the use of gold and silver lace, and for several years male attire was of drab cloth, the upper classes being distinguished mainly by the use of swords and spectacles. The effect of Ericeira's controls is seen in a decline in the number of English merchants in Lisbon between 1670 and 1690.

The traditional Portuguese trade with the East was now much reduced. Not more than three ships were sent every year, though they were large vessels of 800 tons. They brought back silks, carpets, cotton, pepper, dyestuffs and diamonds. The capital required was large and the risks high, but the profits were still considerable. The trade to Brazil consisted of an annual fleet of eighty-eight ships escorted by six warships. These were smaller vessels of 250–500 tons, but the freights and profits were now low. However, in the time of Pedro ii, the royal control of Brazil-wood, tobacco and pepper were important sources of revenue.

In Portugal itself, most of what might be called luxury manufacturing was directed towards the needs of the church—which was also a considerable consumer of imported textiles. When the sumptuary laws were relaxed—after the death of Ericeira in 1690—silks, ribbons and fancy cloths were obtained from France (often indirectly), and sheets and butter from Holland. But these imports were accompanied by a large range of staples —cloth from England, timber from Scandinavia, metals and rope from Holland, and dried cod from Newfoundland, which had become a usual article of diet, as it still is. The Portuguese ingredient in the dried-cod trade was salt, produced at Alcácer and Aveiro, but English ships took the salt to the fisheries, visiting the Atlantic Isles and the American colonies on the way.

6

THE EIGHTEENTH CENTURY

Having turned her back on integration with Spain, Portugal must inevitably look outside the Peninsula. What she could acquire was limited by what she could export—fruits, olive-oil, salt and a few other items. The prospect of a substantial increase in sales of wine became discernible in 1678, when the English prohibited the entry of French wine: after 1690 Portuguese wine, first the fortified wine of Oporto, and later wines from the centre and from Lisbon, were bought in increasing quantities for the English market. When Portugal adhered to the Grand Alliance, the English negotiator, John Methuen, whose family had interests in the cloth-trade, perceived that the opportunity to send the new English worsteds to Portugal depended on a guarantee of the English market for Portuguese wines, and rapidly concluded the treaty that bears his name in December 1703.

The simplicity of the Methuen Treaty, which consisted of only two articles, and the speed with which it was concluded, make it remarkable in the annals of diplomacy. Its consequences have been discussed by economists, and Portuguese writers have often seen in it the sacrifice of their nascent industry, perhaps overlooking the benefits to the renascent wine-trade. But in 1703 Ericeira's protectionism had already been abandoned, and the Portuguese woollen industry was not flourishing. Neither party at that time could have foreseen the vast influx of wealth which would again dilate the Portuguese economy during the following years.

This was due to the discovery of gold in central Brazil. The pioneers of São Paulo, known as *bandeirantes*, since they travelled under the banner of their leader, combed the interior for treasure in expeditions that sometimes lasted for years. It was only in 1692 that river-gold was discovered in the Mato Grosso. The great strikes of the 'General Mines' (Minas Gerais) began two

years later. Thousands of prospectors were drawn from São
Paulo, Northern Brazil and Portugal. They flocked to the region
of Ouro Preto, which by 1705 had a population of 50,000 . The
Paulistas, hitherto few and poor, attempted to control the diggings, but the interlopers or *emboabas* outnumbered them and
could afford slaves, thus giving rise to the 'wars of the *emboabas*'.
The crown itself did not engage in mining, but claimed the royal
fifth which was deducted as the gold passed through the royal
smelting-house. Most of the mines were small undertakings,
consisting of the owner and his party of slaves. In 1705 a fleet
brought about 16,000 lb of gold to Lisbon. In 1728 diamonds
were discovered in the same area: this trade was much more
closely controlled by the government, which constantly feared
lest the market, centred at Amsterdam, should become satur-
ated.

Aided by this wealth, John V was able to play the part of the
absolute monarch. It was unnecessary for him to apply to cortes
for subsidies, and they were not convoked at all during the
eighteenth century. Much of the new wealth was applied to
ceremonies, royal weddings and munificent gifts. The massive
palace of Mafra was raised as if to match Versailles and the
Escorial. A considerable part of the gold passed to the church.
John himself desired that his chapel should be raised to a patriarchate and detached the whole of western Lisbon—Lisboa
Ocidental—to make a new see. The patriarch was granted all
the honours enjoyed by cardinals, and from 1737 the patriarchs
of Lisbon always became cardinals. John was often led on by a
desire to match other courts: in France, Spain and Austria, the
papal nuncios were cardinals, and he embarked on a long struggle
with Rome to gain the same privilege. But John also established
the Aqueduct of Free Waters to supply the fountains of Lisbon,
and he endowed the University of Coimbra with its magnifi-
cently decorated library. Some of the splendid products of the
age are exhibited in the Coach Museum in Lisbon. The king also
figured as the patron of culture, founding a Royal Academy of
History and lending his sponsorship to such works as Bluteau's
Vocabulário, and *Biblioteca Lusitana*, the *Corpus Poetarum Lusitano-
rum* and Caetano de Sousa's Genealogical History of the Royal
House.

John remained at peace with his neighbours. He himself had

been married to Maria Ana, the Emperor's sister, during the war of the Spanish succession. In 1728 their children José and Barbara were married to the Spanish prince and princess, the children of Philip v. Barbara and her husband, Ferdinand (vi), were devoted to one another, to music and to neutrality: there was therefore no danger from the neighbouring kingdom. The Portuguese heir, José, divided his time between riding and the opera, without experience of or interest in public affairs. John v relied chiefly on the secretaries, who in 1736 were three in number, the senior of them handling internal affairs, or State; the second taking foreign and military affairs, and the third the colonies and navy. The first secretaryship, or ministry of state, was long held by Cardinal da Mota until his death in 1747, when it passed to his nephew Pedro, an invalid. Marco António de Azevedo Coutinho directed foreign affairs until his death in 1749, when the place was given to Fr. Gaspar da Encarnação. As his private adviser, John had a Neapolitan Jesuit, Padre Carbone. In the later part of the reign, John himself grew indolent and lethargic, and surrounded himself with ecclesiastics.

The flow of wealth lasted the whole reign. The value of gold and diamonds entering Portugal was:

1711–15	£728,000	1731–5	£1,113,980
1716–20	£315,168	1736–40	£1,311,175
1721–5	£1,715,204	1741–5	£1,371,680
1726–30	£693,465		

The immediate effect of this circulation of treasure was to stimulate Portugal's capacity to import, particularly from England. The commerce between the two countries developed as follows:

	UK Imports into Portugal	Exports from Portugal
1711–15	£610,000	£242,000
1721–5	£816,000	£387,000
1731–5	£1,024,000	£326,000
1741–5	£1,115,000	£439,000
1746–50	£1,114,000	£324,000

Even in 1703 the 'Portugal trade' had accounted for 11 per cent of England's overseas trade. It was now rendered even more attractive by the flow of gold which financed the growing imbalance. Although the Portuguese share in total English imports of wines increased from 40 per cent at the beginning of the century to 70 per cent in 1751–5, English imports to Portugal expanded much faster.

In Portugal it was not at first appreciated that while the country was swimming in gold the new situation did not stimulate industry or alleviate poverty. Until this time all Portuguese industrial production with only insignificant exceptions was in the hands of small workshops with few craftsmen. More than a third of the population of Lisbon was engaged in industry, but the economic strength of each unit was very limited. By tradition, artisans were poor, and only merchants acquired wealth. It was therefore necessary for the crown to provide the stimulus for industries on a larger scale. It already had some experience in certain directions, such as silk-making and undertakings of military interest, the casting of iron for artillery and the introduction of English advances in shipbuilding. Between 1720 and 1740 it gave its support to industrial paper-making, produced at Lousã from about 1717, the glass-factory at Coina on the Tagus, 1722–7, and the processing of leather. But there was no general plan of development nor any official apparatus to make good the lack of skilled management. Not all the new industries were successful. The glass-industry failed and was shifted to Marinha Grande in 1748. Even the Royal Silk Factory was operated at a loss at the end of the reign.

John V died, pious and penitent, in 1750. His heir, the indolent José, was now thirty-six. But scarcely had he succeeded than Fr. Gaspar's secretaryship was conferred on Sebastião José de Carvalho e Melo, the future Marquis of Pombal. The new minister was a member of the minor nobility, and a nephew of the late Azevedo Coutinho. He had served as Portuguese minister in London and Vienna, where he married a daughter of Marshal Daun, a connection which brought him access to the Austrian queen-mother. He quickly made himself indispensable to his idle master and remained so for the twenty-seven years of the reign.

Pombal found the flow of Brazilian gold in decline and the mechanism of the state almost paralysed. His first task was to improve the revenues from Brazil. He proposed to accept a fixed levy from the gold-miners, rather than a tax on the number of

Negroes employed, which discouraged prospecting. He could do little to reverse the downward movement of production, but he could enforce the ancient laws which prohibited the export of gold, despite the objections of the English merchants. He directed their protests away from their judge-conservator to the ordinary courts, which upheld him. He blamed the system of annual fleets for depressing the prices of sugar and tobacco which arrived all at once and flooded the market. He lessened duties to stimulate the re-export of tobacco and sought to encourage sugar-refining in Portugal. The diamond-trade had been let out to contractors who were saddled with large stocks: Pombal challenged the Jewish monopoly of distribution by setting up a marketing agency in Amsterdam, but it was not conspicuously successful. While in England, Pombal had realized that the market for Portuguese wines was much larger than his compatriots imagined, but that the fortified wine of the Douro, port, was confused with cheaper products from central Portugal and Lisbon: the pipe of wine worth 60,000 reis at the beginning of the century now fetched 6,400. He created the General Company for Wine-Culture in the Upper Douro (1750) which had powers to define the port-wine area, assure the quality of wine, buy it and sell to the merchants. Its directors must be Portuguese, and its judge had precedence over other courts. Pombal hoped much from such national companies, and launched a Company for Trade with Asia in 1753, and the Grão-Pará Company in 1755; the latter with Portuguese directors and a monopoly of the export and wholesale trade. Evidently Pombal wanted Lisbon to imitate under his direction the City of London. He transformed the loosely organized Mesa do Bem Comum, or mercantile association, into a new Junta do Comércio, which had direct control over trade, had its own court and could forbid the import of luxuries.

In 1755 the capital was shattered by the great Lisbon earthquake. On the morning of All Saints' Day a series of shocks threw down temples, palaces and dwellings and filled the air with dust. A tidal wave flooded the waterfront and Terreiro do Paço. Perhaps 5 per cent of the population of 270,000 perished. The palaces near the port were destroyed, and so were the Patriarchate, the Inquisition and the churches of São Domingos and the Carmo. Pombal was the only active minister, and the crisis enhanced his authority. He became minister of state on the death of Mota, and chose his own candidate to fill the vacancy. The concentration of authority was not achieved without making enemies, especially among the senior nobles, the Jesuits and some merchants. When a group of his rivals presented a memorandum to the king, José showed it to Pombal, who arrested them. He took the opportunity to make his brother, who had been governing Pará, minister for the colonies. In 1757 when the people of Oporto rioted in protest against the high price of wine, which they blamed on the new company, Pombal set up a special court to try them and caused seventeen to be hanged and twenty-five sent to the galleys. A year later he struck at the nobility. This was a small and exclusive class: the dukes claimed kinship with the king, and there were only nine marquises and thirty-three counts. Most of them dwelt in or near Lisbon, and were employed in the offices of court, on embassies or as governors. The Duke of Lafões had already been sent to Vienna, where he was to spend twenty years in exile. In September 1758 an attempt to shoot the king afforded Pombal with a motive to arrest the Duke of Aveiro, his son the Marquis of Gouvêa, the Marquis of Távora and the Count of Atouguia. They were given a form of trial and barbarously executed at Belém. Other members of their families were kept under arrest until Pombal fell. In the trial Pombal was careful to associate the judge of the people and the Lisbon guilds with his actions.

There remained the Jesuits. The missionaries in Pará had opposed Pombal's monopolistic company, and four of them were deported. On their return they approached José, who requested that the Spanish Jesuit, St Francis Borja, should be made protector of Portugal. But the Jesuits regarded the earthquake as a divine punishment for the wickedness of the Portuguese. In particular, Gabriel Malagrida, who had gained such a reputation by his preaching to the Brazilian Indians that John v regarded him as a saint, composed a work on the subject. Worse still, he had been in close touch with the persecuted aristocrats and had addressed a bitter criticism of Pombal to the Pope. In September 1759 the Jesuits were outlawed and expelled from Portugal by royal decree, being transported to Rome. Malagrida was tried for treason and executed in a spectacular *auto-da-fé*. About one hundred and twenty-four Jesuits were confined near Lisbon, and forty-five were still there when José's death released them. Pombal's defence of regalism was soon taken up by the courts of France and Spain, which also expelled the Jesuits, and pressed for the extinction of the Society.

Pombal had closed the Jesuit University at Évora, and in 1761 he founded the College of Nobles, which was intended to replace Jesuit influence in the preparation of the aristocracy, who were to be introduced to modern languages, mathematics and the sciences. In 1768 the Royal Board of Censorship was set up with exclusive rights to censor all periodicals and books. In 1771 the same body was given control of lower education, and in 1772 Pombal made himself 'lieutenant-general' of the University of Coimbra and set about rooting out Jesuit influence and reorganizing the teaching by adding faculties of natural sciences and mathematics, and creating laboratories, an observatory, a botanic garden and museum of natural history.

Pombal's most lasting achievement was the reconstruction of central Lisbon after the great earthquake. It was the first and grandest piece of town-planning in Portugal since Roman times. In June 1775 it was sufficiently advanced to erect an equestrian statue—the first in Portugal—of José I in the Terreiro do Paço, the 'Black Horse Square'. Pombal took the opportunity to describe the achievements of the reign for the king's benefit. He asserted that he had made Portugal literate, by which he meant that merchants who needed clerks could now find plenty of applicants. He believed that he had made Portugal self-supporting in many articles that had once been imported, and that he had revitalized and modernized Portuguese culture. He also told the king that the country was in the highest state of prosperity.

If the great earthquake had shaken established assumptions, the great minister had succeeded in shaking the old order. Absolute government claimed to dispose of all the resources of the state. It began to be systematized and to acquire its own ideology. Absolutism implied equality before the crown, and this was but a single step—though a long one—from the equality before the law proclaimed a generation later: the theorists of liberalism were to proceed from the reformed University of Coimbra. Many of its champions were the descendants of that mercantile middle class whose want Pombal had hoped to supply.

But his belief that he had created a new prosperity was exaggerated. The volume of gold received from Brazil continued to decline. During 1736 to 1751 it averaged 125·4 *arrobas* a year. From 1752 to 1787 it fell to 86·1, and from 1788 to 1801 to 44·5. The demand for Brazilian sugar also dwindled as England, France and Holland found alternative sources of supply. Brazil's total exports were worth £5 million in 1760, but only £3 million in 1770. The shrinking of the supply of gold was necessarily mirrored in Portuguese imports, which fell from a peak of £1,200,000 after 1750 to £635,000 and £532,000 in 1771–3. The commercial crisis is reflected in Pombal's policies. During the first half of his regime, his principal object had been to create large trading organizations and to stimulate the ambitions of merchants, but in his last decade, as Portugal's capacity to import shrank and trade stagnated, he turned rather to the encouragement of manufactures which would replace imports. A French report of 1764 noted that Portuguese imports included staple foodstuffs such as grain and dried fish, as well as textiles and other manufactures, and added with palpable exaggeration that Portugal had neither agriculture nor manufacture, nor highways, nor navigation: it knew of the importance of Brazilian gold, but not that it was declining. A similar report of 1778 noted the fall in the supply of gold and the reduction of the royal revenues.

Pombal's administrative reforms included the centralization of the tax system by the creation of the Real Erário in 1761. Until this time there was no central agency to record collections and payments. The Casa dos Contos confined its activities to auditing the accounts of every custom-house, receiver and paymaster. The lack of a uniform procedure tolerated much confusion and irregularity. The new Erário was supervised by an inspector-general—Pombal himself—and a treasurer-general. It was divided into four sections, each under a comptroller-general: (1) the court and Estremadura, (2) the rest of continental Portugal and the Atlantic Isles, (3) Bahia, Maranhão and West Africa, and (4) Rio de Janeiro, East Africa and the East. The first of these officials were merchants. The system of double entry book-keeping was introduced.

Pombal's power depended entirely on the king, on whose death he was at once dismissed. His victims were liberated from the prisons, and a revulsion against his regime swept the country.

José was succeeded by his daughter Maria i, who had been married to her uncle Pedro (iii). She was torn between attachment to her father's memory and the pressure of the rehabilitated aristocrats, and eventually lost her reason. Yet Pombal's son remained president of the municipality of Lisbon, and few of the changes he had made were abruptly undone. He had created the Intendancy of Police in 1760, and his nominee, Pina Manique, remained in office. Although Maria chose her ministers from among the noble families, she also called on José Seabra da Silva, one of Pombal's most promising protégés from Coimbra, and also one of his victims. The Jesuits applied for restitution, but the queen refused to readmit them, though she sent them relief. The business of censorship was restored to the church, until in 1794 the onset of the French revolution made it necessary to set up a political tribunal.

The belief that Pombal had left a full treasury was soon disproved. The property seized from the persecuted nobles and the Jesuits had been dispersed. Salaries and pensions were in arrears and the armed forces neglected. It was necessary to reduce sharply the expenses of the royal household. The lavish operatic and equestrian performances dear to José were given up, his singers dispersed and his horses sold. Maria and Pedro held court in the rococo palace of Queluz. The queen was timid, benevolent and conscience-ridden. It was said that her heir, José, had advanced ideas, but on his death the succession passed to his brother John, a man as mild as their mother. The domestic virtues were in fashion, and the royal family regarded its subjects with benign paternalism.

Pombal's cult of the merchant had led to the emergence of some considerable fortunes, and new palaces began to rise in Lisbon. The Grão-Pará and Pernambuco Companies, which had long been in difficulties, were wound up. A board of administration was set up to take over the state enterprises. It cut subsidies to the silk-industry and sold off the woollen-factories to private persons. In the last decade of the century trade began to revive and prices moved sharply upward. In 1764 only one ship a year had sailed for Goa: now twenty vessels were engaged in trade with the East and six of them reached China. Appreciable quantities of Portuguese wine were exported to Russia: the produce of the silk-factory went to Brazil—though because of its high prices this was its only overseas market. Trade became so brisk that a French reporter thought that a tenth of the population of Lisbon was engaged in contraband.

From 1782 the general rise of prices was in train. Thus wheat which stood at 395 *reis* the *alqueire* in Lisbon in 1750, was 375 in 1760, 405 in 1770, 577 in 1780, 560 in 1790, 893 in 1800 and 1,000 in 1801. In Oporto the same commodity was 560 *reis* in 1750, 550 in 1760, 600 in 1770, 650 in 1780, 750 in 1790, 1200 in 1800 and 1,800 in 1810. Other goods followed a similar course. As prices rose, the supply of gold decreased, and the currency, which had been $95\frac{1}{2}$ per cent gold until 1772 became increasingly silver. In 1796 the state for the first time issued paper-money, which became legal tender in the following year. The new currency was soon exchanged at a discount, though this remained moderate until 1807, when the notes lost half their value under the shadow of the French invasions.

The revenues of the state, which had amounted to 3,582 *contos* in 1716, reached 11,045 *contos* in 1804. The part played by the tax on gold fell from 350 *contos* (1719) to 100 *contos* in 1800. Receipts from the custom-house were still by far the largest item in the revenues of the state: they had mounted from 1,777 *contos* to 4,631 *contos*. But whereas they had formerly represented 60 per cent of the whole, they were now only 39 per cent. To some degree the new situation reflects more efficient means of collecting taxation, but it also covers new sources of taxation. Royal revenues from the monopolies ('exclusive commerce') nearly doubled from 760 *contos* to 1354 *contos*. Even the *sisa* or sales-tax nearly doubled.

The statistics for foreign trade show a similar movement. From the low levels of 1774 imports increased sixfold and exports eightfold, and in 1800 the unfavourable balance was cancelled. In particular, imports from the United Kingdom were substantially reduced, while exports were increased. Exports to Brazil multiplied tenfold in the last quarter of a century, and exports to other parts of Europe tripled, rising from about 6 per cent to 11 per cent of the whole. There were corresponding increases of trade with Spain.

To some extent this development reflects an increase in traditional activities. Exports of port-wine reached new heights, to the advantage of Oporto and its district. An innovation was the rapid development of Brazilian cotton. As late as 1776 this had little importance. By 1789 it was considerable, and in the last years of the century it exceeded 300,000 *arrobas*, and prices were rising: much of this went to the new factories in Britain. But to a large extent the new situation reflected a rapid growth of activity in Portugal itself. The fall of imports from the United Kingdom was not accompanied by a rise of imported manufactured goods from other parts, but by a substantial increase in Portuguese production. The Junta do Comércio was busy with the licensing of new undertakings and the issue of new privileges. Perhaps not many of these represented entirely new activities, but these were now more persistent and better co-ordinated.

The wave of industrial enterprise was accompanied by increased imports of raw materials, metals, wood, leather, and cotton. This in turn gave further advantages to the ports, and particularly to Lisbon and Oporto, where most industrial production took place. The manufacture of woollens tended to concentrate at Covilhã in Beira and between Portalegre and Elvas, using wool from the Serra da Estrela and Beira Baixa. Outside the areas immediately affected by international commerce and specialized industry, Portugal was still a collection of local economies. There was a wide variation in weights and measures, even between Lisbon and Oporto. In most places the roads were extremely bad, indeed it was sometimes held that bad roads were a means of defence. Except where recourse could be had to coastal shipping or river traffic, the local economies were linked by carriers (*almocreves, recoveiros*) and carters. Every city or town had its body of carriers under the supervision of the *almotacé*. They travelled in groups, carrying chiefly fish, wine, oil, salt, honey, and wax. The freights were fixed, but usually increased by a quarter in winter. The increasing circulation of goods in the eighteenth century is marked by the revival of the practice of licensing fairs. The rulers conceded a large number of annual or semi-annual fairs, usually in response to requests by the '*fidalgos* and people', who drew attention to their difficulty in obtaining supplies.

Lisbon itself drew most of its fresh supplies from market-gardens, often surrounded by high walls bordering the roads and paths, which had therefore a rather gloomy appearance. The suppliers of the city were *saloios*, a term still applied to the inhabitants of the district. But wheat was brought from the Alentejo, which now became the granary of Portugal. It was gathered at Évora and carried overland to Setúbal and conveyed thence by sea to Lisbon, where the main market for cereals was the Terreiro de Trigo. As a result of this cumbersome journey prices in the capital were high and the rewards of the peasants low. The constant deficiencies were made up by the import of wheat from the north and from the Mediterranean countries, which sold at lower prices.

The need for improvement in agriculture was realized in the eighteenth century. Alexandre de Gusmão noted the need for increased production and the importance of road-building. The Academy of Sciences, founded in 1779, drew attention to rural problems, performing the same function as the Spanish Economic Societies. But the importance of alleviating the lot of the peasants, still overburdened with taxation and feudal dues, was appreciated particularly by the administrators who had graduated from the reformed University of Coimbra, and whose influence was paramount in the liberal movement of the early nineteenth century.

A report on the Alentejo noted that the land was badly farmed because landowners shared the crops of the tenants, and made no provision for improvement: the nobles also owned large flocks of sheep and goats which invaded the land of the peasants. The province was full of vagabond beggars: eighty or a hundred might appear at a wedding or a christening. It was perhaps the only part of Portugal where travellers were not safe from robbery. Link, entering Portugal at Elvas, thought the experience pleasing, and the common people polite and friendly, and better dressed than their Spanish neighbours. The houses were better than in Spain, and the inns supplied food and drink. About a quarter of the Portuguese army was stationed in the Alentejo. The troops were good, but miserably paid: they lived on bread, sardines and wine. Recruits were rounded up like criminals by the *juiz de fora*.

From the War of the Spanish Succession until 1761, Portugal had avoided direct entanglement in the strife of Europe. Then France, at war with England, had drawn in the new king of Spain, Charles III, and planned to invade Portugal. Pombal had invoked the English Alliance, and Count William of Schaumberg-Lippe had reorganized the Portuguese army. Peace had been made in February 1763, after which the forces were neglected.

Pombal's educational reforms made new ideas more accessible, but he had also provided the means of controlling them. The board of censorship suppressed offending publications and the intendancy of police, established by him in 1760, and still directed by the redoubtable Pina Manique, smelt out revolutionaries. The first of the revolutions, that of North America, probably inspired the abortive Inconfidência of Minas Gerais in 1789, in which a very small group of intellectuals were punished for having ventilated independence as an alternative to higher taxation. The first stirrings from France elicited some sympathetic interest, but news of anti-monarchical or anti-religious excesses alarmed the great majority of Portuguese. In 1793 the Portuguese government made treaties with England and Spain and contributed to the Pyrenean campaign. The victory of the French Republic caused Spain to make the separate Peace of Basle (1795), by which she consented to bring pressure on Portugal. French royalists, formerly received in Spain, now passed on to Portugal. With the rise of Napoleon, the French government again sought to use its influence over Spain to force Portugal to break the Alliance with Great Britain and to close her ports to British shipping. In 1801 Godoy invaded Portugal, but negotiations were at once begun, and Portugal was required to pay 25 million francs as an indemnity. For the following five years Portugal was under strong pressure. In 1802 the French sent General Lannes to Lisbon to demand the expulsion of the royalist refugees and the removal of Pina Manique in order to facilitate revolutionary penetration. In July 1803 the Duke of Sussex, the grand master of the English masons, saw the Prince Regent, hoping perhaps to check Jacobin infiltration in the police. Opposing secret forces sought to have the Prince replaced by his aggressive Spanish wife, Carlota Joaquina. It was at this time that the idea of removing the royal family to Brazil was first broached.

Portugal attempted to maintain a formal neutrality as long as possible. French efforts to cut off British trade bore little fruit. Between 1802 and 1807 Portuguese trade with England was consistently high. About half of it was with Brazil, and the largest Portuguese export was now Brazilian cotton—after the United

States Brazil was the leading supplier to the British market. Some 40 per cent of Portuguese exports went to Britain, and 45 per cent of Portuguese imports come from Britain. These included large quantities of textiles produced by the new mechanical methods. French interests remained small until 1804, when purchases of cotton in Lisbon suddenly increased. In 1805 Napoleon sent General Junot to Lisbon to demand a Portuguese declaration of war on Britain. But Nelson's victory at Trafalgar showed clearly the cost of Spain's subservience, and it was only in November 1806, after his triumphs in Prussia, that Napoleon finally proclaimed his continental blockade, declaring any ship that touched at a British port lawful prize. This attempt to drive a wedge between Britain and the neutrals directly threatened Portuguese trade. The connivance of Spain was secured by offering Godoy a'principality in Portugal, and in July 1807 Talleyrand demanded that the Prince Regent close his ports to the English. French armies were assembled at Bayonne, and the command was entrusted to Junot. Napoleon's ultimatum (12 August) required Portugal to declare war on Britain, arrest British merchants and close the ports. The Portuguese government offered only to 'adhere' to the blockade, and Junot set out on the long march across Spain. The two predatory powers meanwhile negotiated the partition of Portugal and of her overseas possessions. In Lisbon, an order to expel British ships was passed on 20 October, but nothing was done to put it into effect. As the French troops entered Portugal, the royal family and court embarked at Lisbon, and escorted by the fleet of Sir Sidney Smith sailed for Brazil, leaving behind a council of seven regents.

The Portuguese crown was to remain for twelve years at Rio de Janeiro, which was thus the temporary capital of the Portuguese world. The court was warmly received. The colony acquired a monarch, a government, courts of appeal, a bank, a printing-press and other institutions. On the death of Maria I, the Prince Regent became John VI, and on 16 December 1815 he declared Brazil a United Kingdom with Portugal and the Algarve. The Brazilian ports were opened to foreign shipping, and the new economic situation was reflected in the Anglo-Portuguese Treaty of Commerce concluded in Rio de Janeiro in 1810. While Brazil prospered, Portugal herself was confronted by enforced European integration.

In Portugal, Junot established himself in the mansion of the wealthy Barão de Quintela and proclaimed himself Protector. He appointed a commission to the regency and took over the treasury. He then dispersed the Portuguese army, with the exception of a force of 9,000 which was sent to serve Napoleon in Europe. It was estimated that 15,000 persons had gone to Brazil: they took such treasure and possessions as they could carry. Junot confiscated their remaining property, and imposed a tribute of 100 million francs. In February 1808 he announced that the House of Bragança had ceased to rule, and replaced the regents with a military committee, presided over by himself, with three secretaries, for the interior, treasury, and war and marine. A Frenchman, Lagarde, was named intendant of police.

Three months later the Peninsula was aflame with revolt. In Spain, the French intrusion precipitated the fall of Charles IV, and Napoleon invited the royal family to Bayonne, where he juggled the crown out of their hands, to bestow it on his brother. The departure of the last members of the Bourbon house from Madrid was the signal for the popular rising of 2 May 1808. A trail of resistance spread far and wide. On 6 June the French general sent to govern Oporto was arrested. Bragança declared for the Prince Regent, and a Provisional Junta was formed in Oporto. In Coimbra the students formed the Academic Volunteers. Appeals were sent to Britain: in July Sir John Moore landed in Corunna and in August Sir Arthur Wellesley in central Portugal. Wellesley's victory at Vimeiro (August 20) exposed the French stronghold in Lisbon, and Junot sued for terms. The agreement, ratified in the Convention of Sintra, by which the French were given ships to depart, with their booty, and without reparations for the havoc they had done, was strongly criticized in both Portugal and Britain.

In September 1808 the Portuguese colours again flew over the castle of St George in Lisbon. The Council of Regency was reconstituted with eight members under the bishop of Oporto. Its first concern was to invite Wellesley to re-create the Portuguese army: instead it received General William Carr Beresford, who arrived with the rank of Marshal (March 1809) and reorganized the artillery and created units of chasseurs and engineers. The heroic campaigns of 1809–12 assured the independence of Portugal. When Soult penetrated the Minho and entered Braga

16. Portuguese baroque. The University Library, Coimbra

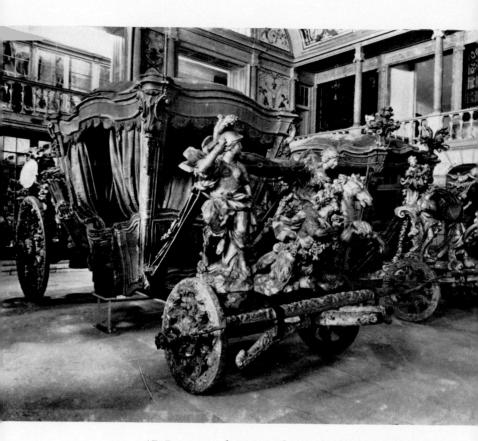

17. Portuguese baroque. The coach of the Marquês de Fontes, ambassador of John v, in the Coach Museum, Lisbon

and Oporto in 1809, Wellesley returned to Lisbon and drove him out. A second French force was expelled from the valley of the Tagus. In 1810 Napoleon entrusted the 'Army of Portugal' of 60,000 men to Masséna, who invaded Beira. He was faced by 52,000 troops, almost equally divided between Portuguese and English. The French were worsted on the heights of Bussaco (27 September), but they continued to advance, and the allies retreated behind the lines of Torres Vedras. With the onset of winter their supplies ran out, and in mid-November they were compelled to depart. They held out at Santarém until February, and then retreated into Spain. With the fall of the frontier fortress of Almeida (May 1811), the invasions came to an end, and the war was carried into Spain and France.

7

THE LIBERAL MONARCHY

I: JACOBIN LIBERALISM

The campaigns had ravaged the Minho, the Beiras, the valley of the Tagus and the district of Lisbon, and memories of destruction and rapine survive in many places. In addition, the country bore the expense of a large military establishment of regular troops, rather than of guerrilleros, as in Spain. The removal of the monarchy to Brazil had been followed by the opening of the Brazilian ports. Part of the British merchant colony had left Lisbon for Brazil, and the treaty of 1810 diverted British trade to the former colony. Thus Portugal ceased to distribute Brazilian goods, and with the disruption of her own industry she ceased to supply Brazil. Portuguese exports of cotton fell to less than a tenth. Just before the war, the introduction of mechanically-produced textiles from Britain had begun to flood the Portuguese market, and it was now clear that the national factories could not compete. In 1813 instructions were given to restore production, but those who received them saw no way of complying. The usual explanation was that the industry was in 'decadence'. But an inquiry into the woollen manufacture at Portalegre in 1817 showed that it was realized that the equipment had been rendered obsolete. The mere revival of protectionism would not suffice. New methods were needed: the work of the eighteenth century had been undone by the industrial revolution.

It was hard to see how the process of recovery could be begun. The institutions of the old regime were either dormant or absent. The regency had requested the return of the royal family at the end of 1813. Canning had gone to Lisbon to welcome John VI, but he had not arrived. The erection of Brazil into a kingdom seemed to reduce Portugal to colonial status. The army, enjoying great prestige after its notable victories, seemed to be the only active national institution in Portugal. Yet even it was still commanded by Beresford and other foreign officers, and it represented a burden that the impoverished country could not carry. Seven years after the war in Portugal ended, it cost 5,128 *contos* (1818) and almost as much, 4,961 *contos*, in 1819. It consumed about three-quarters of the national revenues. There was therefore a large deficit and no visible means of offsetting it. The sudden decline of customs-revenues directly affected the finances and the prosperity of the ports. If agriculture had recovered from the invasions, it now suffered from the fact that the cities could not afford to buy its produce.

This was the background of the revolution of 1820 and the entry of liberal constitutionalism. The leaders of the movement were a small group of lawyers and merchants, and its makers a more numerous band of army officers. The interests of the two groups were not identical. The army was essentially conservative: it desired the return of the royal family, the removal of the English commanders, and pay and promotion. The civilian party was led by a magistrate of Oporto, Manuel Fernandes Tomás, who with a small group of friends had formed a society known as the Sinédrio. It proposed more far-reaching changes.

Constitutionalism had been brought to the Peninsula by Napoleon, who, on granting the crown of Spain to his brother Joseph, had provided his Spanish subjects with the 'constitution of Bayonne'. This was patently a foreign imposition, and in 1810 an assembly of Spaniards meeting at Cádiz, then the only piece of Spain free of French control, began to elaborate a national reply, the Constitution of 1812. At this time, the Spanish Bourbon, Ferdinand VII, was in exile in France, but when he returned at the close of the wars in 1814, he at once abrogated a system of government about which he had not been consulted. In the following years the Spanish liberals were persecuted or exiled, and their clubs and societies suppressed. Only in the army were they secure from police investigation. In Portugal, masonic lodges were active in 1816. General Gomes Freire de Andrade, an adventurous officer who had commanded the Portuguese contingent serving under Napoleon in Russia, had returned and become grand master. In March 1817 Spanish officers made contact with him with a view to a simultaneous uprising in both countries. At a moment when a rising in Pernambuco was put down with some difficulty, the Lisbon conspiracy was reported to Beresford and the Portuguese authorities. Gomes Freire was arrested and executed, with twelve of his followers. He thus became the martyr of Portuguese liberalism. A foreign officer, Baron Eben, was pardoned, supposedly at the request of the Duke of Sussex. The suppression of the plot did nothing to enhance the popularity of Beresford, but the malcontents contained themselves until 1820. At the beginning of the year, Spanish officers launched a liberal revolution at Cádiz and obliged Ferdinand vii to restore the Constitution of 1812. They soon after sent agents to Portugal and Naples, supplying copies of the Spanish constitution for use as propaganda. Meanwhile, Beresford went to Rio de Janeiro to inform John vi of the state of affairs and to seek instructions.

In Oporto, the magistrate Fernandes Tomás and his friends had little difficulty in making contact with officers in the garrison, and in August 1820 the northern city came out in favour of a constitution. The Portuguese regency at first condemned the liberals of Oporto for the 'horrible crime of rebellion', but on 1 September they declared their readiness to consult the nation by convoking cortes. After this, the armies of the north and south united and replaced the regency with a provisional government, which entered Lisbon amidst general rejoicings. It received the support of the *juiz do povo* and of the guilds and obtained an oath of allegiance from the two dukes, Lafões and Cadaval, and other nobles, and drew up a loyal address to John vi. But when Beresford returned from Brazil, without the king, but with new orders, he was not allowed to land.

The idea of resuscitating the cortes was not new. During Junot's rule, Pombal's former favourite, Seabra e Silva, had recommended consultation with the three estates. Junot in fact added to his ruling committee members of the clergy, nobles, magistrate and people, selected by himself. They included the *juiz do povo*, who asked for a constitution and a deliberative body composed of representatives of the municipal *câmaras*. But Junot had rejected the proposal, probably fearing any real expression of national autonomy. When John vi's council of regency was restored, it took no further action. It was now nearly a century and a quarter since cortes had been celebrated, and there were some doubts about how it should be done, but in October 1820 it was suggested that the summons be sent to twenty-three mem-

bers of the clergy, thirty nobles, and one hundred and fifty commoners, procurators of cities, towns and other *concelhos*. This
assembly would vote as a whole, not by classes. However, this
plan was opposed by the judge of the people, who demanded that
representatives be elected by the nation, not merely designated
to attend. Liberal army officers gave this suggestion their support, and on 31 October the government issued a manifesto
which denounced the traditional cortes as 'feudal' and announced instructions for elections. On 11 November the judge
of the people asked Marshal Gaspar Teixeira to apply the
Spanish constitution of 1812, and after a brief struggle the more
radical faction prevailed and new instructions were issued for
elections on the Spanish pattern. There would thus be indirect
elections by parishes, *comarcas* and provinces. In the parishes, all
Portuguese males over the age of twenty-one would elect one
elector for every two hundred hearths. A week later, all the
electors would assemble at the centre of the *comarca* and choose
eleitores de comarca. A week after that, these electors would meet
at the provincial capital to pick one deputy for every 30,000
souls in the province. The resultant cortes would meet on
6 January 1821.

The moving spirit behind this was Fernandes Tomás. He had
been a judge of the court of appeal at Oporto and had written a
work on the agrarian question which was critical of the crown
and nobles. He was a member of the Provisional Government
(which administered, but did not legislate), and also minister
of the Interior (*Reino*) and Finance (*Fazenda*), in which capacity
he wrestled with the public debt and the lack of revenue. But the
process of reform began only with the assembly of the new
cortes in 1821. The deputies included provincial nobles,
bishops, clergy, academicians, professors, officers, magistrates,
lawyers, civil servants, landowners, doctors and merchants.
Only the craftsmen (who had spoken through the judge of the
people) and the country-people were absent. The strongest
representation came from the church and the courts, the
oratorical classes. Most, but not all, were strongly liberal in
their views. They professed to worship liberty and believed in a
constitution as a panacea for all ills. This accepted, they were
loyal to the church and crown. For them, liberty meant the rejection of absolutism and freedom of expression: they were also

vehemently critical of all privileges except their own. There were as yet no parties or party organization.

The deputies assembled in Lisbon and elected five regents and five ministers. They then began to elaborate a draft constitution. The key issue was the question of sovereignty. The 'sovereignty of the nation' was held by some as an article of faith. The desire to proclaim it was strengthened by the fact that they had met without the express sanction of the crown. This point had enabled Ferdinand vii of Spain to overthrow the Constitution of 1812 on his return from France: another revolution had been necessary to oblige him to accept the constitution in 1820. In Portugal, there was no doubt that the crown had always retained the right to convoke the traditional cortes. The question of the 'sovereignty of the nation' was therefore a delicate issue. The more conservative deputies succeeded in modifying what might have seemed an act of defiance, and it was accepted that 'sovereignty resided *originarily* in the nation'. Having decided this, the deputies voted by an overwhelming majority that the king could have no absolute veto, but only 'suspensive' powers. They were divided about the need for a council of state. On the question of parliament, a large majority favoured a single chamber rather than two. Great importance was attached to freedom of expression. A minority favoured censorship of religious works, but only a handful were for any other control, and most favoured only small penalties for abuses of freedom of the press.

The deputies abolished the Inquisition and the courts of Inconfidência, all privileges of *aposentadoria* (free lodging or keep), and all salaries and pensions not sanctioned by law: they declared for freedom to teach. However, they showed no enthusiasm for free trade, and wished to forbid the import of wheat, oil, wines and pigs. Evidently, their denial of absolute power most directly concerned the king, long absent in Brazil, and their dislike of privilege went against the crown, the nobles and the church. Of the nobles, some were sympathetic, some absent with the king in Brazil, and some discredited as collaborators. The decision to abolish the Inquisition and to end novitiates for the monasteries displeased the Papacy and the Patriarch. All Lisbon was illuminated to celebrate the passage of the draft constitution, but the nuncio remained in darkness and had his windows broken. The Patriarch refused to take the oath, and the deputies decided with only one dissentient vote that those who refused to swear ceased to be Portuguese citizens, and with only five that those who ceased to be Portuguese citizens must leave Portugal. The assembly was elated by a message from Jeremy Bentham. Tidings of these events, together with the prospect of troubles in Brazil, finally resolved John VI to return. At the end of April it was learned that John would accept a constitution. He himself reached Lisbon on 3 July. The deputies, remembering the action of Ferdinand VII on his return to Spain in 1814, forbade several of John's advisers—including the Count of Palmela—to land. But on 4 July the benevolent king appointed his first constitutional ministry, and the discussion of the draft constitution was begun.

The impassioned debates of the Constitutionalists set many against them, and the even more extreme views of their Spanish contemporaries did little to help. But their intransigence was nowhere more evident than in their treatment of Brazil. Portugal and Brazil now formed a united kingdom, and Brazilian deputies therefore arrived to participate in the new cortes. In June 1822 they proposed additional articles which would have resulted in the setting up of three consultative bodies, one in either country and one for both. The plan was rejected by sixty-six to twenty-two, but the refusal seriously to discuss it strengthened the determination of the Brazilians to set up their own institutions. John had left his elder son, Pedro, as his representative in the New World, and the prince now anticipated a tide of feeling in favour of independence which might have put an end to the rule of the Braganças in Brazil by himself uttering the Cry of Ipiranga, 'Independence or Death'. The intransigent radicals in Lisbon were too intoxicated with their own authority to realize that others might entertain similar sentiments against them. The sudden separating of Brazil left them unperturbed, but it widened the gulf between them and other Portuguese.

In November 1822, the constituent cortes having dissolved, the first and only regular cortes under the new constitution assembled. The radical majority now included many demagogues. Death had removed the firm hand of Fernandes Tomás. The moderate opposition was weak, and the right-wing brave, but heavily outnumbered. Although John himself accepted the constitution, his Spanish queen, Carlota Joaquina, refused to take the oath and was deprived of Portuguese citizenship by a vote of seventy-seven to four, with forty-nine abstentions (4 December). But instead of leaving Portugal, she had ten doctors certify her inability to travel and retired to the palace of Ramalhão, where she became the centre of absolutist reaction. The programme of the cortes included the production of a budget, the restoration of industry and trade, the reform of education, the remuneration of the clergy and the question of military service. The reports of the ministers presented a gloomy picture. The minister of justice declared that crime was rife. The minister of war stated that there were few troops and no funds to raise more. The minister for foreign affairs drew attention to the failure to secure recognition by the great powers which were even reluctant to accept commercial *chargés*—the Portuguese diplomats in Madrid, Paris, Berlin and the Hague had all dissociated themselves from the radical regime. A proposed defence pact with Spain had not been concluded. Meanwhile, the deficit continued at 3,000 *contos*, though cortes cut their own allocation by a quarter, those of the patriarchate and Public Works by a half, and abolished the College of Nobles and the military schools.

Russia, Prussia and Austria refused to recognize any revolutionary regime, and as the Spanish revolution spread to Naples, Piedmont and Pará in Brazil, many Portuguese moderates reacted against it. In January 1823 Louis xviii announced his intention to intervene in Spain, and in April his armies began the task of overthrowing the radicals in the name of monarchy and religion. The Portuguese government asked cortes for a special session to deal with questions of public order. On 23 February the Count of Amarante rebelled in Trás-os-Montes, and there was growing tension throughout the country. When cortes resumed on 15 May, it was already clear that the Spanish radicals could not resist the French armies, which entered Madrid on 24 May. This time, there was no patriotic rising against the French invader.

Portuguese traditionalists were already conspiring, and not only in Trás-os-Montes. Some wished to depose John vi in favour of his wife, making their younger son, D. Miguel, head of the army. On 23 May a sizeable part of the Lisbon garrison troops and militia deserted to Vila Franca, where Miguel placed himself at their head. The radical government resigned and a moderate ministry was formed. Cortes, in permanent session, was no more than a rump, most deputies having ceased to attend. On 30 May the king, advised by the Marquis of Loulé, overcame his hesitations, placed himself at the head of the only regiment left in Lisbon and drove to Vila Franca to identify himself with the royalist revolt. The radical cortes carried a last vote of protest, by sixty-one of two hundred and eleven members. On 1 June John formed a new government which included General Pamplona (Count of Subserra) for War, the Count of Palmela at Foreign Affairs, and Mousinho da Silveira at Finance.

The radical regime had succeeded in antagonizing the royal family, the church, the nobility and conservative classes, the diplomatic service, the Brazilians and most foreign governments. Many of its adversaries regarded the whole episode as a masonic intrigue. But not all enemies of the late regime were adverse to cortes in any form, and in June 1823 John vi entrusted Palmela with the task of heading a committee of fourteen to recommend a new system. In fact, no new constitution was produced. In Spain, Ferdinand vii was in much more reactionary hands, but he too maintained a state of constitutional suspense. John vi countenanced the repeal of the laws of the radical period (19 December 1823), restored the queen to her rights, and bestowed a marquisate on the Count of Amarante. But he remained surrounded by moderates, and the absolutist faction which clustered round his wife and son was not satisfied. In October a plot was uncovered by which Miguel would have seized power with the aid of the Lisbon garrison and made his mother regent. It was scotched, but at the end of February 1824 John's adviser, Loulé, was murdered in mysterious circumstances at the hunting-box of Salvaterra: there is little doubt that Miguelite bullies were the perpetrators. In April Miguel made yet another attempt to take over the Lisbon garrison, arresting Palmela and forcing Subserra to seek refuge in the French legation. Once more John pardoned his reckless son, but the coup was only frustrated when the diplomatic body escorted the king to shelter on a British ship, the *Windsor Castle*. He then sent Miguel abroad to learn prudence in Vienna. With the prince out of the way, the queen's party was leaderless, and the country became calm.

John declared his own preference for the traditional cortes of three estates—that is, for the separate representation of the nobles and clergy—avoiding the pitfalls of radical Jacobinism on one hand and Apostolical absolutism on the other. But he took no steps to convene cortes, old or new. The most urgent task was now to resolve the problem of Brazil, where his elder son, Pedro, had proclaimed independence and asserted the title of emperor. If John was anxious not to lose at least the title of ruler, the Brazilians were no less anxious to prevent a Portuguese restoration. In 1823 British mediation was sought, and the two parties presented their cases at a conference. Finally, John accepted the independence of Brazil, saving for himself the title of 'Senior Emperor', but recognizing the exercise of sovereignty by his son. A few months later, in March 1826, John VI died, and the whole question was reopened in a new form, since Pedro was heir to both crowns.

In the absence of his two sons, John set up a regency under his daughter Maria Isabel. A deputation went to Rio de Janeiro to recognize the succession of D. Pedro, who on 2 May made a conditional abdication in favour of his infant daughter, Maria da Glória, later Maria II. He also produced his own constitution for Portugal, the Charter, which he entrusted to Sir Charles Stuart for delivery in Lisbon, where it arrived on 7 July 1826. The conditional abdication required that D. Miguel should swear to observe the Charter and to accept the hand of Maria da Glória, thus, it might be hoped, healing the dynastic rift and the breach between liberals and absolutists.

D. Pedro's Charter was closely modelled on that which had been adopted as the constitution of Brazil. Its appearance took the Lisbon regency by surprise and rudely ended the delicate period of constitutional suspense. Many liberals did not consider an 'octroyé' or granted constitution acceptable: absolutists did not want one at all. The decision to publish it was attributed to the minister for war, João Carlos de Saldanha e Daun, a grandson of Pombal who had distinguished himself against the French and again in Brazil. Maria Isabel now formed a moderate ministry under Trigoso de Aragão Morato, a moderate constitutionalist of 1820, and Saldanha.

D. Pedro's Charter was to remain the constitution of Portugal until the fall of the monarchy in 1910, with the exception of one short period, and with the addition of a number of amendments. It provided for the appointment and dismissal of the prime minister, or president of the council of ministers, by the ruler. In this task, the ruler would consult with a Council of State. The government usually consisted of six ministers, for interior (*Reino*), finance, war, justice, navy and colonies, and foreign affairs. The Charter provided for two chambers; the first, the House of Peers, would be selected by the ruler from among the aristocracy; the lower house would consist of one hundred and thirty-eight deputies, including eleven for the Atlantic Isles and seven for the overseas provinces, chosen by indirect election. It thus broke with the radicalism of 1820 by instituting a higher chamber and rejecting the principle of national sovereignty, though it accepted the liberal concept of representative government and reserved for the ruler the right to exclude the recalcitrant nobility from the upper chamber. When elections were held, the absolutists or Miguelites abstained, and on 23 November, Amarante, now Marquis of Chaves, occupied Bragança and set up a provisional government with the support of the Spanish Apostolicals. Another absolutist, Teles Jordão, entered Beira but was checked by the Academic Volunteers of Coimbra. A third party crossed from Spain into the Alentejo, and was driven out. Although Miguel, still at Vienna, had pledged his word to uphold the Charter (4 October), his followers clearly looked forward to the day when he would return and overthrow it. The government itself was divided, for Saldanha, the strongest supporter of the Charter, fell ill, and in a new ministry the conduct of internal affairs was entrusted to the bishop of Viseu, who had Miguelite leanings. The main danger was that the Spaniards might intervene. In response to Palmela's request, Canning sent General Clinton with 5,000 men to guard the forts of the Tagus.

When cortes resumed in January 1827, some of the weaknesses of the Charter were already apparent. The connection between the government and the two chambers was not clear and relations between peers and commons were soon strained. But the survival of the regime turned on the completion of Pedro's abdication and the return of Miguel. By now Pedro's own situation in Brazil was becoming precarious, and he was less anxious to cede his rights in Portugal. He added five members to his sister's council, all moderates, and named more peers with a view to tempering the conservatism of the nobles and prelates.

The recovery of General Saldanha led to a strengthening of the liberal side. He promoted liberal officers, sent liberal generals to govern the provinces, increased the army and settled arrears of pay. Thus a system of liberal patronage was set up in the army. But in July 1827 the government was reconstituted, and the ministry of the interior passed to the erudite Viscount of Santarém, a moderate absolutist whose historical researches threw light on the traditional cortes. The appointment as intendant of police of Rodrigues Basto, a Jacobin in 1820, but now an absolutist, provoked Saldanha's resignation.

The instability of the government arose from the fact that the little Maria da Glória would not come of age until April 1837, and according to the Charter the regency must be exercised by the member of the royal house nearest in line of succession and over twenty-five. D. Miguel would thus qualify to replace his sister as regent in October 1827. As the date approached, there was a considerable transfer of support. The peers favoured him, and the deputies saw no sure way to oppose him. Saldanha urged that Pedro should extend his sister's term or himself go to Portugal. But Miguel repeated the oath to the Charter and was betrothed to his niece: his mother again became a centre of attention. He himself left Vienna and reached Lisbon in February 1828. But in spite of his oaths, he at once appointed a new ministry under the Duke of Cadaval, a moderate but unregenerate absolutist. The ministry of the interior went to another absolutist, and a new chief of police increased the force at Lisbon to 2,000 and at Oporto to 600. There began a general dismissal of liberals from office. On 13 March cortes were dissolved. Passions were further inflamed when a delegation from the University of Coimbra, on its way to express loyalty to Miguel, was ambushed and two of its members were murdered and five wounded. The assailants were students, members of a secret society, nine of whom were captured and executed.

Early in May 1828 the Duke of Lafões gathered the nobility and urged them to petition Miguel to abrogate the Charter and convoke the traditional cortes. The foreign diplomats protested, and the leading Portuguese diplomats resigned. Then the municipal *câmaras* were instructed to send subservient procurators to confirm Miguel's supposed rights. Only Oporto, the home of liberalism, was omitted, and there the garrison rebelled and set up a liberal junta. Saldanha and other leading liberals had already left the country, but they now chartered a ship, the *Belfast*, in England and sailed to Oporto. As they arrived, the movement was already failing. The leaders reboarded the *Belfast* and left, while their troops marched northwards and sought refuge in Galicia: some then returned to their homes, but the rest, 2,389 in number, emigrated to England.

Meanwhile, in Lisbon the 'traditional' cortes had assembled, the nobles in São Roque, the clergy in São António da Sé, and the procurators of the towns in the monastery of St Francis. They all declared that Miguel had been the legitimate king since his father's death—notwithstanding that Lafões and others had made submission to D. Pedro. The moderate absolutists such as Cadaval did little to restrain the wilder elements that gathered round Carlota Joaquina. An inquiry was held into the events at Oporto, and about 2,000 suspects were held under arrest: in May 1829 ten were sentenced to death. The rebellious liberal generals were also sentenced, but they were safe in exile.

Pedro had already sent his daughter to Europe, but on receiving news of Miguel's usurpation, her guardian took her to England, where Palmela, who presided over the liberal refugees, took a house for her at Laleham. The little queen remained there until her father denounced the marriage-contract and recalled her to Brazil. The liberal refugees in England were divided into six classes, the generals and politicians living in some style, while the soldiers and students occupied a disused warehouse at Plymouth. Although Miguel now seemed to be firmly in possession of Portugal, one piece of territory remained liberal, Terceira in the Azores. The captain-general of the islands acknowledged Miguel in May 1828, but the battalion of Caçadores 5, which had been sent to the islands because of its liberal opinions, opposed him and appealed to Palmela. This led to ideas of transferring the refugees from Plymouth to Terceira, but Wellington's government had little confidence in a liberal revival, and when Saldanha sailed he was intercepted by British ships and diverted from the Azores, putting in at Brest (January 1829). Hyde de

Neuville, who had been French minister in Lisbon at the time of Miguel's coup, gave the Portuguese liberals protection.

In London Palmela acted as universal minister in the name of Maria da Glória until June 1829, when a regency was set up, of Pamela, Vila Flor, governor of the Azores, and Guerreiro, secretary to D. Pedro. But the diplomatic boycott of the usurper was weakening. Spain recognized Miguel in October. The Papal nuncio followed suit, but was disowned by the Vatican. In England, Aberdeen thought that Canning had been mistaken in recognizing Pedro's claim. But the turning-point for Maria's cause was the liberal revolution of July 1830 in France, the effects of which were soon felt in Spain. Wellington would have been disposed to recognize Miguel if he had been prepared to grant an amnesty to the Portuguese liberals. But Miguel did not respond, and Wellington and Aberdeen were replaced by Grey and Palmerston, who dropped any idea of recognizing the usurper.

Miguel's regime had shown itself lamentably lacking in diplomatic skill, and indeed in cohesion and purpose. Once the dislodged supporters of the old regime recovered their places and privileges, they did nothing, unless perhaps oppress their opponents. In February 1831 a revolt in Lisbon was followed by the condemnation of seven participants; one of these was a Frenchman, whose fate elicited the concern of the new liberal regime in Paris.

Events in Portugal waited on those of Brazil. Pedro, for all his liberalism, was by nature an autocrat: he had grown increasingly impatient of Brazilian parliamentarians. On April 6, he attempted to appoint a cabinet of his own choosing, but it was so badly received that he abdicated in favour of his infant son Pedro II and left for Europe, where he was to devote the last three years of his life to establishing Maria da Glória on the throne of Portugal.

He made first for England, seeking funds for mercenaries. He found little response and repaired to France, where he negotiated a loan with Ardoin and the Spanish liberal financier Mendizábal, as well as Sanson and Ricardo. The nominal sum was £2 million, though heavy discounts reduced the cash payment. The bankers also stipulated that the mercenaries should be put under an English captain, G. R. Sartorius.

In the Azores, the liberal regency had extracted some money from the wealthy islanders (who were by no means favourable to their cause), and in August 1831 they annexed the island of São Miguel. This brought their forces to 7,746. There was now no danger of their being dislodged from the islands, and the former Emperor made them his base. On 7 July 1832 the liberal fleet sailing from the Azores appeared off Oporto and made a landing at the beach of Mindelo. The city was evacuated by the Miguelites and converted into a liberal stronghold. Pedro appointed a military and a civil governor, and replaced the bishops of Oporto and Braga, thus giving rise to a schism in the Portuguese church. In addition to the 7,000 men who had been landed Pedro called up all males between eighteen and fifty for the defence of Oporto. But it soon became clear that if Oporto was disposed to resume its old role as the citadel of liberalism, the neighbouring countryside was not enthusiastic for the cause. The Miguelites had raised a large body of volunteers throughout the country, and were said to be able to call on 80,000 men, though many of these were very inadequately armed. In April 1832 Miguel raised a loan of 40 million francs (of which he received only 69 per cent) with Outrequin of Paris.

In material terms, Pedro was little better off than his brother. When he removed his commander Vila Flor, he could only reward him with the title of Duke of Terceira (the first of many titles distributed by the bankrupt liberals) with 100 *contos* in 'national property'—lands seized or to be seized when the liberals were victorious. Nevertheless, the liberals possessed a fund of idealism. The great historian, Alexandre Herculano, who was among the heroes of Mindelo, was convinced that liberalism was the greatest renovation Portugal had experienced since the Middle Ages and was comparable in significance to the French Revolution. For him it was a struggle against obscurantism and self-interest. The great reformer of the regime was Mousinho da Silveira (1780–1849), to whom Pedro had entrusted the finances. Mousinho had studied law at Coimbra and been *juiz de fora* at Marvão and Setúbal, becoming administrator of customs in 1820. He was not stirred by the radical policies of the first liberal regime, but he had conceived an abiding passion for the land and the people of the countryside. While in the Azores he had signed decrees to abolish tithes and the innumerable seignorial dues and tributes which he regarded as 'feudal'. His law of 4 April 1832 extinguished the numerous small *morgados* which he considered the chief burden of the countryside. His honesty and bluntness, which had endeared him to John vi, made him inconvenient in a regime constantly reduced to shifts and straits. He soon left office, but he also left his mark on his country.

As 1833 opened, the liberal invasion appeared to have lost its impetus. Its treasury was exhausted, and Palmerston thought of inviting Pedro and Miguel to withdraw in favour of a compromise regency of Palmela, Terceira and Cadaval. But Pedro dismissed Terceira, and Palmela soon resigned. Saldanha's star rose again: he was promoted marshal. The naval command was given to Admiral Napier, who replaced Sartorius. Napier proposed either to force the Tagus and take Lisbon or to land in the Algarve. The liberal council of war decided for the Algarve, and a liberal army was duly transported to Tavira. So in July 1833 Terceira was able to enter Lisbon. Miguel continued to hold much of Beira and the Alentejo, but he finally capitulated in the treaty of Évora-Monte (March 1834) and left the country, never to return.

Liberalism was victorious, but bankrupt. On 28 May 1834 Pedro himself enacted a decree extinguishing all religious orders and confiscating all their property save sacred vessels and ornaments. In theory, the state would pay an annual pension to those who were displaced, provided that they had not helped Miguel. The draft of the measure had been submitted to the Council of State, which had rejected it. Pedro had published it on his own initiative, evidently convinced that the monks had been among the bitterest opponents of the constitutional regime. While therefore a bulwark of absolutism was destroyed, arrangements were made to bring back elected cortes. The number of deputies was now to be 132, or one per 25,000 in each province.* Scarcely had the Charter thus been put into effect when Pedro fell ill, resigned the regency and died (August 1834). Despite the provision of the constitution, it was decided to declare Maria ii of age, and not to institute another regency.

* Minho 16; Douro 27; Trás-os-Montes 11; Beira Alta 14; Beira Baixa 14; Estremadura 20; Alentejo 9; Algarve 9; Azores 8; Madeira 4.

18. The Douro: vine-terraces
19. The grapes are loaded into 'cestos' and carried coal-heaver fashion

20. Oporto: Avenida dos Aliados

11: THE CHARTER

Maria 11 was now fifteen. Her first cabinet was presided over by Palmela, the experienced diplomat who had trodden the difficult path of moderation since the inception of the first liberal regime. He was accompanied by Terceira at War and Silva Carvalho at Finance. This was still the most difficult ministry. The cost of the war was calculated at 6,059 *contos*. It had been covered by loans at a real rate of interest of about 20 per cent, and therefore required a service of 1,200 *contos* a year. The loans contracted by Miguel in Paris were repudiated, to be revived as a political issue at the end of the century. But the debts of the victors alone were sufficient to dog the liberal monarchy until its fall, and to distort the plan of progress that its champions had predicted. The only means of rewarding the victors was by grants of confiscated land, the award of titles and the distribution of offices. Terceira was already a duke with 100 *contos* of land. Palmela would soon also became a duke and proprietor of great estates at Arrábida. Already in August 1831 António José Freire had prepared a 'law of indemnization' which authorized every municipal council to confiscate the property of Miguelites: it fell to José Passos, one of the most prominent liberals of Oporto and then president of the city council, to reject the implication that municipalities could thus usurp the place of courts of law. As we have seen, Pedro himself had insisted on the seizure of monastic properties, which became 'national property'. But the greater part of the liberal army had to be content with appointments in the military or civil service, both of which were suddenly flooded with Chartist clients.

The first cortes of the new reign devoted much of their time to discussing the conversion of paper-money and the fate of Miguel. Although the prince had been promised an annuity on leaving Portugal, he himself provided a pretext for cancelling it by reasserting his claims from his place of exile. By the end of the year almost the only achievement of the cortes was a law declaring freedom of the press. There was soon tension between Palmela and Freire within the ministry, and between the ministers and cortes. There were still no political parties within the Chartist movement, though Saldanha adopted an attitude of opposition in the Chamber. The year 1835 saw a series of small conflicts due partly to personal differences and partly to the nature of the Charter, but aggravated by the prevailing financial crisis. The government's most valuable acquisition was the *lezírias* or irrigated islands and banks of the Tagus, once owned by the Military Orders and now expropriated. The proposal to raise money by selling this land was bitterly opposed. Some reformers wished to grant them to small farmers, but the government was desperately in need of ready money, which only large capitalists could supply. When Palmela resigned, Saldanha formed an administration which lasted only a few months.

Chartists filled the cortes as they filled the public service. Although there were no formal parties, there was a tendency towards aristocratic Chartism, led by such figures as Palmela and Silva Carvalho, and this was offset by a more popular faction, in which Sá da Bandeira and the liberals of Oporto were prominent. At the end of 1835, the Queen called on this wing to govern, but it achieved little beyond a general reduction of salaries. When cortes opened in 1836, the treasury had no money and receipts were committed for years ahead. The queen's appeal to the Count of Farrobo, the wealthiest man in Lisbon, was unheard. The government was finally forced to fall back on the sale of the *lezírias*, which its members had formerly opposed. In April, it was unable to vote a budget and fell. The exponents of orthodox or conservative Chartism, Terceira, Silva Carvalho and Freire, returned to office.

The more radical elements now gathered in a club, the Patriotic Society of Lisbon. It was closed, as the government regarded its activities as seditious. When new elections were held, a property qualification was introduced. The electorate was thus reduced, and this enabled the conservative wing to win in most parts of the country, though Oporto and the Douro were less amenable and remained radical. They indeed were now disenchanted with D. Pedro's Charter and looked for a return to the Constitution of 1822. On 9 September the deputies of Oporto arrived in Lisbon by sea, and on landing were greeted with demonstrations in favour of the radical regime. The National Guard joined in, and the government, being unable to dominate the situation, resigned. Thus on 10 September the radicals took power with the ostensible object of rejecting the Charter and resuscitating the first constitution. The new movement was known as Septemberism. Its most prominent leader was Passos Manuel (or Manuel Passos), the brother of José Passos, a compelling orator who passed like a comet across the Portuguese political scene. The Septemberist regime strove manfully to curtail expenditure by reducing salaries and pensions and dismissing the Chartist placeholders. Passos remarked that his arm ached from signing dismissals. He and his friends had inherited much of the radicalism of 1820. They proposed to abolish the Chamber of Peers and to restore the doctrine of national sovereignty, though embodied in a new constitution : until this was ready they planned to govern by decree for some two years. The proposed change involved the position of the crown, for the radical constitution would not be 'octroyée' like the Charter. Maria II regarded the Charter granted by her father as the foundation of her throne, which she thought would be undermined by a return to the sovereignty of the people. She had been married at sixteen to Augustus of Leuchtenberg, who died a week after reaching Portugal. Her second husband was Ferdinand of Saxe-Coburg, a cousin of Prince Albert. He arrived in Portugal, accompanied by a German tutor, Dietz, to become King-Consort and Commander-in-Chief. The young rulers and their circle regarded the Septemberists as dangerous radicals, and Maria, who had inherited her father's dash, summoned the ministers to Belem and dismissed them, and herself appointed successors. When news of her coup reached the city, the National Guard came out in support of the Septemberists, and Maria was finally obliged to climb down and countenance the radical regime.

Among the reforms of the Septemberists were the institution of the civil register of births, marriages and deaths and the adoption of new administrative and penal codes. Portugal was divided into districts, *concelhos* and parishes. At each stage there was a government representative who presided over an elected council. Thus the district was under an appointed administrator-general, who was accompanied by an elected general junta. In the *concelho*, the *administrador do concelho* was head of the municipal chamber (*câmara municipal*), and in the parish the appointed *regedor* had his parish junta. The system was intended to carry government by consent throughout the national life, though its effect was rather to strengthen the grip of the central authority throughout the country. In 1837 Portugal was divided into twenty-seven electoral regions, which were to return one hundred and thirty deputies, one hundred and ten for the mainland, twelve for the Atlantic Isles and eight for the overseas provinces. All male citizens over twenty-five were entitled to vote, unless living with their families or servants. Graduates, clergy or officers under twenty-five but over twenty were also voters.

There was now a danger that, instead of a single constitution under which two or more parties disputed for power Portugal would have two incompatible constitutions, each supported by its partisans. The Septemberists had made numerous enemies by their drastic dismissals and their declared opposition to vested interests. The Chartists made several attempts at revolt. In July the Charter was proclaimed in the north, and Saldanha and Terceira came out in favour of it. But the radicals took special powers and the 'Revolt of the Marshals' fell flat. However, the Septemberists themselves were now divided, and a small majority favoured a second house, in the form of an elected Senate. Sá da Bandeira even favoured life senators nominated by the crown. Although the Revolt of the Marshals failed, it had the effect of disuniting the existing regime. The Civic Association, the Septemberist club, now stood in the centre, and the Arsenalists, a society based on the Lisbon Arsenal, took an extreme position. In 1838 the issue was between those who wanted order and feared anarchy, and those who were prepared to use popular disturbances to force the government to pursue a radical line. The administrator of Lisbon, who controlled the National Guard, was an extremist, and Sá da Bandeira was obliged to call out regular troops. The Guard soon gave in, and the governorship of Lisbon was given to A. B. da Costa Cabral, who had begun his political career as an extreme radical, but who was essentially an ambitious and authoritarian opportunist.

Although the new Constitution was sanctioned by Maria II in April 1838, the split in the government was soon beyond control.*

---

* The Constitution of 1838 provided for a senate of seventy-one and a lower house of one hundred and forty-two deputies, of whom seven senators and fourteen deputies represented the overseas territories. They were all to be chosen by direct election.

Sá da Bandeira had emerged as the leader of the moderates, while Passos continued to enunciate the pure principles of democracy, heedless of the threat of anarchy. In April 1839 the last purely Septemberist ministry resigned and was replaced by a centre group under the Count of Bomfim and including Costa Cabral. In February 1840 cortes were dissolved, and the new system, as practised by Costa Cabral, produced a majority for the government, while the radicals formed the minority. By 1841 the ministry had been modified to include Chartists, and the country was only Septemberist in the sense that the Constitution of 1838 had not been abrogated. Even this was seen as a neutral or transitional stage. Early in 1842 Oporto elected a new municipal council which was openly Chartist. In the army, the Chartist officers of Pedro's force returned to prominence: the Chartist magistrates who had been removed under the Septemberists were restored by Costa Cabral, and in the church new bishops held conservative views—even those appointed by Miguel were permitted to return.

But Costa Cabral's attempt to place himself at the head of the general swing to Chartism was too brash for most of his colleagues. He went to Oporto and publicly supported the Charter while still a minister under the Septemberist Constitution. The senators and deputies meeting in Lisbon disowned him, and he was dismissed from his post as minister of Justice. Nevertheless, the ensuing governments were evidently transitional, and it was not long before Chartism was restored and Costa Cabral was again a minister. The country was tired of radical oratory and anxious for economic recovery. Costa Cabral promised financial reforms and the long-desired system of roads that would link the district capitals with Lisbon and advance material progress. In view of the continued financial crisis and the lack of money outside Lisbon and Oporto, it seemed certain that only a strong government could supply the necessary impetus. The democratic ideas of Passos and the radicals had subjected governments to urban pressure-groups organized by politicians much less high-minded than he. Costa Cabral, a 'tyrant in the midst of anarchy', was able to organize a system of political clientage of a kind hitherto unknown. In 1842 no fewer than sixty of the deputies were public employees. By 1845 indirect suffrage had been res-tored, and the deputies were in effect chosen by the municipal chambers. Thus the role of the administrator of the *câmara* was that of a political chief or agent of the government. If the *câmara* failed to respond, it might be dissolved. In effect, in 1845 only six members of the opposition were returned.

The rebellion against Costa Cabral was to begin not in the cortes, or in the capital, but in the rural north. Local defiance of the government began in the Minho, and was said to have been launched by a countrywoman, whence its name, 'Maria da Fonte'. When it spread into Trás-os-Montes, Costa Cabral sent his brother to impose order, but neither the people nor the local authorities would obey, and in May 1846 the government resigned, and Costa Cabral left for Spain. A rich lore grew up about Maria da Fonte. Almeida Garrett thought that the movement 'renewed the glories of Aljubarrota', and Passos described it as 'the most glorious deed in the history of the universe'. This was hyperbole. At the time the movement was ascribed to Miguelites or attributed to the new health laws which forbade burials in churches. In fact, many of the riots took the form of attacks on local administrative and tax-offices, and expressed the resistance of the countryside against paying for the new road system. The countryside had never been liberal, but Mousinho da Silveira had gained its consent with his reforms. The country-people were prepared to tolerate the new political system as an affair of the towns, and were resigned to living on the margin of political life provided that they were left alone. In Costa Cabral they seemed to recognize a return to a seigniorialism of the state.

With Costa Cabral gone, Maria entrusted the government to Palmela, whose moderation and loyalty to the throne were beyond doubt. But the popular movement had spread to Oporto where the dispossessed Septemberists now set up a junta. The growing revolt against the Chartist establishment was known as the 'Patuleia'. It seemed to some as if the people had at last spoken, as it had not in 1820 or 1837.

With this popular reinforcement, the radicals again began to demand the restoration of the Constitution of 1822 or constituent cortes. But the queen, as in the past, was alarmed at the prospect of any departure from her father's Charter. She abruptly dismissed Palmela and called on the soldier Saldanha to form a government (6 October 1846). She regarded Saldanha as the pillar of the monarchy and of the Charter, and he considered himself to be a national figure, above party issues. On this occasion he suspended elections, dissolved the National Guard and instituted censorship of the Press. To the radicals it seemed as if the queen had by her intervention snatched a legitimate victory at the polls from their hands. The junta of Oporto, headed by José Passos, decided to defy Maria, and when she sent Terceira to be her governor in Oporto, it promptly arrested him. The country thus came to the brink of civil war. Saldanha, for all his prestige, had few political followers, and the junta of Oporto controlled the larger part of the army. The Patuleias even published propaganda in Lisbon under Saldanha's nose.

Prince Albert, alarmed at Maria's predicament, sent his aide, Colonel Wylde, to mediate. The colonel went to Oporto, but Passos and Sá da Bandeira refused to compromise. Finally in June 1847 the convention of Gramido was arrived at, by which Saldanha was to form a transitional ministry and organize elections. Hopes of a settlement were dashed when Saldanha permitted the arch-manipulator Costa Cabral to return to Portugal. The Patuleias then withdrew from the elections with loud protests. Saldanha proceeded to convoke cortes without them, and some of the radical Patuleias, blaming Maria for the whole situation, began to speak of an abdication.

Meanwhile, the civil strife was estimated to have added 30,000 *contos* to the national debt. Saldanha was never the leader to consider expense or grudge favours, yet pay was in arrears and army contractors cut off supplies: many soldiers lacked cloaks or uniforms—only rebellious Oporto had a surplus. In June 1849 Maria made the bold gesture of calling on Costa Cabral to head what she hoped would prove a strong and enduring government. It was hazardous, not simply because the Patuleias hated Costa Cabral, but because many respectable Chartists felt no less strongly: the air was full of accusations of peculation and of illicit dealings with the queen. The Chartist aristocracy was entrenched in the House of Peers, but Costa Cabral created a majority for himself by making eight new peers. His methods drove Saldanha to oppose him, and Costa Cabral retorted by stripping the marshal of his offices of chamberlain to the queen, first adjutant to the king and counsellor of state. In February 1850 Costa Cabral attempted to silence all criticism by measures of strict censorship, the 'law of the corks' (*lei de rolhas*).

Finally in April 1851 Saldanha rebelled against his former ally. At first there was little response, and the famous soldier travelled north to Coimbra and Viseu without arousing much response. But as he approached Oporto, the garrison of the citadel of liberalism acclaimed him, and two days later Costa Cabral again resigned, departing to occupy the Portuguese legation in Madrid.

The movement of 1851 was the Regeneration, i.e. of liberalism. Seventeen years had passed since the triumph of D. Pedro and his Charter. They had been years of conflict and confusion, but some of the illusions of constitutionalism had been dissipated. If the Charter could not bring felicity, neither could the dogma of national sovereignty. Both sides must learn to compromise. By its struggles Portugal was merely impoverishing itself at a time when other countries were advancing in the wake of the industrial revolution. Costa Cabral had pointed the way, but his methods were intolerable, and it was therefore necessary to adjust the existing system so as to produce a stable government.

III: THE PARLIAMENTARY REGIME

The Regeneration brought together all those who were prepared to accept the Charter, with necessary modifications, as the basic law of the constitutional monarchy. The modifications were embodied in the Additional Act of 1852. The Upper House remained a hereditary peerage, while the Lower House was chosen by direct elections. The conduct of treaty negotiations with foreign powers, which D. Pedro had reserved to the crown, was transferred to cortes, but the prerogatives of the crown and the nation were excluded from further discussion, thus ending the vain debate on sovereignty. Only a small number of 'pure' Chartists and intransigent radicals remained dissatisfied, though there were still absolutist Miguelites who wanted no part of the liberal regime. However, the electoral law now required a property qualification of 400,000 reis for a deputy and one of 100,000 reis for an elector, so that the number of those eligible to sit as deputies was reduced to 4,569 and the number of registered electors was only 36,000. The essential problems of the country were political and economic, first to establish and set in motion an effective party-system and then to reform the cortes and the electoral law in a more liberal sense. The core of the economic problem was the application of a programme of development at a time when the commotions of the first half of the century had saddled the country with a heavy burden of debt. The supporters of Saldanha constituted the movement of the Regeneration and governed the country for five years. The Marshal and Duke regarded himself as the patriarch of liberalism and of the Regeneration, a figure above party politics. His chief followers, Rodrigo da Fonseca Magalhãis and António Maria Fontes Pereira de Melo, became the leaders of the Regenerator or conservative party, the strongest political force in the country, particularly under the long leadership of Fontes. At first the opposition was based not on a party organization but on personal grounds, such as the resentment between Costa Cabral (now Count of Tomar) and Saldanha. When the first Regenerator ministry resigned, the Marquis of Loulé formed a government with Sá da Bandeira and other former moderate Septemberists: they were known as Historicals. Loulé was the son of John VI's adviser, and had married one of John's daughters. He was a liberal aristocrat rather than a notable parliamentarian, and his followers were not at first sharply distinguishable from the Regenerators on matters of policy. Such was the source of the party system.

In November 1853 Maria II died in childbirth at the age of thirty-four. She and Ferdinand had set an admirable example of domesticity. Their family was large and their court small. Their only extravagance was the building of the Pena Palace at Sintra, a monument to Ferdinand's eclectic taste in art. Maria's excursions into politics had been venturesome. Ferdinand, after the conflict with the Patuleias, for which his German tutor was blamed, gained in discretion. He now became regent until their son Pedro V attained his majority at eighteen in September 1855. The young prince had been carefully educated at home and thoroughly inculcated with the responsibilities of the constitutional monarch. He interested himself in every aspect of national life and carefully scrutinized every paper that was submitted to him. His idealism and industry inspired feelings of devotion in those who knew him, many of whom believed that he had the makings of a great king. But he carried his sense of duty almost to the point of morbidity. He married a German princess, Stephanie of Hohenzollern, who died of diphtheria soon after her arrival in Portugal, and he himself, together with two of his brothers, succumbed to typhoid fever in 1861.

The Portugal of Pedro v had grown from less than 3 million at the end of the Napoleonic invasions to about $3\frac{1}{2}$ million. The average density (56 per sq. km.) was above the European average (38). It exceeded ninety-five in the districts of Oporto, Braga, Viana and Aveiro. Lisbon, Leiria, Coimbra and Viseu exceeded fifty-six, but the Alentejo (Évora, Portalegre, Beja) had less than twenty-eight. The whole country was still predominantly rural, and the urban population was only 15·8 per cent of the total—less than half that of Europe as a whole. Two-thirds of the urban population was concentrated in Lisbon (with 356,000 inhabitants) and Oporto (167,000). Forrester, writing in 1853, noted that the Miguelite nobility had returned from expatriation, but played no part in political life, remaining in dignified seclusion: it mingled with the new nobility, but did not amalgamate. The new aristocracy had been created by a lavish distribution of honours and titles. Most of its members were engaged in the stock or wine exchanges of Lisbon or Oporto: some had benefited from speculation in church or crown lands and others thrived on government monopolies. The old aristocracy was noble in character and conduct: the new was shrewd and diligent and never lost sight of the main chance. All the middle classes had become involved in the civil struggles and revolutions, and all were politicians. Politics was the order of the day. Everyone read the political sheets: there was relatively little interest in literature. In the cities, politics were discussed in the squares, cafés and newsrooms: elsewhere, in the apothecaries' shops. There was much talk of constitutional liberties and little satisfaction with any government. The middle classes were kind, hospitable and loyal, but suspicious. They rose early and walked out with their families before going to business. In the winter the men wore cloaks and the women thick shawls: few of the houses had fireplaces, since the climate was usually mild. Food was simple. Dinner-parties were rare, but evening gatherings with tea and biscuits frequent. The lower classes worked hard and lived poorly. They toiled under burning sun or drenching rain, and lived on maize bread and pottage, with occasionally dried fish, but no meat. Yet they were cheerful, honest, persistent and unaspiring.

In the countryside the average rent of cultivated land was a third of the yield. Weekly wages were 5s. 6d. (as compared with 9s. 6d. in England). Nearly half the country's maize came from the Minho: there it had been predominant since the eighteenth century. Trás-os-Montes and Beira mingled maize with rye. Half the country's wheat and barley came from the Alentejo. Agriculture was done with the hoe and wooden plough. Only the wealthier farmers had cattle and sheep: the rest kept pigs, goats and poultry. Even in Lisbon flocks of goats were brought into the public squares to supply milk. In the north chestnuts were used to make bread. The use of the potato was not yet widespread. An agricultural association existed; but in the countryside custom justified everything and there was little desire for change.

In the whole of Portugal there were 1,600 manufacturing establishments employing about 20,000. They produced iron and brass-work, arms and shot, tin, glass, porcelain, earthenware, cottons, woollens, silk, shoes, hats, tallow and candles, soap, soda, ships and cordage. A single family, the Pinto Bastos, produced corn, olives and fruit, reared horses, cattle and sheep, made bread, wine, oil, butter and cheese, refined sugar, tanned leather, fabricated glass and porcelains, built carriages, contracted public works and lent money, but this was exceptional. Communications were poor. Outside the cities there was little carriage road. Between Lisbon and Oporto there was no coach, omnibus or diligence, the mails being sent on horseback at three miles an hour. There were still no railways, though one had been contracted for from Lisbon to Santarém.

In view of the passivity of much of the countryside, it was possible to believe that Lisbon and Oporto were Portugal. Lisbon was the court, the centre of administration and the source of patronage. Industrial activity was closely linked with the concession of privileges. It was generally agreed that priority should go to schemes for producing articles of prime necessity, and that luxuries should be imported—whence a sense of inferiority about Portuguese goods. Oporto enjoyed economic independence because of its wine-trade. It had possessed a bank of issue since 1834, and prided itself on its liberal tradition and its commercial acumen.

During the first half of the century the preoccupation with

political abstractions had led the country to fight itself to a stand-still, and had saddled a rather stagnant economy with a formidable burden of debt. After 1834 the country had little capital and nothing to lend to the Treasury. Silva Carvalho had maintained that only foreign capital could regenerate the economy. But dividends fell into arrears and were added to the debt, which by 1840 exceeded £12 million. Much of it had been discounted, and only a small part was received in Portugal: most of this had been used to amortize paper-money and to pay troops. Costa Cabral had attempted to consolidate debt and arrears of interest at a higher rate (5 per cent instead of 3 per cent) and an increased nominal value, thus adding 540 *contos* to the annual service. In 1841 the administration of the debt was entrusted to Junta do Crédito Público, with the object of ending arrears of payment and accumulating capital to provide roads and railways. But in the following years a new round of civil disturbances compounded the existing difficulties. In 1851 the Regeneration, with Fontes as its finance minister, capitalized outstanding dividends at 4 per cent and abandoned the pretence at amortization. In the following year the existing debt at 4 per cent and 5 per cent was replaced by a single funded debt bearing 3 per cent, no distinction being drawn between internal and external creditors. This was a form of bankruptcy, and the London Stock Exchange retaliated by refusing to quote Portuguese funds. Fontes, the 'fanatic for communications', firmly believed that the only solution for Portugal was a policy of economic modernization, which would require new foreign loans. The new ministry of Public Works was created in August 1852 to execute Fontes's programme of development. He succeeded in convincing the London bondholders of his purpose and reopened the money-markets in order to 'irrigate the country with sterling'. In consequence, the debt continued to accumulate.

The first Regenerator ministry fell in 1856. Saldanha had had no difficulty in obtaining a majority in the Lower House, but he had been obliged to make one in the House of Peers by creating twenty new titles. The process of 'baking a batch' (*fornada*) of peers became a usual method of securing support in the Upper House, since governments could rarely function without the backing of both chambers. The end of the first Regenerator ministry was probably due to disagreement about Fontes's policy, which could not be realized without higher taxes. Loulé and Sá da Bandeira formed a government of Historicals, but when they in turn fell in 1859 the total debt had increased by about a third, from 96,000 *contos* to 120,000, requiring a service of 3,600 *contos* a year instead of 2,900. The Regenerators under Terceira and Fontes returned in 1859. Terceira died in 1860, and the Historicals were entrusted with power.

The young king and two of his brothers succumbed to disease in 1861, and the crown passed to the second son of Maria II and Ferdinand, Luis. Because of the close relationship between the crown and the Charter, the character of the monarch was not without influence on the political evolution of Portugal. Luis (1861–1889) had little of his brother's self-consuming desire to control the wayward politicians: he had thoroughly digested the principle that constitutional monarchs reign, but do not govern, and devoted himself to literary and artistic undertakings, which included the translation into Portuguese of the works of Shakespeare. Pedro had found Fontes overweening and maintained some reserve towards the Regenerators, but Luis scarcely concealed his preference for the conservatives, to the annoyance of the opposition. As the parties developed, power was concentrated in the hands of the professional politicians. In 1863 the demolition of the *morgados* begun by Mousinho da Silveira was completed: thereafter there were no entailed estates except the House of Bragança, which occupied a lonely eminence unsupported by a hereditary landowning class. The liberal Civil Code of 1866 altered the law of inheritance, abolishing primogeniture and requiring that at least two-thirds of estates be divided equally among heirs. This law probably encouraged the fragmentation of land, for within two generations the average holding fell from 1⅔ hectares to about half as much.

During these years the annual deficit remained high. It was 7,858 *contos* in 1862–3, and although it fell to 3,780 in 1864–5, it then rose to 6,120. The opposition clamoured for economies; but the government again attempted higher taxation and on 1 January 1868, the members of the Commercial Association of Oporto refused to pay new taxes and the government fell. In July 1868 Sá da Bandeira's Historicals formed a new administration with the support of the bishop of Viseu, the austere leader of the small Reformist party. They drastically reduced the civil service and cut the civil list and salaries, but they were not strong enough, or did not have sufficient control over their supporters, to put through tax reforms. In 1870–1 the revenues of the state were 16,636 *contos* and expenditure 21,931, of which the service of the public debt accounted for no less than 9,153. It was calculated that a property tax of 8 or 9 per cent would suffice to redress the balance, but after the merchants of Oporto—the traditional home of Septemberism—had successfully defied the government, the Historicals and Reformists could not muster a majority for such a purpose.

Thus Fontes and the Regenerators returned to power with a policy of strong government and a programme of economic development intended to dwarf the deficit by sheer force of expansion. Fontes reduced the deficit to 2,800 *contos* in 1875–6, and Portuguese funds rose from 37 to 52$\frac{1}{2}$. Railways and steamship services were inaugurated and the modernization of the port of Lisbon was begun: with the introduction of steam navigation and the intensification of the trade of western Europe with Africa, South America and the Pacific its future seemed assured. The year 1873 was one of opulence and saw the launching of new banks throughout the country. The boom came to a sudden end with the Spanish banking crisis, and in 1876 three Lisbon banks were forced to close their doors: a moratorium was declared and a new loan raised in London.

The crisis scarcely shook the personal predominance of Fontes, but it precipitated the fusion of the opposition parties, whose leaders joined in the Pact of Granja of September 1876, out of which emerged the Progressist party. It took its stand on an extension of the suffrage and the provision of popular education, advocating a revision of the Charter and a decentralized administration, so as to loosen the grip of the central government on the electoral process. The opposition was irritated by the long tenure of Fontes (from 1871) and for a time expressed its displeasure by abandoning the chamber. When it returned and Fontes at length resigned, King Luis called upon Ávila, the leader of a small group of deputies with no defined programme. This stopgap government negotiated a loan of £6·5 million to liquidate the floating debt before falling after less than a year (March 1876–February 1877).

The apparent exclusion of the opposition party gave a certain stimulus to republicanism. Until the Spanish revolution of 1868, republicanism was professed by a handful of belated radicals, who seemed to look back to the French revolution for inspiration. Their leader was José Elias Garcia, of whom Fontes remarked that if he had not existed, it would have been necessary to invent him: his presence enabled the monarchist parties to demonstrate their own broadmindedness. The republican paper the *República*, though well written, failed for lack of readers. However, another generation had arisen which, under the influence of Proudhon and others, set about organizing the working class. The most striking figure of this group was the poet Antero de Quental (1842–1893), the son of an Azorean *morgado*. As a result of their efforts, there were soon eighty-five mutual aid societies with 30,000 members and some three hundred and sixty unions. The strongest group was the Fraternidade Operária of Lisbon, which included some forty-three federated bodies, ranging from tobacco-workers to barbers, and had its own paper. Such associations were socialist and co-operative rather than republican, but events in Spain drew some of their leaders into politics. It was only in 1871 that Elias Garcia and others launched the Democratic Republican Centre, from which the republican party was to issue.

On the fall of Ávila, D. Luis again invited Fontes to form a Regenerator government. The Progressists regarded themselves as passed over and attacked the king for flouting the constitution. In 1878 the government held elections, which it duly won. Nevertheless, the opposition carried the cities of Lisbon and Oporto and the republicans put forward candidates for the first time, obtaining one seat at Oporto. However, the Regenerator ministers disagreed among themselves and when Fontes resigned in May 1879, Luis called on the Progressists to assume power. They had no majority in cortes, and therefore dissolved the lower house and organized elections, obtaining ninety-six seats to nineteen Regenerators and seven non-Regenerator oppositionists. This result was largely the work of their Minister of the Interior, José Luciano de Castro, who removed most of the existing civil governors and replaced other officials: he was destined to occupy as dominant a position in the Progressist party as the ageing Fontes among the Regenerators. It was also necessary to create twenty-six peers in order that the

Progressists should have a majority in the Upper House. In May 1878 a bill had been passed for the reform of the peers, which would gradually be converted into a form of senate: as existing peers died, they would be replaced by persons chosen by the king from among twenty categories (i.e. former ministers, generals, diplomats, magistrates, professors, landowners, capitalists, etc.). But this did not resolve the difficulty for a new government to find support in the Upper House. It became necessary for the Progressists to bake a second batch, thus creating forty peers in a year—more than their rivals had elevated in the previous eight years. In spite of this, the Progressists could not muster the unity necessary to pass a tax-reform, and when they resigned in March 1881, D. Luis again called on the Regenerators. They had no difficulty in arranging a majority in the Lower House, and regained the Upper by creating twenty more new peers (making sixty in two years).

At this time the Progressists began to press for a reform of the constitution to end the 'personal regime'—i.e. to limit the royal prerogatives. Part of their press made unflattering remarks about the king. The Portuguese press had enjoyed almost unlimited freedom for over thirty years and few steps were taken to curb its personal attacks or scurrilities: the arrest of a pamphleteer for sedition caused a general outcry, and the government gave way. The question of freedom of expression thus returned to the political agenda.

The Progressists had long talked of reforms, but in their short tenure of office they had failed to enact a tax-bill and the rest of their programme remained unfulfilled. Thus in 1883 Fontes took the opportunity to put forward a comprehensive reform bill. It provided for the abolition of the hereditary principle in the Upper House and limited the number of peers. The life of parliaments would be reduced from four to three years. In the event of dissolution new cortes must be convoked within three months. It was proposed to adopt a system of minority representation: thus the country would be divided into forty-two 'circles', of which twelve would return a majority and a minority. In a total of one hundred and fifty-four deputies, the minority would be assured of twenty-two members, and six more would be elected by accumulation of votes. The Progressists accepted this reform, which was passed by large majorities.

21. Alentejo: a street in Arraiolos
22. Algarve: a *chaminé*

23. Eça de Queiroz (1843–1900) *ref.* p. 172.
In later life he mocked his contemporaries with urbane humour

Elections were held later in the year, and the Regenerator government as usual won a large majority. The Progressist opposition took ten seats in the ordinary circles, fifteen in the minorities, and all six of the seats awarded by accumulation. The republicans took two minority seats for Lisbon. The attempt to form a new party, the Conservative Liberals, in order to attract the Miguelites, met with little success. In 1885 the first elections for the Upper House were held. The new bill provided for fifty elected peers, twenty-five chosen by the Lower House, twenty-one by the administrative districts and four by educational bodies. For the administrative districts special electoral colleges were created of delegates of the district juntas, the municipalities, the forty highest tax-payers on the property roll and the forty highest contributors to industrial tax. A special college of the University, Polytechnics, Academy of Sciences and medical and other schools chose the educational peers. In addition, the prelates remained peers by right of office. Existing peers would retain their seats for life: until their numbers fell to one hundred, the king would fill only one of every three vacancies that occurred, limiting his choice to the twenty categories established in 1878.

These changes recognized the fact that the hereditary aristocracy had long been superseded by a commercial and administrative oligarchy, but they did little to stimulate a wider participation in political life. A vociferous political press enabled the urban population to follow the doings of the politicians like the audience of a play whose action was becoming well known. But the limited electorate impeded the transition from audience to actors. In the countryside, most of the population was out of earshot, and had to rely on what it heard of the performance from local pundits.

In the Portugal of the 1880s there was an appearance of prosperity and activity, especially in the two large cities, which were certainly rich by comparison with the countryside. But there were very few large accumulations of wealth. New fortunes were emerging from banking and communications, but they were outnumbered by the lawyers, politicians, administrators and others who lived from the state and its concessions. Fontes's policy of contracting loans for development had created a mesh of interests around the government, but he had laid more emphasis on communications than on production, and the revenues of the state had not risen in proportion to the rate of borrowing. In particular, the practice of contracting foreign loans had become a habit, the extension of which was made possible by the receipt of remittances from Portuguese emigrants to Brazil. All politicians were aware of the existence of the chronic deficit, but inclined to regard it as a surprising novelty and disagreed about its seriousness. Fontes himself continued to believe that it would be gradually remedied by expansion, though experience had shown that the economy was vulnerable to external events, both by reason of its dependence on foreign credit and of the traditional predominance of customs-dues as an item of revenue. It had long been plain that the loss of Brazil could be compensated for by the development of Portugal's vast possessions in Africa, but this could only be achieved by a substantial expansion of administration and by the attraction of capital. Hitherto the Africanists had been few—the most prominent being Sá da Bandeira—and African and other overseas problems had been thrust aside by more pressing domestic matters, among them railways and ports.

The problem of Portugal's rights in Africa was still unresolved. The peace treaties after the Napoleonic Wars had recognized Portuguese claims in Mozambique as far as Cape Delgado, but in Angola the possession of the mouth of the Congo was undecided, and the interior of Africa, between the two provinces, remained largely unexplored, though the continent was crossed by Portuguese Africans as early as 1815. But relations with Britain had been strained by the long discussions about the slave-trade: even when these were resolved, British governments refused to allow Portuguese claims in northern Angola without giving reasons or admitting arbitration, causing Sá da Bandeira to suppose that they were seeking a pretext to seize territory which the Portuguese supposed to be theirs. The question was brought to a head by the travels of Livingstone, whose philanthropic but tendentious reports were accepted by a wide public in Britain. In 1867 Sá da Bandeira had published a map reserving much of the Zambesi system for Portugal, and ten years later a basis was given to the claim to a coast-to-coast colony by the expeditions of Capelo, Ivens and Serpa Pinto from Angola to Mozambique. But the scramble for Africa was now under way: Leopold II had launched the 'International African Association' and Stanley had obtained land in the Congo for it in 1878, while the French founded Brazzaville in 1880 and the Germans began to conceive colonial designs. In 1884 Britain offered to recognize the Portuguese claims to both banks of the Congo in return for guarantees of freedom of navigation and trade. But it was now too late for a division of central Africa between the British and Portuguese. The Germans opposed the new treaty, and when the British attempted to appease them they demanded a protectorate over South West Africa, where they had no historical or other claims. Leopold aligned himself with the Germans and the French, and Bismarck seized the opportunity to announce an international conference at Berlin. This meeting adopted the doctrine of 'effective occupation' (February 1885), which undermined Portugal's historical claims and licensed what were in effect mere seizures.

In Portugal, Fontes had resigned in 1885, and died in February 1887. The disappearance of a figure who had dominated the scene for a generation weakened the Regenerators, and enabled the Progressists, now led by José Luciano de Castro, to establish themselves. Despite their plans for reform, they used the now consecrated methods of manipulating elections and obtained a substantial majority in parliament. But African affairs soon overshadowed all others. Their minister for foreign affairs, Barros Gomes, proposed to claim for Portugal a block of territory joining Angola and Mozambique, embodied in a document known as the 'Rose-coloured Map'. It was clear that this conflicted with British expansion to the north, but he was sufficiently impressed by the German success at the Conference of Berlin to hope to secure his object with German backing. In 1886 he concluded treaties with France and Germany, both of which powers promised their good offices to secure recognition of Portuguese claims, though in language which committed them to nothing. When he published the 'Rose-coloured Map', Lord Salisbury protested, but showed no haste in opening negotiations or in stating British claims. In June 1887 he declared that he could not recognize Portuguese sovereignty in territories not occupied with sufficient forces to maintain order: Barros Gomes pointed out that both the Belgians and Germans had obtained recognition without either historical claims or occupation.

The Portuguese drew the conclusion that they must employ their slender resources to achieve occupation as rapidly as possible. The British had occupied Bechuanaland in 1884, and in 1888 a treaty was concluded with Lobengula, the king of the Matabeles, who claimed, on somewhat dubious grounds, sovereignty over Mashonaland. This conflicted with Portuguese claims to the middle course of the Zambesi, the Shiré and Lake Nyasa, which Barros Gomes prepared to make good with a series of expeditions to obtain the submission of the local chiefs. Although Salisbury sent a mission to Lisbon in 1889, his warnings to Barros Gomes were lacking in precision. Serpa Pinto arrived on the Shiré, where the British consul at Blantyre informed him that the Makalolos were under British protection. In consequence of a skirmish near Ruo, Salisbury delivered a demand for the immediate withdrawal of Portuguese from the lands of the Makalolos and Mashonas. This was the famous Ultimatum of 11 January 1890, which shook the Anglo-Portuguese Alliance and with it the throne of the Braganças.

Luis had died in October 1889, being succeeded by his son Carlos, an earnest but inexperienced prince of twenty-six. The publication of the Ultimatum was followed by an extraordinary outburst of emotion in Portugal. This took the form of demonstrations, attacks on British institutions, public meetings, the formation of patriotic societies and the launching of a public subscription to acquire warships. At first all classes were carried away by the excitement, but the republicans sought to throw the blame for the national humiliation on the monarchy, and in January 1891 a small body of disaffected troops seized the city hall at Oporto. The movement was easily suppressed, but public opinion was so inflamed that the chamber dared not approve a treaty with Britain and the government resigned. An elderly general, João Crisóstomo de Abreu e Sousa, was asked to form an all-party ministry.

The sudden crisis arose from a variety of factors. The founding of the Lisbon Geographical Society in 1875 had done much to stimulate pride in Africa. The government had published the Rose-coloured Map, but had given little publicity to opposition to it. There was moreover a long record of opposition by the Ancient Ally to Portuguese claims in Africa. British governments had claimed places generally considered to be Portuguese, and had shown reluctance to go to arbitration: when they did, two cases had gone in favour of Portugal. Resentment against the English derived also from the long dependence on the London money-market: the very word '*inglês*' was a synonym for 'creditor'. It was popularly believed that the English manipulated the Portuguese economy—it was, of course, true that the English had lent considerable sums to the Portuguese state and these sums had been heavily discounted, but in recent years much of the debt had been transferred to German and other foreign bondholders. The financing of the Portuguese railways was done largely with French capital, and recent governments had looked to Paris for aid. In Paris speculators had brought up the disowned Miguelite loan, and attempted to oblige the Portuguese government to honour it.

The upsurge of republicanism arose in part from the consolidation of the French Republic in 1876 and, more directly, from the overthrow of the Brazilian branch of the Braganças in 1889. Pedro iv had been Emperor of Brazil when he conferred the Charter on his Portuguese subjects, and the Brazilian rejection of his son could not fail to be felt in Portugal. The declaration of the Brazilian Republic was soon followed by a financial crisis in the daughter-nation which immediately affected Portuguese remittances and contributed to the ensuing tensions.

But Portuguese republicanism also reflected the shortcomings of Chartism. The historian Herculano, the great proponent of the liberal renewal, had stressed the historic importance of the autonomy of the *concelhos*. A younger generation including Henriques Nogueira (1825–1858) saw the centralizing tendency of the Portuguese liberals as reducing the *câmaras* to a new form of feudalism, the antithesis of what Herculano had hoped for. Moreover, since 1860 the students of Coimbra had begun to reject the values of the previous generation. The romantic ideology of exalted patriotism and the cult of the individual made way for the concept of universal progress, the advance of humanity and faith in the capacity of society to improve itself. Traditionalist religion yielded before idealist philosophy. Antero de Quental, disdained the romantics ('tiny sensibilities tinily told by tiny voices'), and his *Odas modernas* (1865) treated life as a social mission. The Spanish revolution of 1868, which overthrew the throne of Isabella ii, was seen as a turning-point in 'the modern movement'. Quental's socialism impinged on the Lisbon association for the advancement of the working-class in 1872. In the previous year the leaders of the younger generation (including Eça de Queiroz) set out to shock their elders by condemning religion and society in the Casino lectures, which were suppressed by the government. But others followed different roads. Oliveira Martins (1845–1894) thought that constitutionalism was leading to real and moral bankruptcy and looked forward to a reorganization of society through a fusion of the workers with the lower middle-class. Teófilo Braga, the historian of Portuguese literature, harnessed himself to Comtian positivism, which carried him to the provisional presidency of the Republic in 1910. The republicans were the chief organizers of the centenary celebrations of Camões in 1880, and they launched the successful paper *O Século* in 1881. At the time of the crisis of 1890 Quental gathered republicans, merchants and nobles in his Northern Patriotic League. The young poet Guerra Junqueiro wrote malevolent verse against the young king. But republicanism was not a necessary ingredient of protest. A monarchist with socialist leanings, A. Fuschini, founded the Liberal League, which for a time flourished in the army, while Oliveira Martins called for a 'new life' in existing politics: he condemned the stifling effects of the politics of plutocracy (i.e. of Fontes) and despaired of the 'bacharéis', graduates who plunged into politics as a career, looking for the emergence of a socialist aristocracy.

Foreign creditors were not likely to wait for this solution, however desirable. Silver money disappeared from circulation, and the Banco Lusitano declared a moratorium for six months. In the midst of financial panic, General João Crisóstomo's finance minister, Mariano de Carvalho, raised a loan in Paris, guaranteed by the tobacco monopoly. When the dust settled, Carvalho admitted having advanced funds to banks and railways without consulting his colleagues and resigned. Dias Ferreira, a successful lawyer on the fringe of party politics, formed a non-party government, bringing in Oliveira Martins to manage the finances. The advocate of the 'new life' cut salaries and expenditures and raised taxes, suspending a third of the payments of interest. But the struggle with vested interests and professional politicians was too much for him: he soon resigned and devoted himself to literature. The old political parties had no intention of permanently giving way to new forces, though they were prepared to use the talents of others to tide them over the existing crisis. The king now called on the Regenerators, who had chosen E. R. Hintze Ribeiro as their leader, but persuaded him to entrust the finances to Fuschini, whose backing by the army was influential. He negotiated with the foreign bondholders, but the old parties were perhaps relieved to find that he had no magic formula. The financial crisis was temporarily resolved by assigning specific sources of revenue to appease the foreign bondholders. Carlos began to visit foreign capitals in order to restore confidence, while Portuguese achievements in Africa, culminating with Mousinho de Albuquerque's capture of the Makalolo king Gungunhana in 1895, obliterated the humiliating memory of the Ultimatum. The Africanists who succeeded in establishing the modern provinces of Mozambique and Angola enjoyed the patriotic support of all parties to a greater degree than any of the contemporary political leaders.

The republican tide soon abated, if only because the two old parties agreed in combating this threat to their own security. The steps they took included control of the press and a strengthening of the powers of the police. But the eclipse of the republicans in the closing years of the century was due in part to dissensions among themselves: it was only after the turn of the century that they began to recover. In 1891, they had accused the crown of failure to defend Portuguese Africa and of complicity in the abandonment of Portuguese claims. The charges were baseless. Nevertheless, there was a danger that the financial situation might lead to bankruptcy which would force the alienation of part of Portuguese Africa. This danger was increased by the success of the foreign bondholders in attaching an important part of the revenues of the state. In 1898 the Germans sought, and obtained, a convention with Britain by which they received the promise of a share in any arrangement to grant Portugal financial aid with the colonies as security. They then tried, unsuccessfully, to thrust a loan on Portugal. In the following year, with the onset of the Boer War, the British found a pressing need to use the ports of Mozambique, and the Anglo-Portuguese Alliance was revived. By the Treaty of Windsor of 1900 Britain undertook to defend and protect the Portuguese possessions.

The burden of debt, if it did not actually bring down the constitutional monarchy, constantly embarrassed successive governments. By 1900 the Portuguese state owed some £177 million, or £35 a head for a population of just over 5 million. The figure per head was the largest anywhere outside of Australasia. France, the most heavily indebted European nation, carried a burden of £28 a head. However, the annual charge on the Portuguese debt was less striking: it required under £4·5 million or 15s. 10d. per head, while France had to find almost £50 million or nearly £1. 6s. 0d. per head. The capital charge was higher in Brazil, and also in Spain and Italy. However, Portugal's taxable capacity was small, and in view of the failure of successive governments to apply effective income or property-taxes, it is probable that much of the burden was passed on to the countryside, and that the situation of the rural labourer was worse than it had been half a century before. The large proportion of external debt imposed a heavy burden on Portugal's limited sources of foreign exchange. Relatively minor incidents could produce serious crises: the interruption of remittances from emigrants to Brazil, the need to compensate foreign speculators for a rescinded railway contract, the import of grain made necessary by bad harvests. The latent economic crisis played its part in undermining the political system, for once a part of the national revenues had been assigned to foreign bondholders, the process seemed likely to continue. The prominence of a small number of foreigners in financial and banking circles lent colour to the impression of foreign control. It was thus that the republicans were able to appeal to popular nationalism, and even to accuse the Braganças of being a foreign dynasty.*

---

* The charge had been made against D. Pedro, who, though born in Portugal, became Emperor of Brazil and issued his Charter from Rio de Janeiro. Maria II was born in Brazil, though she was as typically Portuguese as her husband was German. Of their sons Pedro V was impeccably Portuguese: Luis rather resembled his father. Luis's son, the stout D. Carlos, presented a Germanic appearance, though he liked to assume the role of an Alentejo landowner and to wear provincial costume. It would seem idle to rebut the republican charges against the Braganças.

Since the Regeneration, the political system had been based essentially on the alternation in power of the two main parties, Regenerators and Progressists. When a party in office could no longer govern, the king offered power to the other. This was the principle of rotativism. On taking over the ministry, a party usually found it necessary to organize elections in order to secure a majority. Each party maintained a network of interests throughout the country, and in most places the issue was not in doubt, since the minister of the interior could count on the collaboration of civil governors and other administrators, local potentates and even the clergy, to obtain the desired result. There were many complaints against the system, but it was not in the interest of either party to put an end to it. But when the parties themselves began to disintegrate, the role of the monarch was no longer simply to indicate the new head of government, but to decide between several possibilities. By the Charter, he was required to consult the Council of State, but as this was composed almost exclusively of ex-ministers, the king was drawn into politics and became the arbiter between the parties. His involvement was increased by the fact that he held the right of dissolution: when he appointed the leader of the opposition to form a government, that leader usually had to ask for a dissolution in order to obtain a majority. In this sense, the king abetted him in the election. Frequent dissolutions made it only too clear that the object of elections was not that the voters should express their wishes, but that the government should acquire sufficient support to govern.

It was now almost a convention that the party heads held their position for life. The Progressists obeyed José Luciano de Castro, an astute lawyer who contrived to retain his command even when confined to his house by illness. After the death of Fontes, the Regenerators had followed Serpa Pimentel, whose authority was nominal: their leader in the Upper House was Hintze Ribeiro, and in the Lower João Franco Castelo-Branco; both were graduates in law from Coimbra, but João Franco was young, ambitious and in quest of reform. At the end of 1894 he obtained the dissolution of cortes and governed by decree (or, according to the current phrase, 'in dictatorship'). Under the Charter, cortes must assemble every year on 2 January for a session of three months. When cortes were not in session, the government could decree legislation, but must then submit it to the next session for approval. To postpone the January session aroused strong opposition, and the Progressists decided to abstain from the elections, aligning themselves with the republicans. When the Regenerators fell in February 1897, Carlos called on the Progressists. But with the death of Serpa Pimentel, Hintze Ribeiro was made head of the party, and João Franco, who had inherited the reformist ideas of Oliveira Martins and Fuschini, formed his own group. In 1900 the Regenerators returned to power: among the Regenerators Hintze had seventy followers, and João Franco twenty-five. Since the Progressist opposition had only twenty-nine, Franco felt free to act independently. Hintze therefore resigned and called elections in June 1901 : in these he set out to destroy Franco's faction and succeeded in preventing it from winning a single seat. Although at first José Luciano and the Progressists supported Hintze in the defence of party discipline, the prospect of crippling the Regenerators by backing Franco was too tempting to be long resisted. Franco launched his Conservative Liberal Party ; and in 1904 he reached an electoral agreement with the Progressists. The resulting combined opposition numbered forty-three, which was sufficient to force Hintze to resign. Carlos then invited José Luciano to form a government, and new elections were held in February 1905.

It was now the turn of the Progressists to divide. José Luciano had entrusted the ministry of justice to José de Alpoim, an ambitious lawyer, intent on succeeding the old leader. At first José Luciano sought to appease him with a seat in the Upper House, but as Alpoim remained dissatisfied, he called new elections, in which the main Progressist party took eighty-six seats and Alpoim's Dissidents nineteen. When Alpoim finally came out in open opposition to his former chief in January 1906, José Luciano asked for another dissolution and a temporary dictatorship. This Carlos refused, and the Progressists resigned. Thus in March 1906 Hintze and the Regenerators returned to office, and promptly sought to perpetuate the Progressist split by offering Alpoim nine seats. In return, Castro retorted with an alliance with Franco : the elections of April 1906 produced a Regenerator majority and an opposition composed of seventeen Progressists and seven supporters of Franco. Thus in a decade the two old parties had each given birth to dissident movements and each nurtured the other's unwanted offspring. Both of the new leaders were energetic and ambitious, but while João Franco was a devoted monarchist who strove to raise the existing regime out of its rut, Alpoim appeared disposed to borrow the programme of the republicans. The republicans had recovered from the decline that followed their successes in 1890, and had won a firm hold on the two great cities. Between 1895 and 1905 they could command a quarter or possibly a third of the votes in the capital; in 1906 they secured over half. They were helped by defections of monarchists, particularly that of Dr Bernardino Machado, a former Regenerator minister, and by renewed contacts with organizers in Paris. They operated partly through secret societies: many of the masonic lodges were monarchist, but the Carbonária, introduced in 1898, was exclusively republican. It was to prove effective in infiltrating the armed forces, in particular the navy. In April 1906 there were mutinies on the warships D. *Carlos* and *Vasco da Gama*: in the first case Hintze made concessions, and in the second the press was forbidden to report the event. However, the rapid spread of republican ideas was due even more to the organization of mass-meetings, which circumvented both the censorship and the illiteracy bar. In view of the closed nature of monarchist politics, few of the old leaders thought it necessary to approach the electorate directly—only João Franco had gone out to seek popular support for his party.

The republican attack was aimed at the king: they accused him of extravagance and thus of responsibility for the financial plight of the country. They also condemned the high level of direct taxes on essential commodities, which in part accounted for high prices and the distress of the poor. They further set out to stir up anti-clerical feeling, in imitation of the French republicans and the radicalism of Lerroux in Spain. Although D. Pedro iv had expelled and banned the religious orders, there had been a tendency to flout the law or to bend it so as to re-admit selected bodies such as the Sisters of Charity and the Jesuits. Finally the republicans had considerable success in exploiting the immediate situation—the attempts of the monarchists to dilute their numbers in Lisbon by modifying the electoral laws, to silence the republican press, and to arm the Lisbon judge with special powers against sedition.

As republican pressure mounted, Hintze asked the king to prorogue cortes by decree: Carlos refused and he resigned. The king then called on João Franco to form a government. Carlos was rightly impressed by the honesty and determination of Franco, and believed him to be the only monarchist politician with the will to make drastic changes and to gain general support. Franco promised a 'liberal concentration', electoral reform, ministerial responsibility and the reorganization of public finances. He had no support in the Upper House, but José Luciano and the Progressists undertook to vote for his programme, though without accepting office with him. Even so, in June Franco could muster only sixty-five votes to the Regenerators' sixty, a majority no Portuguese government considered secure. He then obtained Carlos's consent to new elections to strengthen his position. But on 12 November 1906 a deputy made a reference to reports of unsettled accounts between the state and the Royal House, and Franco admitted that advances had been made to the king without the consent of parliament. Hintze urged Franco to be prudent, and José Luciano denied that Carlos had ever asked for advances, but the damage was done, and the republican leader, Afonso Costa, demanded a full statement. The question of the unauthorized advances was exploited with ruthless persistence.

Franco endeavoured to calm the situation by means of new press laws. The Progressists supported these, but when he asked that they should enter his government, they refused: neither Franco, nor Carlos could move them. Thus in May 1907 João Franco dissolved cortes and announced that he would govern by decree. He had already publicly condemned his own former dictatorship as an error he would not repeat, but Carlos now pressed him not to resign, and publicly placed himself behind the dictatorial regime. José Luciano urged the king to consult the Council of State, but Carlos would only meet its members individually. The Progressist peers and deputies then protested against the infringement of the constitution, as did the municipality of Lisbon. João Franco had decreed a number of salutary reforms. But in September he published a decree which liquidated the advances to the Royal House. Soon after, Carlos gave an interview to a French paper in which he pledged support to João Franco and openly criticized the other politicians. All this was grist to the republican mill. Both monarchist parties were now opposed to the dictatorship, and in December João Franco announced that elections would be held in April 1908: however, he also took steps to suspend the provincial electoral commissions, suggesting that he intended to manipulate the results. On 6 January 1908 the royal family left Lisbon for Vila Viçosa. In Lisbon, the Progressists decided to fight the election as opposition monarchists. The Dissidents of Alpoim moved even further to the left, and were involved in a republican plan for a revolt. This conspiracy was uncovered by the police on 28 January, and Costa and other republican leaders were arrested: Alpoim fled to Spain. João Franco replied by drawing up a decree which applied the penalty of transportation for crimes against the security of the state. It was taken to Vila Viçosa to receive the royal signature. Carlos decided to return to Lisbon; and on 1 February, as the royal party crossed the Terreiro do Paço, the king and his heir were murdered by assassins. Two of the assailants were shot by police: they were a teacher and a clerk, but their accomplices, if any, were never arrested, and no report on the crime was published.

Carlos was succeeded by his younger son, Manuel ii, a youth of eighteen, who had survived the regicide with only a graze. He was, not unnaturally, much shaken; but his mother, Queen Amélia, a daughter of the French pretender, the Count of Paris, showed considerable courage in the crisis. The Council of State was summoned to the palace. It recommended Manuel to dismiss Franco, who went into exile. Power was again in the hands of the leaders of the old parties. But José Luciano, though too infirm to govern, was unwilling to surrender control of the Progressists, or to support Júlio de Vilhena, who, on the death of Hintze, had been chosen to lead the Regenerators. It was therefore decided to appoint a non-party prime minister, supported by a cabinet with equal representation of Progressists and Regenerators. The new prime minister, Admiral Ferreira do Amaral, successfully negotiated the immediate crisis, though he proved so non-party that he later adhered to the Republic.

The republicans, far from denouncing the regicide, seemed to condone it, and the graves of the assassins appeared strewn with flowers. Ferreira do Amaral did not forbid this demonstration and seemed intent on appeasement. In June the list of unauthorized advances to the royal family was published: it compromised most recent finance ministers. The publication seemed to guarantee that the republicans would win the municipal elections in Lisbon on 1 November. Although José Luciano proposed to postpone them on a legal pretext, Ferreira do Amaral insisted that they be held: as anticipated, the Lisbon republicans swept into power.

It was soon clear that Manuel II was too inexperienced to steer his way through these troubled waters. He at first relied on the advice of José Luciano, the veteran Progressist, whose shrewdness was beyond doubt. But though José Luciano was confined to his house, he loved power and clung to the congenial role of royal mentor and political manipulator. Vilhena, the new leader of the Regenerators, desired to govern, and after the Lisbon elections he withdrew his support of Ferreira do Amaral, who in consequence resigned (December 1908). Vilhena expected to succeed, but his party was not solidly behind him, and José Luciano seized the opportunity to divide the Regenerators: eventually Manuel called one of the Regenerator ministers, Campos Henriques, who obtained the postponement of cortes until March 1909. Meanwhile, Vilhena, the elected leader of the Regenerators, considered himself slighted and formed a block with Alpoim and the Dissidents.

When cortes opened, there were tumultuous scenes as accusations were tossed to and fro. Manuel was aware that his father had incurred blame by conceding dissolutions too readily: he therefore decided not to grant requests to dissolve cortes. But it was difficult to find a majority in cortes so divided between different factions. Campos Henriques resigned on being refused a dissolution, and Sebastião Teles' cabinet lasted only three weeks. His successor, Wenceslau de Lima, a Regenerator much in the king's confidence, lasted only until December 1907. Meanwhile Vilhena, mortified at being passed over in favour of his own lieutenants, resigned the headship of the Regenerator party, which passed to Teixeira de Sousa, a doctor from Trás-os-Montes: he was to preside over the last ministry of the monarchy.

The opponents of the regime were now entrenched in Lisbon and extending their influence far and wide. In particular, infiltration in the navy and in the garrison of Lisbon prepared the way for insurrection. The monarchical parties, divided and devoted to mutual recriminations and accusations of corruption, did much of their enemies' work for them. In August 1910 elections gave the republicans seven seats in Lisbon and four elsewhere. They had now recruited an admiral, Cândido dos Reis, who planned the revolution of October 1910. The appearance of a Brazilian cruiser with the president-elect of the daughter-nation, Marshal Hermes da Fonseca, on a visit, gave the republicans the opportunity to demonstrate. The Portuguese government did not order its disaffected fleet to sea, and Admiral Reis planned to go out to the ships anchored in the Tagus and bombard the palace of Necessidades. His launch did not appear, and he committed suicide. But a Carbonarist naval second-lieutenant, Machado dos Santos, seized an infantry barracks and occupied the Rotunda (Praça do Marquês de Pombal). Two rebellious warships began to bombard the palace at 11 a.m. on 4 October. Loyal troops were concentrated in the Rossio, but the head of the government, Teixeira de Sousa, remained in his house with a strong guard and no one undertook the active defence of the young king. As the palace was threatened, he was advised to leave by car for Mafra. Early on 5 October Machado Santos advanced from the Rotunda down the Avenida da Liberdade and the royalist defences crumbled. Manuel ii and his family went to the fishing-village of Ericeira and boarded the royal yacht. There was some idea of going to Oporto, but the ship eventually sailed to Gibraltar. Manuel settled at Fulwell Park, Twickenham, where he formed a splendid collection of Portuguese books: he died in 1932.

8

THE REPUBLIC

Visitors to Lisbon were surprised at the ease with which the long-established monarchy was overthrown: they overlooked the events that had undermined its prestige and the tenuous support for the parties on which it had rested. The propaganda of the republicans had never been effectively countered—indeed, it was refuted only by their victory: the palace was searched for documents that would justify the accusations of malversation and treason, but none were found; the governments of the Republic soon proved even more chronically unstable than those of the monarchy; and the financial situation, if it seemed for a moment to improve, became more chaotic than before. The leaders of the Republic were graduates of Coimbra, like their monarchist counterparts: only the proportion of lawyers was slightly reduced. Their ideas harked back in part to the French revolution, in part to Comte, in part to the Second Republic. Yet their attitudes were doctrinaire, like those of the Portuguese radicals of 1820, reformist, like the Septemberists, and popular, like the Patuleias. As the lower middle and working-class of Lisbon calmly rejoiced in the victory of the new regime, it seemed clear that they welcomed the opportunity to participate in the affairs of the nation, a right they had scarcely enjoyed since the Regeneration. The Provisional Government set about removing symbols of privilege, leaving the task of setting up new institutions to a constituent assembly. The negative phase—the suppression of titles of nobility, the royalist arms and flag and so forth—was extended from the monarchy to the church. The new leaders were persuaded that their views were 'modern' and 'scientific'. Afonso Costa, now minister of justice, was firmly convinced that religion was about to disappear, and that he must help it on its way. The Provisional Government

24. King Carlos I (1863–1908)

25. António de Oliveira Salazar (1889–1970)

banished theology from the University, religious education from the schools, and the religious orders from the country. The army was forbidden to participate in religious ceremonies, and the state ceased to recognize ecclesiastical festivities. On 11 April 1911 a Law of Separation turned the churches over to lay associations and forbade bequests to them. In theory, the state would provide pensions for priests until they found an alternative livelihood.

Elections were held on 28 May 1911, for a constituent assembly of two hundred and ten deputies. About half the deputies were returned unopposed. The monarchists ceased to participate in political life, and the old parties became inactive. The assembly elected a president for four years and decided on a bicameral legislature. When the Constitution was approved, the assembly designated seventy of its members as senators, and the remaining one hundred and forty as deputies to form the first republican parliament. The ministries remained as under the monarchy, with the addition of a portfolio for Development. The republicans had already committed themselves to the freedom of the press and the right to strike, and they amended the tenancy laws in favour of tenants. They also created new universities at Lisbon and Oporto and suppressed the payment of fees.

The republicans had repudiated the Braganças as a 'foreign' dynasty, the Jesuits as a foreign order, and the monarchist parties as dominated by foreign designs on Portuguese Africa or the interests of foreign bondholders. The quest for evidence of tremendous scandals was abortive: the court had been small and unpretentious, and the question of the advances arose less from royal extravagance than from the exiguousness of the civil list. The suppression of payments to the monarchy and its appanages afforded a temporary relief. The financiers and bankers, some foreign, who had had close associations with the politicians of the old regime, accommodated themselves to the new situation. The Republic also had its clients, less pretentious, but more numerous than those of the monarchy. The Republic was 'for republicans', though as most of the officials of the old regime adhered to it there was some difficulty in rewarding aspirants.

The republican movement, hitherto unified in opposition, now divided into three factions, the Evolutionists of A. J. de Almeida, the Unionists of Brito Camacho, and the Democráticos of Afonso Costa. The first two were moderates who combined to elect an elderly lawyer, Dr M. Arriaga, as first president. The third was radical and doctrinaire. Almeida's oratory had converted many to the cause: his single-minded pursuit of his aim derived from the crisis of 1890 when as a medical student he had been imprisoned for an article against the Braganças: there was no doubt of his sincerity. Afonso Costa, a lawyer and demagogue, had learned anti-clericalism in the French school and imitated the radical fanaticism of Lerroux in Barcelona. He was the spearhead of the anti-religious campaign.

Although Lisbon and the south adhered to the Republic, the north remained luke-warm. The bishop of Oporto defied Costa's legislation, and was deposed. There were also monarchist stirrings in the north, and the decision to try officers who were implicated led to the resignation of the two soldiers in the cabinet, the elderly General Pimenta de Castro (War) and the young Major Sidónio Pais (Development). The army had been divided over the change of regime; its defence of the monarchy had been less than adequate, and it now attempted to preserve a theoretical unity above political systems. However, as the republican party machine fell into the hands of the extremists and the Carbonária, now transformed into a secret police, spied on the military, it sided with the moderates.

President Arriaga sought to bring in a ministry of concentration, but he could not prevent the return of Costa to the ministry of Justice and the resumption of the anti-religious policy. By 1912 the monarchists of both lines, Manuelite and Miguelite, had reached agreement, and a royalist officer, Captain Paiva Couceiro, attempted a counter-revolution in the north. It was overthrown, but was followed by many arrests and by legislation for the defence of the Republic, which included limitation of freedom of speech and of the press. In addition to the arrested royalists, the prisons were filled with labour leaders and syndicalists who had taken too much advantage of the right to strike. Relatives of the political prisoners began to agitate for their release by writing letters abroad. Protest meetings were held in London at which many charges of left-wing persecution were voiced, but an inquiry showed that they were much exaggerated.

It was now no longer possible to govern by coalition and in 1913 Costa and the Democráticos took power. His main claim to fame was a balanced budget, but his arbitrary methods led to his resignation a year later. The events of 1914 demonstrated that no other republican group was strong enough to govern, and in January 1915 President Arriaga appealed to General Pimenta de Castro to form a government, exercising dictatorial powers until new elections could be held. The Democratic deputies, finding the chamber closed, met elsewhere, denounced the dictatorship and began to prepare a revolution. It broke out on 14 May 1915: Pimenta de Castro was arrested and banished, and President Arriaga removed from office. In consequence, the Democráticos recovered, and by November Afonso Costa was prime minister.

It was at this time that Portugal entered the Great War. Although republicans had habitually denounced the monarchy and Great Britain for the crisis of 1890, they were forced to recognize the fact that the real peril lay in German designs on Portuguese Africa and the possibility of a policy of appeasement by Britain. It was now held therefore that the Ancient Alliance was not between monarchs, but between nations, and had thus survived the change of regime. Since Spain had declared neutrality, there seemed to be no direct danger of military involvement in Europe. Most of the republican leaders had ties of sympathy with France, and the government had rendered services to the allies even while non-belligerent. Reinforcements had been sent to Angola and Mozambique, both of which bordered on German possessions. However, the republican parties were not at one: the Unionists held that Portugal should not enter the war unless her colonies were invaded. The Democráticos decided that the time had come for intervention: they seized German ships in Portuguese ports and Germany declared war on 9 March 1916.

The Democráticos then formed a 'sacred union', offering the premiership to the Evolutionist leader, Dr A. J. Almeida. An Expeditionary Force left for France early in 1917: it consisted of 25,000 men, later raised to 40,000, who were soon heavily engaged in Flanders. The consequences of the war rendered the Democráticos extremely unpopular, since agriculture and trade were disrupted and acute shortages of food developed. When the unions struck for higher pay, the government retorted by mobilizing the workers. The opposition formed a committee under Major Sidónio Pais, who was backed by the Unionists and the many enemies of Afonso Costa. On 5 December 1917 they overthrew the Democrático regime.

The Republic had now existed for seven years, yet the essential conditions of parliament—short-lived ministries, personal quarrels, belief in oratory, failure to pursue a coherent economic policy—repeated and in some ways aggravated the errors of the monarchy. Some monarchists still awaited the turn of the wheel, but in Lisbon they were evidently a minority. So long as the Republic continued to persecute the church, there was a chance that the two pillars of the old regime might be restored together. But there were now new political thinkers who hoped rather to reform the Republic. Sidónio Pais had taught mathematics at Coimbra, served in the army and been Portuguese minister at Berlin. To many he was a magnetic figure. He was rapturously received in the north. His 'New Republic' rested on the more conservative and nationalist forces, the Unionists, independents and the army. It abolished the lay associations and allowed exiled religious leaders to return. Sidónio Pais combined the offices of president of the Republic and prime minister in a 'presidentialist' regime. Since the old republicans abstained, he obtained a majority in both houses, the minority going to the monarchists.

But in 1918 the Portuguese troops in Flanders suffered heavy losses and at home the government could only pay its way by recourse to the printing press: the *escudo*, the new currency of the Republic, lost nearly half its value. The president dismissed his finance minister. The regime began to form local military committees like those which had lately swept Spain. On 5 December there was an abortive attempt on his life, and on 14 December he was assassinated as he entered the Rossio station in Lisbon. The New Republic at once collapsed.

Dr Almeida was elected President of the Republic, becoming the first of six to complete the term of office of four years. The Democráticos returned to power, but governments succeeded one another with bewildering rapidity: there were four reshuffles in 1919, seven in 1920, and five in 1921. As the Germans unleashed a communist regime in Russia, and communism briefly succeeded in Germany and Hungary, the tide of confusion reached the Iberian Peninsula. In neutral Spain the collapse of the wartime boom gave rise to a violent economic crisis. In Portugal, the currency continued to depreciate and prices to rise. There were repeated strikes in almost every branch of industry and service. In the Democrático governments former

Carbonarists were now ministers, but they had little control over new secret societies and political gangsters. In October 1921 one of these bands assassinated a group of former ministers, including Machado Santos, the hero of the revolution of 1910. The cost of Portuguese operations in Africa had been met by printing money, while the Expeditionary Force in Flanders had been supplied by Britain against a sterling account in London. This mounted to £80 million, which would have been 400,000 *contos* in 1916, but now reached 8 million *contos* as the *escudo* descended from 4*s*. 5½*d*. to 2½*d*. The fiduciary circulation rose from 87,767 *contos* to 791,024. Prices had far outstripped wages, thus giving rise to constant social unrest. The general confusion was illustrated by the 'Portuguese Bank-note Case' in which a band of swindlers placed an order with the London firm of Waterlow for 580,000 500-*escudo* notes, which they put into circulation by launching a bank.

The only institution capable of putting a term to this state of affairs was the army. In Spain, General Primo de Rivera had taken power and resolved the existing labour disputes by simple expedients. In Portugal, three attempts at a military coup were unsuccessful, in March, April and July 1925. Special courts were set up to try the officers concerned, but they were finally acquitted. On 28 May 1926, General Gomes da Costa, the best-known general of the Great War, issued an appeal to all citizens of goodwill from Braga. Two days later President Bernardino Machado resigned and the Democratic regime was overthrown.

II: THE NEW STATE

The military leaders themselves had no concerted programme. Some wished simply to remove the Democráticos: others to reform the parliamentary system. Gomes da Costa was soon deposed, sent to the Azores and later promoted marshal. By July 1926 the head of the government was General António Oscar de Fragoso Carmona, who became acting-president of the Republic in November: he was elected in March 1928 and re-elected in 1935, 1942 and 1949.

Apart from the army, the only Portuguese institution to survive all regimes was the budgetary deficit. The total deficits between 1919 and 1926 reached 1,548,760 *contos*: in 1923 a loan was taken at 13 per cent. Although negotiations in London led to the scaling-down of the war-debt to £23 million, even this could not be paid. When the government applied to the Finance Committee of the League of Nations for a loan of £12 million, one of the conditions demanded was supervision of the Portuguese customs-duties. This was only too reminiscent of the former subservience to committees of foreign bondholders. The military government considered that Portugal's allies were placing her on a par with the defeated powers. They therefore rejected the terms.

In April 1928, when General Carmona had formed a mixed cabinet of soldiers and civilians, the portfolio of finance was offered to Dr António de Oliveira Salazar. Dr Salazar was born at Santa Comba Dão, near Coimbra, in 1889, graduated at Coimbra just after the advent of the Republic and lectured there on political economy. He was a member of the Coimbra centre for Christian democracy and had been elected a deputy in 1921, but returned to Coimbra after one day. He was therefore unknown as a politician, and came into the government as an economic expert. He insisted on being given full control of all government expenditure; and by rigid restriction of all disbursements and applying new taxes, he produced a budgetary surplus. In the course of time, his surpluses were to become as much a national institution as the former deficits. The deficits of 1917–28 had reached 2,574,000 *contos*: the surpluses of 1928–39 yielded 1,963,000 *contos*. The public debt, which stood at 692,000 *contos* in 1910 and reached 2,574,000 in 1927, was steadily reduced. Interest rates paid by the state fell from $6\frac{3}{4}$ per cent to $3\frac{1}{2}$ per cent. The surpluses were devoted to public works, development, social assistance and rearmament, and long-range plans were introduced for communications, ports, electrification and education.

Dr Salazar held that the solution of basic economic problems was an indispensable preliminary to social and political stability. This belief led to a radically different concept of the Republic. He became prime minister (president of the council) in 1932, and was largely responsible for the Constitution of 1933, the statute of labour and the Colonial Act. The President of the Republic was now given a term of seven years: he was elected by popular suffrage until 1961, when a return was made to the old system of election by parliament. The President of the Republic appointed the prime minister, and successive presidents continued to appoint Dr Salazar until he was incapacitated by a stroke in September 1968. The cabinet, which had numbered six or seven under the monarchy, was usually eleven (president, interior, justice, finance, war, marine, foreign affairs, public works and communications, overseas, education and economy), though different groupings occurred from time to time. It was Dr Salazar's practice to change ministers at varying intervals: he worked with each in turn rather than through frequent cabinet meetings. He devoted himself entirely to his 'peaceful revolution'. He lived simply as a bachelor with two adopted children. He made few public appearances and never went abroad, apart from an occasional encounter with his neighbour, General Franco. His infrequent speeches were usually couched in rather technical language.

The experience of cortes both during the monarchy and the republic was ample justification for an overhaul of the representative institutions. The lower house was replaced by a National Assembly, at first of ninety members, increased in 1945 to one hundred and twenty and later to one hundred and thirty. Members were elected by block-list for four years. Suffrage was direct, but limited to heads of families and a few other categories. The block-list system meant that the official list was rarely opposed and the electorate merely ratified the chosen candidates. The Assembly might pass or amend legislation and was required to discuss the budget in detail, but it might not initiate money-bills. It might criticize the government's actions, but not the government.

In place of political parties, the regime relied on a loose league, the National Union. Other groups were tolerated only at election times, and rarely succeeded in presenting candidates. Dr Salazar made no secret of his distrust of elections. There was no upper house: the old peerage had long been deprived of any political standing, and the republican senate had enjoyed no special prestige. Dr Salazar hoped much of his Corporative Chamber, a consultative body in which the economic activities of the nation would be represented through twenty-four corporations and the professional and intellectual classes through 'orders'. The corporations could come into existence only slowly. They depended on the creation of guilds of employers and syndicates of workers. These were set up only when half of those engaged in a particular activity in a particular region consented. Once guilds and syndicates existed, they negotiated collective contracts which were binding on members and non-members alike. An under-secretary responsible to the prime minister supervised the negotiation of contracts: strikes and lockouts were forbidden. Communal welfare centres, Casas do Povo and Casas dos Pescadores, were set up for labourers and fishermen.

The rigid discipline of the New State enabled it to survive the economic crisis of 1929–32, though in neighbouring Spain the monarchy, which had associated itself with the dictatorship of Primo de Rivera, disappeared. The emergence of the Spanish Republic encouraged the Portuguese Democráticos to make a last bid for power: a number of politicians and professional revolutionaries rebelled in the Azores and Madeira, but the shortlived 'Atlantis republic' soon collapsed, and the New State was not thereafter seriously endangered from within. For twelve years, Dr Salazar had to contend with problems of foreign policy. Not a few of the Spanish republicans favoured some form of annexation of Portugal in the guise of a Pan-Iberian federation. This danger decreased during the more conservative period in Spain (1934–5), but the success of the Spanish Popular Front in February 1936 revived Portuguese apprehensions. When General Franco rebelled against the crumbling government of the Popular Front, Dr Salazar suspended relations with Madrid and finally recognized the Burgos government when Britain did so. He had no difficulty in arriving at a treaty of friendship with the new Spanish regime, each agreeing to respect the other's independence, to assist the other in case of attack by a third party, and not to enter into any treaty aimed against the other (March 1939). Although Spain's temporary dependence on Germany and Italy caused the Portuguese some difficulties, Hitler's alliance with Russia and their partition of Catholic Poland weakened his influence in Spain. Even his conquest of France and the appearance of German troops at the Pyrenees failed to pull Spain into the Axis camp, and Dr Salazar was able to exercise his influence to maintain the neutrality of the Peninsula. The most critical moments were at the end of 1940 when Hitler decided to invade, but changed his mind, and in 1941, after his invasion of Russia. This cut off his supplies of wolfram from the East, and German agents forced up prices of the mineral in order to stimulate prospectors in Portugal. The price reached £6,000 a ton, and there was danger of disruption of the rural economy. As the Portuguese attempted to control production, the Germans openly sank a Portuguese merchantman in October 1941 and another in December: in January 1942 Dr Salazar was obliged to continue to supply wolfram.

The involvement of the United States gave a new importance to the Atlantic islands. In June 1942 Hitler planned to meet an American landing in the Azores by the use of submarines, but a year later the situation had changed. Britain invoked the Ancient Alliance and requested facilities in the Azores. When these were granted, the Germans protested, but took no action. Under the Azores agreement, Portugal received guarantees of the integrity of her possessions from both Britain and the United States. As late as 1944 the Germans held up a Portuguese liner in mid-Atlantic as a threat in order not to lose the supply of wolfram, but Dr Salazar finally declared a total embargo on production and closed all mines.

During the long conflict sales of wolfram to Germany had been paid for in cash or goods, while Portugal extended credits to Britain which reached about £76 million. The war had caused shortages of fuel and industrial equipment which seriously affected the railways and other forms of transport, but essential supplies of food were maintained and prices fixed. After the war it was at last possible to re-equip the railways and obtain trucks and buses. The war had underlined the weakness of the merchant navy, and the accumulated credits were used partly to purchase ships. By 1953 £40 million had been invested in fifty-one new ships, giving an increase of 70 per cent in total tonnage.

The creation of the Technical University at Lisbon provided economists, scientists and technicians. The large-scale production of hydro-electricity was the basis of a programme of industrialization. The damming of rivers in the north and centre made power generally available, and finally the harnessing of the international stretch of the Douro supplied the isolated interior of Portugal as well as northern Spain. Thermal electricity which required imported coal disappeared, as hydro-electric production doubled between 1940 and 1950 and multiplied by seven between 1940 and 1960. Over the same period the general industrial index rose from sixty to ninety-two and one hundred and fifty-seven. The growth of construction was accompanied by the rapid development of cement and similar industries. The rate of industrial expansion reached 11 per cent in 1953–6, and production doubled in a decade. However, most enterprises were still small, and in 1959 there were still only thirty-six employing more than 1,000 persons. The industrial sector formed between a third and a half of the population in Oporto, Braga, Lisbon, Setúbal and Aveiro.

But in 1950 nearly half the total population depended directly on agriculture for its livelihood, and a decade later the proportion was still over 40 per cent: in Trás-os-Montes, Guarda, Beja and Viseu about two-thirds of the inhabitants were agricultural. The total population had doubled in the course of the nineteenth century, and doubled again in the first two-thirds of the twentieth. The productivity of the countryside had also been expanded. Between 1874 and 1957 the cultivated area had increased from 4·6 million hectares to 6·6 million. The area under olives had doubled, that under wheat tripled, and that under rice quintupled: there was nearly six times as much pine-forest. Much had been done to increase productivity by the use of artificial fertilizers. But now barely 8 per cent of the total land area was classified as uncultivable, and part of the new production of wheat had been gained from marginal land on large estates and was not necessarily permanent. Afforestation, particularly of pine and eucalyptus, made timber a principal product and served as a basis for resin, pulp, paper and plastics industries. Some relief was also gained by irrigation. Nevertheless, there remained a large proportion of peasant agriculture, and in places the rural diet was sober to the point of meagreness, and the average holding too small to give an improved livelihood or to support the initial cost of new methods. The countryside tended to persevere with beans, potatoes, oil and wine, for which demand only kept pace with the growth of population, rather than venture into more profitable crops. Such hazards as irregular rainfall reinforced the natural tendency to avoid the risks of change. More efficient methods reduced the demand for rural labour.

Substantial transfers of population were inevitable. The main movement was to Lisbon and Oporto. The capital was transformed by the addition of new suburbs, and acquired an extensive industrial concentration on the south side of the Tagus. This included the country's first steel-mill and plants for the assembly of motor-vehicles: the maritime tradition was revived with the extension of shipbuilding and the construction of docks for the repair of the largest tankers. The building of the Salazar bridge across the Tagus linked Lisbon directly with the industrial belt and the whole of southern Portugal. A parallel, if less rapid, development occurred at Oporto, where the old city was extended to engulf the neighbouring townships. The other district capitals, which had remained small during the nineteenth century, began to attract and to fill out: here there was room for considerable development.

Overpopulation had traditionally been alleviated by emigration. The Azores had long been overcrowded and sent a stream of emigrants to the United States, receiving income from their remittances. Migration to Brazil was rendered more difficult and less attractive by currency and immigration restrictions. Despite the national interest in Africa, few Portuguese country-people possessed the resources or experience to embark on African farming without substantial support and training. There was an increase in emigration to Canada, and the shortage of labour in Europe opened opportunities, especially in France.

But these movements, though important, did not disguise the fact that a larger proportion of the population must be accommodated in industry or services. It had long been a Portuguese preference to invest in property, and the construction industry accounted for a considerable proportion of industrial activity during the Salazar regime. It was necessary for the state to participate in order to attract investment to other fields. The predominance of construction and electrification accounted in part for a somewhat slow pace of capital formation. The state therefore tended to direct interest towards activities requiring relatively small inversions of capital and a high labour component. A wide range of products, formerly imported, was produced for home consumption, and, where possible, for export. However, industrialization did not necessarily decrease the need for imports, which tended to grow faster than exports. Since the beginning of the century, Portugal's export trade had consisted largely of wine, cork and sardines: diversification added some new items, and progress was made with the tourist industry. But the reserves were maintained chiefly by the development of the economies of Angola and Mozambique, which now at length began to reward the efforts of the small body of early Africanists. After the Great War, the Republic had conceded to Angola a measure of autonomy and encouraged rapid development, which brought the province to the verge of bankruptcy. Dr Salazar had granted Angola a loan, but instituted a commission to control its exchange operations. The weakness of the Angolan economy had formerly been its dependence on poor crops such as maize. The war opened new perspectives: cotton and coffee became the staples, while the production of diamonds provided an important source of wealth. Luanda, the oldest European city in Africa south of the equator, became an important capital, while advances in tropical medicines made it possible to introduce white settlers into areas formerly considered unhealthy.

The first threat to the overseas provinces was posed by the creation of the Indian Union, which desired to annex Gôa, Damão and Diu. The Goans showed little desire to join India, though some political expatriates and descendants of Goans in India did. Agitators organized in India entered Portuguese territory by force and overran the enclaves of Dadra and Nagar Aveli: in September 1954 Mr Nehru stated that India would not tolerate Portuguese rule in Goa even if the Goans wanted it. Shortly afterwards the Russian leaders, Bulganin and Khrushchev, visited India and egged Mr Nehru on, but when the American secretary of state declared that 'all the world regards it (Gôa) as a Portuguese province', Indian attacks ceased for four years.

The adoption by the Marxists of 'anti-imperialism' as their chief propaganda weapon followed the success of China in forcing the partition of Indo-China. They now sought to fan nationalism and to turn the newly created nations against the Western powers, using the substantial voice in the United Nations given to the newly created flock of Afro-Asian territories. By the use of this block of votes the constitution of the international body was altered in order to make colonies 'illegal'. The less responsible the United Nations became the more the North American states clung to it. In October 1960 Khrushchev appeared in New York to bang the table with his shoe in the cause of anti-colonialism.

For Dr Salazar and for the majority of Portuguese the separation of the African provinces was inconceivable. The French in 1958 gave their African possessions the chance to convert themselves into an economic and cultural union. The British negotiated independence with each colony separately. One French territory, Guinea, opted out of the union under Marxist influence, and one British territory, Ghana, adopted a Marxist regime, drawing delegates from the Belgian Congo to a conference. One of these, Lumumba, provoked riots in the Congo to force a change of government: Belgian rule ended, and the territory fell into anarchy, making it necessary for the United Nations to intervene with troops. French Guinea sheltered a handful of communists from Angola, and both Ghana and the Congo gave facilities to small independence groups from Portuguese territories. In 1960 American agitators tried to create disturbances in Angola, but without success.

A month after Khrushchev's performance in New York, J. F. Kennedy was elected to the American presidency. He and his group were quite lacking in experience and chose a simple formula for an African policy, which in effect aligned it with the Soviet Union. Thus nothing was done to put into execution the findings of the International Court at the Hague which supported the Portuguese claim to have access to the enclaves occupied by India. When the Afro-Asian bloc declared Angola a 'threat to peace' and bands of armed men from camps in the (Belgian) Congo invaded it, the American delegate voted for the first time with the Russians. A massive press campaign was mounted to present the invasion as a rising in Angola. Many Angolans had long before been attracted by boom conditions to Leopoldville under Belgian rule. The separation of the Belgian Congo had brought much unemployment, and it had not been difficult to recruit them as 'liberators'. Many Angolans, black and white, were slaughtered by the intruders, but the authorities gradually regained control.

Meanwhile, Ghana brought accusations against Portugal before the Internation Labour Office, and these led to an investigation, and were disposed of by a report published in April 1962. In the summer of 1961 the Indian government sponsored a so-called seminar at New Delhi to study the partition of the Portuguese possessions: it was attended by a representative of the

Labour party. In December preparations were made in New Delhi for an invasion: they were attended by the Russian president. The conquest of Gôa was soon completed, and the Russian delegate to the United Nations promptly stifled discussion by using his veto. Dr Salazar had expected a reaction of world opinion against the aggression, but Western policy was so confused that nothing was done.

The intensity of Portuguese feeling about Africa had been amply demonstrated in 1890. Dr Salazar committed his regime to the defence of the overseas provinces, and met with little opposition. If hitherto his African policy had laid much stress on trade, it was now diversified to embrace all forms of economic, social and educational development. Dr Salazar's assertion of traditional concern for Africa was supported by a demonstration of half a million people in Lisbon in August 1963. However, the support of various African states for liberation or terrorist movements made it necessary to reinforce the African provinces. The garrisons in Africa were increased from 30,000 in 1964 to some 120,000, and the total cost of defence accounted for two-fifths of the budget.

Dr Salazar never modified his view that a return to party politics was undesirable. The National Assembly was elected without competition and produced no opposition. Only the presidential elections aroused political conflict. In 1949 Marshal Carmona was opposed by the octogenarian Democrat, General Norton de Matos, who however withdrew at the last moment. Two years later, Marshal Carmona died, and General Craveiro Lopes was elected: both opposition candidates withdrew before the election. The government insisted on accusing opposition movements of communism, and so dissolving them. At the elections of 1958, the National Union withdrew its support of General Craveiro Lopes and put forward Admiral A. Rodrigues Tomás. He was opposed by Brigadier H. Delgado, who declared his intention of dismantling the New State. Admiral Tomás received $77\frac{1}{2}$ per cent of the votes cast and Brigadier Delgado $22\frac{1}{2}$ per cent. Delgado was later accused of illicit political activities and was arrested, but escaped to Brazil: his fate, apparently murdered in Spain, has remained mysterious. In 1960–1, the alignment of the United States with Russia over the colonial issue was the context of attempts to overthrow the Portuguese government. Captain H. Galvão, a former member of the National Assembly, who had parted company with the regime, went to Venezuela and seized the liner *Santa Maria*, murdering the first officer: the object was to broadcast attacks on Dr Salazar and announce troubles in Angola. After the Indian conquest of Gôa, a band of armed men attacked army barracks at Beja, killing the under-secretary of the army: they were tried in 1964 and received moderate sentences. By the end of 1964 the only visible opposition was in the form of student disorders.

When Dr Salazar celebrated his seventy-fifth birthday in 1964, he was already a legendary figure. His economic achievements had acquired a kind of consecration: the repressive aspects of his regime were blamed on the unpopular state-defence police. Portugal possessed a wide array of new industries: her communications included a growing airline and a restored merchant marine, a modernized railway system, good roads and bridges. These had not been attained without considerable sacrifice. The need to build up an investing class had perpetuated the uneven distribution of wealth. The government obliged industrial undertakings to provide housing and other facilities for their employees, but such schemes could scarcely be all-embracing. Not unnaturally, as its creator grew older, the system became somewhat inflexible and immune to change. Dr Salazar was incapacitated by a stroke in September 1968. When it was clear that he would not be able to govern, President Tomás, after consulting his advisers called upon Professor Marcelo Caetano, a former minister and rector of the University of Lisbon, to form a government. Dr Caetano paid tribute to his predecessor, who had done so much for Portugal, and maintained the New State in its general outlines, though he clearly differentiated himself from Dr Salazar's methods, not least by his frequent broadcast speeches and his travels to Portuguese Africa.

INDEX

208   INDEX

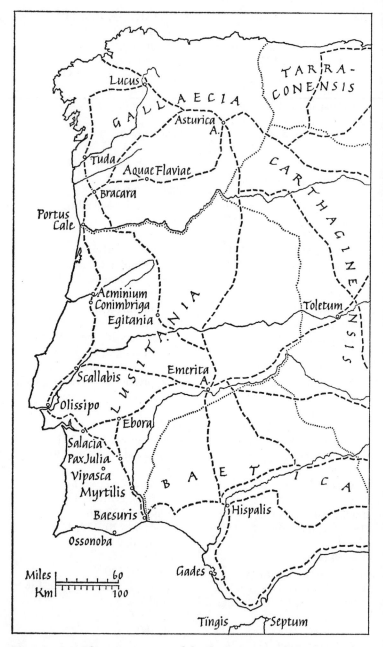

Map 1. (a) The western part of the Iberian peninsula in ancient times. The dashed rule indicates the Roman roads. The classical provinces are outlined.

Map 1. (b) The modern equivalents of the classical names in 1 (a) are shown with a solid circle.

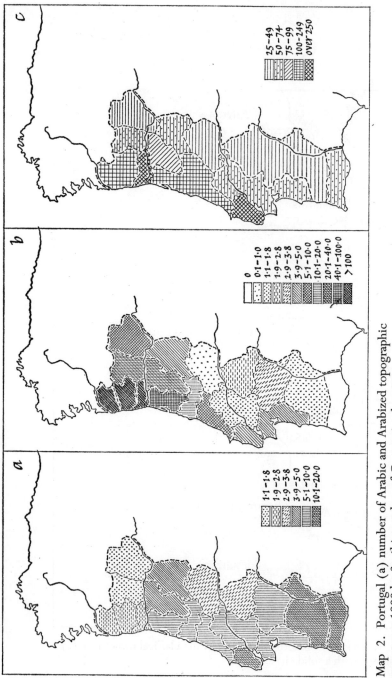

Map 2. Portugal (a) number of Arabic and Arabized topographic names per 1000 km²; (b) number of Germanic place names per 1000 km²; (c) Population density (number of inhabitants per km²). ((a) and (b) after Lautensach; (c) after Luis de Hoyos Sáinz).

a

	1·1 – 1·8
	1·9 – 2·8
	2·9 – 3·8
	3·9 – 5·0
	5·1 – 10·0
	10·1 – 20·0

b

	0
	0·1 – 1·0
	1·1 – 1·8
	1·9 – 2·8
	2·9 – 3·8
	3·9 – 5·0
	5·1 – 10·0
	10·1 – 20·0
	20·1 – 40·0
	40·1 – 100·0
	> 100

c

	25 – 49
	50 – 74
	75 – 99
	100 – 249
	over 250

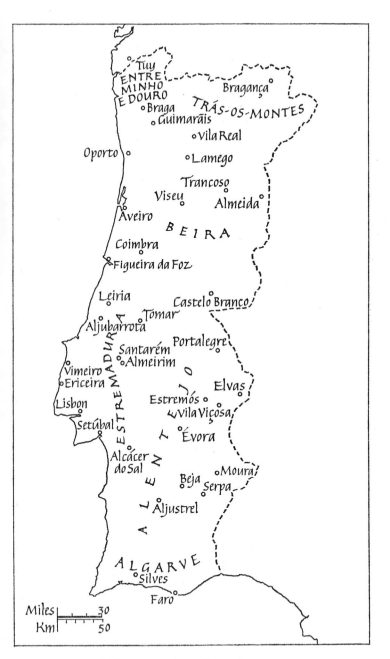

Miles, Km scale: 30 / 50

Map 3. Portugal: showing traditional provinces.

Map 4. Portugal: showing modern regional groupings.